HANDBOOK of LITIGATION FORMS

With Annotations

STUART J. FABER
Member, California Bar

lega-Books
A Division of the Charing Cross Publishing Company
658 S. Bonnie Brae Street / Los Angeles, Calif. 90057 / (213) 483-5832
California's Largest Publisher of Legal Texts in Paperback

Printed in the United States of America

Handbook of Litigation Forms

ISBN-0-89074-052-6
11782

TABLE OF FORMS

This collection of forms does not include any of the printed forms provided either by local courts or by the Judicial Council. If a desired procedural form cannot be found in this book, the selection at the appropriate court should be consulted.

CAPTION)
)
)
)
_____________________)

Case No.______________

COMPLAINT FOR DAMAGES FOR ABUSE OF PROCESS

Plaintiff complains:

1. At all times herein mentioned, defendant was and now is a resident of the County of_________, State of California.

2. On or about_______, 19___, defendant filed against plaintiff three complaints for____________. Each of the complaints was identical to the other and each was filed in a different county, to wit; ______________,______________and ___________________Counties. This abuse of the process was not authorized in the regular course of the proceeding.

3. Defendant's ulterior purpose and motivation in so misusing the process was to obtain a collateral advantage over the plaintiff by requiring plaintiff to respond to three identical pieces of litigation and to coerce plaintiff into settling the disputed claim, hoping that plaintiff would settle rather than undergo the expense of defending three separate actions.

4. As a proximate cause of defendant's actions hereinabove described, defendant has been damaged generally in the sum of $_______________.

5. Defendant's conduct hereinabove described was committed maliciously and willfully and with the intention of injuring plaintiff and harrassing him. Plaintiff is therefore entitled to punitive damages in the sum of $____________.

WHEREFORE, plaintiff prays:

1. For general damages in the sum of $___________.

2. For punitive damages in the sum of $__________.

3. For costs of suit and such other relief as the court deems just.

____
Attorney for Plaintiff

****

Barquis vs. Merchants, 7 Cal. 3d, 94.

White vs. Wolfson, 68 Cal. 2d, 336. Czap vs. Credit Bureau, 7 C.A. 3d, 1. Templeton vs. Ralston, 69 Cal. 2d,461.

Two essential elements for abusive process are an ulterior purpose and a willful act and the use of the process of the court which is not proper. Spellens vs. Spellens, 49 Cal. 2d, 210.

A cause of action for intentional infliction of emotional distress and/or injunction may be alleged if the facts warrant. Czap vs. Credit Bureau, 7 C.A. 3d, 1.

Defenses: Advise of counsel, Templeton vs. Ralston, 69 Cal. 2d, 461.

Statute of limitations: McFaddin vs. Crocker, 219 C.A. 2d, 585.

No collateral advantage alleged: Golden vs. Dungan, 20 C.A. 3d, 295. Spira vs. Superior Court, 41 C.A. 3d, 537. Younger vs. Solomon, 38 C.A. 3d, 289.

CAPTION	)	Case No.______________
	)	
	)	COMPLAINT FOR ACCOUNTING AGAINST JOINT TENANT
____________________	)	

Plaintiff complains:

1. At all times mentioned herein, plaintiff was and now is, an owner and entitled to possession of an undivided one-half interest in that certain real property in the County of______________, described as follows, (describe).

2. Defendant at all times mentioned herein was, and is, the owner with plaintiff, in joint tenancy, of an undivided one-half interest in said property.

3. On________, 19____, defendant leased the property to tenants and has collected and retained from said tenants, all rents, profits and income from said property since ________, 19____. Defendant has refused to account to plaintiff for any portion thereof, although plaintiff has made numerous demands on defendant for such an accounting. Defendant has all books, papers and records with reference to the income from said property and has refused plaintiff access to said records.

4. Except by an accounting through this court, plaintiff has no means of obtaining an accounting of said rentals and income and has no means of ascertaining what his interest therein may be. Plaintiff has no adequate or speedy remedy at law.

WHEREFORE, plaintiff prays:

1. That defendant be required to account to plaintiff for all rents, issues and profits obtained by him from said tenant, or other tenants of said real property from__________, 19___.

2. That when the amounts so collected and obtained by defendant are ascertained, judgment be entered thereon in favor of plaintiff for one-half of said amount.

3. For costs of suit and such other relief as the court deems just.

____
Attorney for Plaintiff

CAPTION	)	Case No.__________
	)	
	)	COMPLAINT FOR ACCOUNTING
	)	
______________________	)	

Plaintiff complains and for cause of action alleges:

1. At all times herein mentioned, the relationship between plaintiff and defendant was as follows: (Set forth relationship such as trustee and beneficiary, attorney and client, broker and client.)

2. In his capacity as above-mentioned, defendant has received money on behalf of plaintiff, a portion of which is due to plaintiff from defendant.

3. The amount of money due from defendant to plaintiff is unknown to plaintiff and cannot be established without an accounting of the receipts and disbursements of the above-mentioned transaction. Plaintiff is informed and believes and thereon alleges that the amount due exceeds $5,000.00.

4. Plaintiff has demanded an accounting of the above-mentioned transactions from defendant and has further demanded that defendant pay plaintiff the amount found due. Defendant has failed and refuses, and continues to fail and refuse to render an accounting and to pay the sum due, or any sums.

WHEREFORE plaintiff prays:

1. For an accounting between plaintiff and defendant.

2. For the amount found to be due from defendant to plaintiff as a result of the accounting.

3. For costs of suit herein and for such other relief as the court deems just.

DATED:____________________, 19___.

____
Attorney for Plaintiff

CAPTION) Case No.________
)
) STIPULATION FOR ARBITRATION
____________________)

COME NOW the parties to the within action, ________________and________________and stipulate that the above entitled cause may be submitted to arbitration pursuant to C.C.P. §1141.10 and Rule 1602, Rules of Court.

DATED:______________, 19____.

____
Attorney for Plaintiff

____
Attorney for Defendant

IT IS SO ORDERED:

____
Judge

****

The parties may stipulate that the proceeding may be submitted to arbitration. The stipulation may be filed at any time after the filing of an At Issue Memorandum.

CAPTION) Case No.________
)
) NOTICE OF PLAINTIFF'S ELECTION TO
____________________) ARBITRATE

TO THE DEFENDANT__________________AND TO HIS ATTORNEY__________________:

YOU AND EACH OF YOU WILL PLEASE TAKE NOTICE that defendant, pursuant to the provisions of 1602, Rules of Court, hereby elects to submit the within matter to arbitration and hereby agrees that the arbitration award shall not exceed the amount of $7,500.00.

____
Attorney for Plaintiff

CAPTION)   Case No.____________
)
)   COMPLAINT FOR DAMAGES
)   (ASSAULT AND BATTERY)
____________________)

Plaintiff alleges:

1. On or about __________, 19__, at ____________, California, defendant assaulted and battered plaintiff by striking plaintiff with a club in various areas of plaintiff's body and about his face.

2. By reason of the acts of defendant, plaintiff was placed in dread fear of his life and well-being.

3. By reason of the wrongful and malicious acts of defendant, plaintiff suffered severe physical and mental anguish and physical pain to his damage in the sum of $_______________.

4. The acts of defendant were willful, wanton, malicious and oppressive and justify the awarding of punitive damages in the amount of $_______________.

5. By reason of the acts of defendant, plaintiff was required to, and did expend money for medical services, drugs, hospital expenses, for the treatment and relief of his injuries. The exact amount of these expenses is presently unknown to plaintiff.

6. As a further proximate cause of defendant's acts, plaintiff suffered tears to his clothing to the extent that a suit, the value of which was $__________was totally destroyed.

WHEREFORE, plaintiff prays:

1. For general damages.

2. For medical expenses according to proof.

3. For loss of personal property in the sum of $__________.

4. For exemplary and punitive damages in the sum of $_______________.

5. For costs of suit herein and for such other relief as the court deems just.

DATED:_____________, 19____.

____
Attorney for Plaintiff

****

Where the action is brought in the Superior Court to recover damages for personal injury, the amount of damages shall not be stated. C.C.P., §425.10.

CAPTION)
)
) ANSWER TO COMPLAINT FOR ASSAULT
) AND BATTERY
____________________)

Case No.______________

COMES NOW the defendant and in answer to the complaint on file herein admits, alleges and denies as follows:

1. Pursuant to the provisions of C.C.P. §431.30, defendant denies generally and specifically each and every allegation of plaintiff's complaint and the whole thereof and denies further that defendant assaulted or battered the plaintiff and denies that plaintiff was damaged in the sum of $___________, or any sum.

AS A FIRST AFFIRMATIVE DEFENSE, DEFENDANT ALLEGES:

2. Plaintiff first violently and viciously made an assault against and on the body of the person of defendant. Defendant defended himself out of necessity and such acts of force complained of, if in fact committed, were done so to protect defendant's body and person.

FOR A SECOND AFFIRMATIVE DEFENSE, DEFENDANT ALLEGES:

3. At all times herein mentioned, defendant was the owner of certain real property located in__________County, California, described as follows: (Set forth description.)

4. At the time set forth in the complaint, plaintiff unlawfully entered defendant's land and attempted to commit the following: (Describe unlawful act of plaintiff.)

5. Defendant ordered plaintiff to leave the premises but plaintiff refused to do so and defendant placed his hands upon the plaintiff to prevent the plaintiff from committing the above-mentioned unlawful act. The force employed by defendant to prevent plaintiff from continuing his unlawful acts was reasonable and necessary.

WHEREFORE, defendant prays:

1. That plaintiff take nothing by his complaint.

2. That defendant be awarded costs of suit and such other relief as the court deems just.

DATED: ____________________, 19___.

____
Attorney for Defendant

****

See Civil Code §50 on the right to use reasonable force to protect real property.

CAPTION)
)
)
_______________)

REQUEST FOR DELAYED PUBLIC DISCLOSURE

TO THE CLERK OF THE SUPERIOR COURT:

Pursuant to the provisions of CCP §482.050, you are hereby requested to keep from public disclosure the following documents:

1. The complaint.

2. The application for a right to attach order and writ of attachment.

It is requested that you keep the above documents from public disclosure for 30 days from the filing of the complaint.

Dated:_______________

____
Attorney for Plaintiff

****

Public disclosure may be prevented against all persons except a party or his attorney. The request can also take the form of a notation or rubber stamp on the top of the first page of the complaint. CCP §482.050(c).

CAPTION	No. ____________ NOTICE OF MOTION FOR AN ORDER EXTENDING TIME OF LEVY OF ATTACHMENT [C.C.P. § 488.510] Date: ____________ Time: ____________ Dept: ____________

TO THE DEFENDANT __________________ AND TO HIS ATTORNEY:

YOU AND EACH OF YOU WILL PLEASE TAKE NOTICE that on ______________________, 19___, at the hour of _________ A.M., in Department ____ of the above-entitled court, plaintiff will move the court for an order extending the levy of attachment on the following-described property: (Set forth description.) An extension will be sought for one year beyond the date at which the attachment is now calendared to expire.

The motion will be made on the basis that the action has not yet been brought to trial and a trial date is calendared beyond the original expiration date of the levy of attachment. The motion is based on the provisions of C.C.P. §488.510 upon an affidavit and points and authorities attached hereto, the papers and records on file herein, and such other evidence, oral and documentary as may be adduced at the hearing on the motion.

DATED: ____________________________.

____
Attorney for Plaintiff

****

The motion must be made not less than 10 nor more than 60 days before the expiration of the 3-year period. Notice must be given to the defendant of the hearing on the motion. At least 5 days' notice must be given.

Enough time should be allowed to enable the court to make the order prior to the expiration of the original period.

The motion should be accompanied by a declaration setting forth the reasons why good cause exists. Points and authorities should also be included.

CAPTION

No. ________________

NOTICE OF MOTION TO DISPOSE OF PERISHABLE PROPERTY [C.C.P. §488.530]

Date: ____________________

Time: ____________________

Dept: ____________________

TO THE DEFENDANT ______________________ AND HIS ATTORNEY:

YOU AND EACH OF YOU WILL PLEASE TAKE NOTICE that on ________________, 19____, at the hour of __________, A.M., in Department _____ of the above-entitled court, plaintiff will move for an order for an immediate sale of the following-described property: (Describe property.)

The motion is being made for the reason that the above-described property is of such a nature that unless it is disposed of immediately, it shall become valueless. The motion is based on the provisions of C.C.P.§488.530, the records and papers on file herein, the motion, declaration and points and authorities attached hereto, and such other evidence oral and documentary that may be adduced at the hearing on this matter.

DATED: ___________________________.

____
Attorney for Plaintiff

****

The motion to dispose of property under attachment where the property is perishable may be made by the plaintiff, defendant, or any third person who has an interest in the property. In addition, a motion to appoint a receiver may be made.

	)	No. ___________
	)	
	)	NOTICE OF MOTION FOR PARTIAL RELEASE
	)	OF PROPERTY
CAPTION	)	Date:___________________
	)	Time:___________________
_______________________	)	Dept:___________________

TO THE PLAINTIFF _________________AND TO HIS ATTORNEY,_______
________________:

YOU AND EACH OF YOU WILL PLEASE TAKE NOTICE that on _____________, 19_____, at ________A.M. in Department ____ of the above-entitled court, defendant will move the court for an order releasing from the attaching heretofore levied on________________, 19_____, the following-described property: (Describe property.)

The basis of the motion is that the amount of property held under attachment is of a value in excess of that necessary to secure the amount of an eventual plaintiff's judgment should such a judgment be rendered. The motion shall be based upon this notice of motion, points and authorities and declarations attached hereto, the records and pleadings on file herein, and such other evidence oral and documentary as may be adduced at the hearing on this motion.

DATED: _________________________.

____
Attorney for Defendant

****

This motion may be made on 10 days' notice to the plaintiff. The motion should be accompanied by a declaration of the defendant setting forth the total value of the property under attachment and the value of that portion of the property for which defendant seeks release. C.C.P. §488.555.

CAPTION

No. ____________

NOTICE OF MOTION TO INCREASE UNDERTAKING

Date: ________________

Time: ________________

Dept: ________________

TO THE PLAINTIFF AND TO HIS ATTORNEY:

NOTICE IS HEREBY GIVEN that on ________________, 19_____, at the hour of _____________, A.M., or as soon thereafter as the matter may be heard in Department ______ of the above-entitled court, defendant will move for an order to increase the amount of the undertaking required on the attachment to $_________________.

The motion will be made on the grounds that the undertaking is insufficient for the reason that the market value of the property exceeds the value estimated in the undertaking. The beneficiary's estimate of the market value of the property is $__________________.

The motion will be based on the provisions of C.C.P. §489.070, this notice of motion, and the declaration of ____________________, memorandum of points and authorities served and filed herewith, and other evidence oral and documentary as may be adduced at the hearing on the motion.

DATED: ________________________.

____

Attorney for Defendant

****

Objections to the undertaking may be made by any person claiming to be the rightful owner of the property.

This notice of motion should be accompanied by points and authorities and a declaration setting forth the declarant's estimate of the value of the property.

Hearing on objections shall be not less than 2 nor more than 5 days after service of the notice of motion.

CAPTION

No. ______________

ORDER INCREASING UNDERTAKING

The hearing on a motion to increase undertaking came on regularly before the undersigned. ___________________ appeared as attorney for plaintiff, and ___________________ appeared as attorney for defendant.

Evidence was introduced by both sides and submitted to the court.

IT IS ORDERED that the undertaking is insufficient in that the court's determination of the value of the property is $_______________.

IT IS FURTHER ORDERED that an increased undertaking in the amount of $_____________ must be filed within 5 days from ______________, 19___. If the increased undertaking is not filed, the sheriff is ordered to release the property held under levy of attachment.

DATED: __________________________.

____

JUDGE

CAPTION	No. ____________
	NOTICE OF MOTION FOR ESTABLISHMENT OF LIABILITY FOR WRONGFUL ATTACHMENT
	Date: ____________ Time: ____________ Dept: ____________

TO THE PLAINTIFF AND HIS ATTORNEY AND TO ____________________, SURETY, AND ____________________, SURETY:

YOU AND EACH OF YOU WILL PLEASE TAKE NOTICE that on ________ ________, 19___, at the hour of _______ A.M., in Department _____ of the above-entitled court, defendant will move the court for an order establishing the liability of the plaintiff and each of the sureties and for an order entering judgment upon such liability for wrongful attachment.

The basis of the motion will be that a levy of writ of attachment was served on the following-described property (describe property) belonging to defendant and that thereafter a judgment in the above-entitled case was rendered in favor of defendant, and as a consequence defendant as suffered damages in the amount of $__________.

The motion shall be based upon the notice of motion, the declaration and points and authorities attached hereto, the records and papers on file herein, and such other evidence oral and documentary that will be adduced at the hearing on the motion.

DATED: ________________________.

____
Attorney for Defendant

****

Defendant may bring an action for wrongful attachment by motion, in which event the amount of his recovery is limited. As an alternative, he may bring an independent action for wrongful attachment. C.C.P. §490.030.

The motion may not be brought until after the entry of final judgment in the original action and after the time for appeal has expired or has been finally determined. The motion may not be filed more than one year thereafter.

Although the statutes do not require it, the better practice would be to include an affidavit setting forth the amount of damages, costs, and expenses. See also C.C.P. §1058(a).

CAPTION	)	APPLICATION FOR AN ORDER REQUIRING THIRD PARTY TO APPEAR
	)	
___________	)	(CCP §491.010)

Application is hereby made for an order requiring __________ to appear before this Honorable Court on a date and time set by the court.

This application is made pursuant to the provisions of CCP §491.010 and it is requested that ______________________ appear to be examined under oath regarding property which he or ________________corporation has in its possession

____________________is the Vice President of ________________ corporation and is familiar with the property of defendant which is held by the corporation.

This application is supported by a declaration of plaintiff which is attached hereto and made a part hereof.

Dated:________________

____
Attorney for Plaintiff

****

The application for the order is obtained ex parte. Plaintiff does not notice a motion. An order should be prepared with space left for the filling in of date by the court.

CAPTION)
)
______________)

DECLARATION IN SUPPORT OF APPLICATION FOR ORDER

I, ______________________________ declare:

I am the plaintiff in the within cause.

A right to attach order and writ of attachment has been issued in the above entitled case. Plaintiff has been attempting to levy the writ of attachment on the following described personal property of the defendant. (Describe property).

The above described property is presently being held in the warehouse of ______________________corporation at ________________, Los Angeles, California. ______________________, the Vice President of said corporation informed me that the property was being held in the warehouse. However, I am informed and believe and upon such information and belief allege that when an attempted levy was made, said ____________________denied possession of the above described property.

WHEREFORE it is requested that an order be issued requiring ________________ to appear and be examined with respect to his possession of the above described property.

I declare under penalty of perjury that the foregoing is true and correct.

Executed at Los Angeles, California on ________________, 19__.

____
Plaintiff

CAPTION)
)
______________)

ORDER FOR APPEARANCE OF ________________

TO ____________________, Vice President of ________________ Corporation, pursuant to the provisions of CCP §491.010, you are ordered to appear in Department ________ of the above entitled court at 110 North Grand, Los Angeles, California, Room ______ on ____________ 19__ at the hour of ___________a.m.

Your appearance is required to secure your testimony with respect to the following described property which it is alleged belongs to ____________________ and which you are holding.

(Describe property).

Failure to appear at the appointed time subjects you to a warrant for your arrest.

Dated:________________ ________________________________
Judge

****

Before a warrant may issue, this document must be served by a levying officer or some other person appointed by the court in the order to make service. CCP §491.010(c).

CAPTION	No. ______________ NOTICE OF EXAMINATION OF THIRD PERSON HOLDING PROPERTY OF DEFENDANT Date: ______________ Time: ______________ Dept: ______________

TO THE DEFENDANT _________________ AND TO HIS ATTORNEY:

YOU AND EACH OF YOU WILL PLEASE TAKE NOTICE that on ___________________, 19____, at the hour of ________ A.M., in Department ____ of the above-entitled court, a hearing will be held in which plaintiff will examine _____________________ on matters concerning his possession of the following described property (describe property) which belongs to defendant.

DATED: __________________________.

____
Attorney for Plaintiff

****

This notice must be served upon the defendant at least three days prior to the hearing.

CAPTION) No. ________________

NOTICE OF MOTION TO SET ASIDE RIGHT TO ATTACH ORDER AND QUASH WRIT OF ATTACHMENT [C.C.P. §492.050]

Date: ________________

Time: ________________

Dept: ________________

TO THE PLAINTIFF________________AND TO HIS ATTORNEY:

YOU AND EACH OF YOU WILL PLEASE TAKE NOTICE that on ____________________, 19___, at the hour of _____A.M., in Department _________ of the above-entitled court, defendant will move the court for an order setting aside the right to attach order,quashing the writ of attachment, and releasing the following-described property (describe property) now held under levy of attachment.

The motion shall be based on the ground that property which is held under attachment is not property which is subject to attachment under C.C.P. §492.040. The motion is further based upon the declaration of defendant and points and authorities attached hereto.

The motion is further based upon the records and papers on file herein, this notice of motion and such other evidence oral and documentary as may be adduced at the hearing on the motion.

DATED: ________________________.

____

Attorney for Defendant

CAPTION)
)
)
_______________________)

CASE NO.______________

NOTICE OF ASSOCIATION OF COUNSEL

TO_______________________AND HIS ATTORNEY OF RECORD:

PLEASE TAKE NOTICE that_______________________has become associated with _____________________, the attorney of record, as attorney for_________________herein. The office address and telephone number of such associated attorney are ____.

For purposes of future services and notices the address and telephone number are:______________________________ ____.

DATED: ____________________, 19_____.

____
Attorney for

****

CAPTION)
)
)
_______________________)

CASE NO.______________

SUBSTITUTION OF ATTORNEYS

COMES NOW_________________, the plaintiff herein and substitutes________________, attorney at law as his attorney of record in place of_______________________.

DATED:______________________, 19___________.

____
Signature

I consent to the above substitution.

DATED:______________________, 19___________.

____
Signature of previous attorney

I accept the above substitution.

DATED:______________________, 19___________.

____
Signature of new attorney

CAPTION) Case No.____________
)
) NOTICE OF MOTION FOR LEAVE TO
____________________) SUBSTITUTE NEW ATTORNEY

Date:______________
Time:______________
Department:__________

TO____________________, THE ATTORNEY OF RECORD OF THE MOVING PARTY, AND TO__________________, THE ATTORNEY OF RECORD OF THE ADVERSE PARTY:

YOU AND EACH OF YOU WILL PLEASE TAKE NOTICE that on _____________, 19____, at the hour of_______ A. M., or as soon thereafter as the matter may be heard in Department_____ of the above entitled court, plaintiff will move for an order substituting _________________ as his attorney in place and in sted of__________, and for an order directing that_______________, the present attorney turn over to the new attorney all the papers and records in connection with the within action which are presently in his possession.

The motion will be made on the following grounds: (describe)

The motion will be based upon this notice of motion, the declaration of__________________and the memorandum of points and authorities served herewith and on such other evidence, oral and documentary as may be presented at the hearing on the motion.

DATED:_______________, 19_____.

*****

The client has an absolute right to discharge his attorney. Fiacasse v. Brente 6 Cal. 3rd 704.

*****

CAPTION	)	Case No.___________
	)	NOTICE OF MOTION TO WITHDRAW AS ATTORNEY
	)	
____________________	)	Date:___________ Time:___________ Department:_________

TO____________________, CLIENT AND TO________________, ATTORNEY FOR THE ADVERSE PARTY:

YOU AND EACH OF YOU WILL PLEASE TAKE NOTICE that on ________, 19____, or as soon thereafter as the matter may be heard in Department____, of the above entitled court,___________, attorney will move the court for an order allowing him to withdraw as counsel of record for___________________.

The motion will be made on the following grounds: (describe grounds).

The motion will be based on this notice of motion, the declaration of____________, and the memorandum of points and authorities attached hereto and on such other evidence, oral and documentary as may be presented at the hearing on this motion.

DATED:____________________, 19____.

____
Attorney

*****

An attorney may not withdraw, absent a client's consent, without order of the Court. Courts have wide discretion in determining whether an attorney should be allowed to withdraw. Hodcarriers vs. Miller 243 C.A. 2nd 391.

A client's failure to cooperate or a lack of confidence in his attorney may be grounds for withdrawal. Heple vs. Kluge 104 C.A. 2nd 461.

See the case of People vs. Prince 268 C.A. 2nd 398, failure to pay attorney's fees as a basis for allowing a withdrawal as an attorney.

An attorney seeking to withdraw must exercise care in not disclosing confidential communications between himself and his client in his Declaration in support of his motion to withdraw. Where there is gross lack of confidence by the client, the rules of professional conduct indicate that the lack of confidence constitutes a waiver of privilege.

CAPTION) Case No.____________
)
) COMPLAINT FOR COMPENSATION FOR LEGAL
__________________) SERVICES

Plaintiff complains and for cause of action alleges:

1. That at all times herein mentioned, plaintiff was and now is an attorney at law duly admitted to practice in all of the courts of the State of California.

2. On or about _______, 19___, plaintiff and defendant entered into a written retainer agreement wherein and whereby it was agreed that plaintiff would perform the following legal services, (set forth description of services) and that defendant agreed to pay for such services the sum of $_______ and to reimburse plaintiff for all costs and expenses including filing fees, deposition fees, investigator's fees and travel expenses.

3. Plaintiff has fully performed all services and conditions required by the agreement to be performed on his part.

4. Plaintiff has incurred the following costs and expenses in connection with the performance of the above mentioned legal services, (describe expenses and cost for each expense).

5. Plaintiff has demanded defendant pay the attorney's fees and has also demanded that defendant reimburse plaintiff for the above mentioned costs. Neither sum has been paid and the sum of $_____remains due, owing and unpaid with respect to attorney's fees and the sum of $_________ remains due, owing and unpaid with respect to costs.

ALTERNATE ALLEGATION FOR REASONABLE VALUE OF SERVICES

6. On or about _________, 19___, plaintiff and defendant entered into an oral (or written) agreement wherein and whereby plaintiff undertook to represent defendant in the following case (set forth the name and nature of the case) and defendant agreed to pay plaintiff the reasonable value of the services.

7. Plaintiff has fully performed all acts and services and conditions with respect to the above mentioned case by expending the following time and performing the following services, (describe fully).

8. The reasonable value of the above mentioned services is $_______________.

ALTERNATE ALLEGATION INVOLVING CONTINGENT FEE

9. On________, 19______, plaintiff and defendant entered into a written contract wherein it was agreed that plaintiff would represent defendant in connection with personal injuries sustained by defendant in the following described case, (set forth the name of the case). Plaintiff was to receive as compensation for his services an amount equal to 40% of any judgment or settlement obtained for defendant.

10. Plaintiff has performed all acts and services required by such agreement and settled the case for the amount of $_________________________40% of which is $_________.

ALTERNATE ALLEGATION IN CONTINGENT FEE CASE WHERE DISCHARGED BY CLIENT.

11. On or about _________, 19____, defendant discharged plaintiff and retained instead_______________as his attorney to represent him in connection with said case. That at no time did plaintiff perform or fail to perform any act which justified defendant discharging plaintiff.

WHEREFORE, plaintiff prays for judgment as follows:

1. For judgment in the amount of $____________, pursuant to the contract.

2. (If a reasonable value allegation) For judgment in the amount of $__________, for the reasonable value of services performed.

3. For costs of suit and such other relief as the court deems just.

____
Attorney for Plaintiff

****

An attorney is entitled to recover the reasonable value of his services. Tracton vs. Youngblood 69 Cal 2nd 17.

Even if the attorney is discharged with cause, he is entitled to recover the reasonable value of his services rendered to the time of discharge, Fracasse vs. Brent 6 Cal 3rd 784.

An attorney may recover for services rendered to the time of discharge unless the attorney violates professional rules of conduct. Hicks vs. Clayton 67 C.A. 3rd 251.

For a case citing the facts to be considered in determining the reasonable value of services see Clejan vs. Reisman 5 C. A. 3rd 224.

An attorney may also sue to enforce a lien for compensation. A lien to be valid must test either by virtue of statute or agreement. Echlein v. Superior Court 13 Cal 2nd 368.

An attorney in most cases may also add a cause of action for an account stated. Fletcher vs. Strauss 16 C. A. 2nd 735.

CAPTION)
)
)
)
______________________________)

Case No.__________________

DEMAND FOR BILL OF PARTICULARS

TO PLAINTIFF AND TO HIS ATTORNEY:

Demand is hereby made pursuant to C.C.P. §454, that you furnish to defendant, a bill of particulars setting forth the following information to be delivered to defendant within 10 days hereafter:

1. Items of account.

2. Material furnished.

3. Costs of material.

4. Costs of labor expended.

5. Costs of services and labor performed.

6. Other items. (Request only those items that are appropriate to the particular action.)

DATED:______________, 19_____

____
Attorney for Defendant

****

A plaintiff, on demand, must deliver to the adverse party within 10 days after the demand a bill of particulars, or be precluded from giving evidence thereof. The court may order a further account if the one delivered is too general. If the pleading is verified, the account must be verified. C.C.P. §454.

CAPTION	)	Case No._______________
	)	
	)	BILL OF PARTICULARS
	)	
______________________________	)	

TO THE DEFENDANT, AND TO_________________, HIS ATTORNEY:

NOTICE IS HEREBY GIVEN that the following is a bill of particulars in response to defendant's demand: (Set forth items.)

DATED:____________, 19____

____
Attorney for Plaintiff

****

If the pleading is verified, the account must be verified. C.C.P. §454.

CAPTION)   Case No.______________
)
)   NOTICE OF MOTION FOR AN ORDER
)   REQUIRING FURTHER BILL OF
______________________________)   PARTICULARS

Date:__________
Time:__________
Department:____

TO PLAINTIFF AND TO____________, HIS ATTORNEY:

YOU, AND EACH OF YOU, WILL PLEASE TAKE NOTICE that on__________, 19______, at the hour of___a.m., or as soon thereafter as counsel may be heard in Department___ of the above-entitled court, defendant will move the court for an order requiring plaintiff to furnish to defendant a further bill of particulars, setting forth the following specific information. (Describe)

The motion is made on the ground that the bill of particulars heretofore furnished does not contain sufficient information.

The motion will be based upon this notice of motion, points and authorities and declarations attached hereto, records and papers on file herein and such other evidence, oral and documentary, as may be presented at the hearing.

DATED:______________, 19____.

____
Attorney for Plaintiff

****

A motion may be made for a further bill of particulars if the one is submitted is too general. C.C.P. §454.

The motion must be accompanied by points and authorities and a declaration setting forth why it is contended that the original bill of particulars is inadequate.

CAPTION) Case No.______________
)
) NOTICE OF MOTION TO EXCLUDE EVIDENCE
)
____________________________)

Date:____________
Time:____________
Department:_____

TO THE PLAINTIFF, AND TO HIS ATTORNEY_________________:

YOU, AND EACH OF YOU, WILL PLEASE TAKE NOTICE that on__________, 19______, at the hour of ______a.m., or as soon thereafter as the matter may be heard, in Department____of the above-entitled court, defendant will move the court for an order excluding at the trial, any evidence concerning ______________alleged in the complaint.

The motion will be made on the grounds that plaintiff has failed to delivered to defendant a bill of particulars setting forth the items requested upon which plaintiff's cause of action is based.

The motion will be based upon this notice of motion, the declaration and points and authorities attached hereto, the records and papers on file herein and such other evidence, oral and documentary as may be presented at the hearing.

DATED:______________, 19____.

____
Attorney for Defendant

****

A motion for exclusion of evidence for failure to file a bill of particulars must be made before trial, otherwise a motion to exclude at trial would be denied. Burton vs. Santa Barbara National Bank, 247 C.A. 2d, 427; Golgua vs. Hagen, 107 C.A. 2d, 313.

CAPTION)   Case No.___________
)
)   COMPLAINT FOR RECOVERY OF BROKER'S
)   COMMISSION
_____________________)

Plaintiff alleges:

1. At all times herein mentioned, plaintiff was and still is a real estate broker duly licensed by the State of California.

2. On or about _______, 19____, plaintiff was employed by defendant by an agreement in writing to procure a purchaser for the following real property owned by defendant. (Set forth description of property.) A copy of the listing agreement is attached hereto as Exhibit "A" and made a part hereof.

3. In consideration thereof, defendant promised, by the listing agreement, to pay plaintiff for his services in securing a purchaser for the property and to pay a commission therefor, in the amount of _____% of the selling price.

4. On or about______, 19____, plaintiff procured___________ to purchase the property for the price and terms as set forth in the listing agreement. Said purchaser was ready, willing and able to purchase the property under all the terms and conditions contained in the listing agreement.

5. Defendant refused, and ever since has continued to refuse to sell the property to the purchaser obtained by plaintiff.

6. Defendant has not paid plaintiff the sum agreed on or any part thereof, for his services and there is now due, owing and unpaid, to the plaintiff, the sum of $____________.

WHEREFORE, plaintiff prays judgment against defendant as follows:

1. For the sum of $___________.

2. For interest on this sum at _________% per annum from _____________, 19____.

3. For costs of suit herein and for such other relief as the court deems just.

DATED: ___________________, 19______.

____
Attorney for Plaintiff

****

A real estate broker has earned his commission when he has brought a ready, willing and able purchaser who will take the property on the terms offered by seller. Seck vs. Foulks, 25 C.A. 3d, 56.

An action for commissions will also lie where a seller accepts terms other than those set forth in the listing agreement and later fails to pay the commission. Webber vs. Ross, 159 C.A. 2d, 77.

If after a listing has expired, the seller encourages the broker to consummate a sale, the seller is estopped from relying on the statute of frauds. Love vs. Gulyas, 87 C.A. 2d, 608.

A sale of real property at the asking price in the listing agreement is not necessary for a broker to receive his commission unless there is a special agreement to that effect. Towle vs. Lewis, 274 C.A. 2d, 376.

On a case where recovery was allowed, absent a written agreement, on a theory of interference with economic advantageous relationships, see Buckaloo vs. Johnson, 14 Cal 3d, 815.

CAPTION) Case No.____________
)
) COMPLAINT AGAINST BROKER
) TO RESCIND SALE OR FOR
____________________) RECOVERY OF PROFITS

Plaintiff alleges:

1. On or about _______, 19___, plaintiff was the owner of that certain parcel of real property described as follows: (Set forth legal description and street address description.)

2. On or about ________, 19_____, plaintiff listed said property with defendant, a real estate broker licensed under the laws of the State of California. The property was listed exclusively for a period of 30 days at a price of $_____________.

3. On or about ________, 19____, defendant presented plaintiff with an offer to purchase said property for the price of $____________ which offer was less than the listing price by the amount of $10,000.00. Unknown to plaintiff at the time was the fact that the purchaser was defendant_______________, the brother-in-law of defendant broker.

4. In an effort to induce plaintiff to accept the offer of defendant________________, defendant broker falsely represented to plaintiff that by reason of the age and depreciation of the property, the market value was rapidly declining and was worth no more than that offered by defendant______________. Defendant broker further represented that he had made a survey of properties in the area and falsely represented that there were three sales of similar property for an amount less than the amount offered by defendant_______________.

5. Defendant was inexperienced in real estate transactions and did not know real estate values and in fact, relied upon information supplied to him by defendant broker.

6. As a result of his reliance in defendant broker, plaintiff agreed to sell the property to defendant______________.

7. On or about ________, 19____, after plaintiff conveyed the property to defendant__________________, defendant____________ sold the property to_________________ at a price of $___________________ which was $10,000.00 more than the listing price and $20,000.00 more than the price which plaintiff received from defendant ____________________.

8. Both defendants knew at the time that the purpose of the sale to defendant ______________________ was to acquire the property to enable defendant broker and________________ to realize a $20,000.00 profit, in addition to the broker's commission which defendant broker received from plaintiff.

9. In doing the foregoing acts, defendants, and each of them, acted maliciously, fraudently and with the intent to extract from plaintiff the profits, which he plaintiff, should have enjoyed.

WHEREFORE, plaintiff prays judgment:

1. For rescission, if rescission can be had.

2. For general damages in the sum of $20,000.00 in loss of profits and $__________ for commission paid the broker.

3. For punitive damages in the sum of $_____________.

4. For costs of suit herein and such other relief as the court deems just.

DATED:____________________, 19_____

____
Attorney for Plaintiff

****

A plaintiff in such an action is entitled to the profit he would have realized. Rodes vs. Shannon, 222 C.A. 2d, 721. Bate vs. Marsteller, 232 C.A. 2d, 605.

The sale may be set aside if possible, or the plaintiff may have damages. Wells Fargo vs. Dowd, 139 C.A. 2d, 651.

CAPTION	)	Case No. _________________
	)	
	)	COMPLAINT FOR DAMAGES
	)	(CLASS ACTION)
____________________	)	

1. The plaintiffs named herein are individuals who have purchased the following described goods for personal use. (Describe goods.)

2. Plaintiffs herein are members of a class of individuals who are similarly situated, in that each of such individuals also purchased the above-described goods for their personal use from the defendants named herein.

3. The facts by which the class may be ascertained are as follows: (Set forth facts from which class may be ascertained.) The exact names and addresses of each of the members of the class are unknown to plaintiffs, but are known to defendant and can be ascertained from defendant's records.

4. The class consists of approximately _________individuals. It is impracticable to bring the members of the class in their entirety before the court for the following reasons: (Specify reasons.) Questions of law and fact, common to the class, are as follows: (Set forth reasons.) The claims of plaintiffs herein are typical of the claims of the class in that each member of the class purchased the above-mentioned items and suffered the following damage. (Set forth damage.) The plaintiffs will fairly and adequately protect the interests of the class.

5. On or about______, 19____, plaintiffs purchased the above-mentioned goods. The establishment of the price for the above-mentioned goods was the result of the following unlawful methods of defendants: (Describe in detail.)

6. On _________, 19____, more than 30 days prior to the commencement of this action, plaintiff notified defendant, in writing, of defendant's violations of C.C. §1770, to wit: (Describe violations) and requested that defendant rectify the violation by doing the following: (Describe) The notice was sent by certified mail, return receipt requested to the place where the transaction occurred at the following address: (Set forth address.) A copy of the notice is attached hereto marked Exhibit "A" and made a part hereof. A copy of the return receipt is attached hereto, marked Exhibit "B" and made a part hereof.

7. Defendants have failed, and continue to fail and refuse to rectify the violation.

8. The violations above-mentioned were committed on all the members of the class herein represented by plaintiffs in the following method. (Describe)

9. By reason of the above-mentioned violations, plaintiffs, and each of the member of the class represented by plaintiffs, have been damaged in the following sums: (Describe the sums and set forth the formula used for ascertaining the damages. Each member of the class has been damaged in the sum of $______________.

10. Plaintiffs have incurred and during the pendency of this action, will incur expenses for attorney's fees and costs. Said attorney's fees and costs are necessary to enable plaintiffs to prosecute this action and the expenditures will result in a benefit to each of the members of the class. $______________is a reasonable amount for attorney's fees herein.

WHEREFORE, plaintiffs pray judgment as follows:

1. For damages in the sum of $________________.

2. For payment of attorney's fees out of the monies recovered.

3. For costs of suit.

4. For such other relief as the court deems just.

DATED:____________________, 19____.

____
Attorney for Plaintiff

****

This procedure is authorized by the Consumer's Legal Remedies Act, Civil Code §'s 1750 through 1784.

The list of proscribed practices which will give rise to a cause of action under the act, are fact in Civil Code §'s 1770.

As a condition to filing suit, plaintiffs must, at least 30 days prior to the commencement of the action, give notice in a manner as required by Civil Code § 1782.

See <u>Outboard Marine vs. Superior Court</u>, 52 C.A. 3d, 30.

The action may be brought for actual damages, injunctive relief and punitive damages. Total award may not be less than $300.00. Civil Code § 1780.

CAPTION	)	Case No.______________
	)	
	)	NOTICE OF PENDENCY OF CLASS ACTION
	)	
______________________	)	

NOTICE IS HEREBY GIVEN that:

1. The plaintiffs named below have brought an action in this court against the following defendants: (Describe defendants' names.)

2. The plaintiffs described below are as follows: (Describe identity of plaintiffs.) Plaintiffs seek the following relief: (Describe relief.)

3. (Set forth the allegations.)

4. Further information relative to this action may be obtained by contacting the attorneys for the parties whose names and addresses are as follows: (Set forth names and addresses of attorneys for plaintiffs and defendants.)

5. The plaintiffs named herein allege that this action is brought on behalf of the following described class. (Describe class.)

6. If you wish to be excluded as a member of this class, you may be excluded by mailing a letter, on or before _______, 19____, requesting exclusion to the following: (Name, title and address of clerk of the court.)

7. The judgment rendered, whether favorable or not, will include all members who do not request exclusion.

8. If you elect to become a member of the class, you may be subjected to a cross complaint or som other affirmative action by defendants.

9. You are further notified that although this action is pending, defendants are not prevented in any way from exercising all remedies available by contract and law.

10. If you fail to request exclusion, the action will be maintained on your behalf by the above-mentioned attorney. You may, however, have your interests represented by any attorney of your choice.

11. It is understood that the court in this action does not at present, express any opinion relative to the merits of the case.

DATED:______________, 19____.

____
Judge

CAPTION) Case No.____________

NOTICE OF MOTION FOR ORDER NOTIFYING MEMBERS OF THE CLASS

Date:____________
Time:____________
Department:________

TO EACH PARTY AND TO THE ATTORNEY OF RECORD FOR EACH PARTY:

YOU, AND EACH OF YOU, WILL PLEASE TAKE NOTICE that on ____________, 19____, at ______a.m., or as soon thereafter as the matter may be heard in Department______of the above entitled court, ____________________will move the court for an order requiring ____________________to notify each member of the class of the pendency of the within action.

The motion will be based upon this notice, the declaration and points and authorities attached hereto, the papers and records on file herein and such other evidence, oral and documentary, as may be presented at the hearing on the motion.

DATED:____________________, 19________.

____
Attorney for

****

If the action is permitted as a class action, the court may direct either party to notify each member of the class. Civil Code § 1781(d).

CAPTION)
)
) NOTICE OF MOTION FOR ORDER THAT CLASS
) ACTION IS PROPER
____________________)

Case No.______________

Date:______________
Time:______________
Department:_________

TO EACH PARTY AND TO THE ATTORNEY OF RECORD FOR EACH PARTY:

YOU, AND EACH OF YOU, WILL PLEASE TAKE NOTICE that on __________, 19____, at _______a.m., or as soon thereafter as the matter may be heard in Department____ of the above entitled court, ______________will move for an order that a class action is proper.

The motion will be made on the grounds that it is impracticable to bring all of the members of the class before the court. The questions of law and fact common to the class are substantially similar and predominate over the questions affecting the individual members, the claims and defenses of the representative plaintiff, are typical of the claims and defenses of the class and the representative plaintiff will fairly and adequately protect the interests of the class.

The motion will be based upon this notice, the declaration and points and authorities attached hereto, the papers and records on file herein and such other evidence, oral and documentary to be presented at the hearing on this motion.

DATED:________________, 19_____.

____
Attorney for Plaintiff

****

If notice of the time and place of the hearing is served on the other parties at least 10 days prior thereto, the court shall hold a hearing on motion of any party to the action, to determine if a class action is proper. The court may also determine whether notice to each member of the class is necessary or whether the action is with or without merit. Civil Code §1781(c).

CAPTION)
)
)
)
__________________________)

Case No.________________

COMPLAINT-OPEN BOOK ACCOUNT

Plaintiff complains:

1. That at all times herein mentioned, defendant was and now is, a resident of the City of___________, State of California.

2. Within two years last past, in the City of _________________, California, defendant became indebted to plaintiff on an open book account for money due in the sum of $_______ for goods, wares and merchandise sold and delivered by plaintiff to defendant at the special request of defendant, and for which defendant agreed to pay the above amount.

3. No part of the above sum has been paid except $_______________, although demand has been made therefor, and there is now due, owing and unpaid the amount of $__________, with interest thereon at the rate of __________% per annum from ___________________, 19____.

WHEREFORE, plaintiff prays:

1. For judgment in the amount of $_____________, with interest thereon at the rate of ________% per annum from _________________, 19_____.

2. For costs of suit herein incurred and such other relief as the court deems just.

____
Attorney for Plaintiff

CAPTION	)	Case No.
	)	
	)	COMPLAINT FOR MONEY
	)	
	)	
______________________	)	

Plaintiff alleges:

1. At all times mentioned herein, defendant was and now is a resident of the County of_________, State of California.

2. Wihtin two years last past, defendant became indebted to plaintiff in the sum of $___________for money had and received by plaintiff for the use and the benefit of plaintiff.

3. No part of said sum has been paid except for $______________, although demand has been made and there is now due, owing and unpaid the sum of $__________, with interest at the rate of ____________% per annum from ______, 19___.

WHEREFORE, plaintiff prays judgment against defendant:

1. For the balance of $_________.

2. For interest at the rate of____________% per annum from__________, 19____.

3. For costs of suit and such other relief as the court deems just.

____
Attorney for Plaintiff

CAPTION) Case No.______
)
) COMPLAINT FOR MONEY LENT
)
____________________________)

Plaintiff complains:

1. That at all times herein mentioned the defendant was, and now is, a resident of the County of__________, State of California.

2. Within two years last past in__________, California, defendant became indebted to plaintiff in the sum of $____________for money lent by plaintiff to defendant, at the request of defendant.

3. No part of the above sum has been paid except for $________________, although demand has been made thereof. There is a balance due, owing and unpaid to plaintiff in the sum of $_______________, together with interest thereon at the rate of _____________% per annum from ________, 19___.

WHEREFORE, plaintiff prays:

1. For judgment in the amount of $_____________ with interest at the rate of _________% per annum from ________, 19___.

2. For costs of suit herein and such other relief as the court deems just.

____
Attorney for Plaintiff

CAPTION) Case No._______
)
) COMPLAINT FOR MONEY PAID
)
____________________________)

Plaintiff complains:

1. At all times herein mentioned, the defendant was and now is, a resident of the County of ___________, State of California.

2. Within two years last past, in the City of_______, California, defendant became indebted to plaintiff in the sum of $___________ for money paid and expended on behalf of defendant at the instance and request of defendant.

3. No part of the above sum has been paid except $______________, although demand has been made thereof, there is left due, owing and unpaid to plaintiff the sum of $_____________, together with interest thereon at the rate of _________% per annum from _________, 19____.

WHEREFORE, plaintiff prays:

1. For judgment in the amount of $___________, together with interest thereon at the rate of __________% per annum from __________, 19____.

2. For costs of suit herein and such other relief as the court deems just.

____
Attorney for Plaintiff

CAPTION)
)
)
)
______________________)

Case No.____________

COMPLAINT FOR WORK, LABOR AND SERVICES

Plaintiff complains:

1. That at all times herein mentioned, the defendant was and now is, a resident of the County of ________, State of California.

2. Within two years last past, in the City of________, California, defendant became indebted to plaintiff in the amount of $____________for work, labor and services rendered by plaintiff to defendant at the instance and request of defendant. The above-mentioned sum was the amount agreed to be paid by defendant to plaintiff.

3. No part of the said sum has been paid except $_____________and there is now due, owing and unpaid the sum of $____________,together with interest thereon at the rate of $____________% per annum from ________, 19____.

WHEREFORE, plaintiff prays:

1. For judgment in the sum of $__________, plus interest thereon at the rate of________% per annum from __________, 19___.

2. For costs of suit herein and such other relief as the court deems just.

____
Attorney for Plaintiff

CAPTION)
)
)
)
______________________)

Case No.____________

COMPLAINT FOR MONEY
(Quantum Meruit)

Plaintiff complains:

1. That at all times herein mentioned the defendant was and now is, a resident of the County of________, State of California.

2. Within two years last past in the City of __________, California, at the special instance and request of defendant, plaintiff performed work, labor and services on behalf and to defendant, for which defendant promised to pay plaintiff the reasonable value of the services.

3. The reasonable value of the services were and are $______________.

4. No part of the above sum has been paid except $___________, and there is now due, owing and unpaid to plaintiff the sum of $_______________.

WHEREFORE, plaintiff prays judgment as follows:

1. For the principal sum of $___________.

2. For costs of suit herein incurred and such other relief as the court deems just.

____
Attorney for Plaintiff

CAPTION	)	Case No.________________
	)	
	)	COMPLAINT FOR WORK, LABOR AND MATERIALS
	)	
______________________________	)	

Plaintiff complains:

1. That within two years last past, in the City of ________________, California, defendant became indebted to plaintiff for work done, materials furnished to defendant by plaintiff at the special request of defendant in the sum of $______________, which defendant agreed to pay to plaintiff.

2. No part of the above sum has been paid except $___________________although demand has been made therefor, and there is now due, owing and unpaid the sum of $____________, with interest thereon at the rate of ___________% per annum from _________, 19____.

WHEREFORE, plaintiff prays:

1. For the principal sum of $__________.

2. For interest at the rate of ________% per annum from ___________, 19____.

3. For costs of suit herein and such other relief as the court deems just.

____
Attorney for Plaintiff

CAPTION	)	Case No.________________
	)	
	)	COMPLAINT FOR GOODS SOLD AND
	)	DELIVERED
______________________________	)	

Plaintiff complains:

1. That at all times herein mentioned, defendant was and now is a resident of the City of________________, State of California.

2. Within two years last past, defendant became indebted to plaintiff in the agreed amount of $___________for goods sold and delivered to defendant by plaintiff in the above price which defendant then and there agreed to pay.

3. No part of the above sum has been paid except $__________, although demand has been made therefor, and there is now due, owing and unpaid from defendant, the sum of $____________, together with interest thereon at the rate of _________% per annum from _________, 19____.

WHEREFORE, plaintiff prays:

1. For judgment in the amount of $___________.

2. For interest at the rate of__________% per annum from________________, 19___.

3. For costs of suit herein and such other relief as the court deems just.

____
Attorney for Plaintiff

CAPTION) Case No.__________

COMPLAINT FOR GOODS SOLD AND DELIVERED (Quantum Valebat)

Plaintiff complains:

1. That at all times herein mentioned, defendant was and now is a resident of the City of_________, State of California.

2. Within two years last past, in the City of_________, California, plaintiff sold and delivered to defendant at the request of defendant, certain goods, the reasonable value of which defendant agreed to pay therefor.

3. The reasonable value of the goods, at the time of delivery was $_______________.

4. No part of the above sum has been paid except $___________________ although demand has been made therefor, and there is now due, owing and unpaid the amount of $_______________.

WHEREFORE, plaintiff prays:

1. For judgment in the amount of $____________.

2. For costs of suit herein incurred and such other relief as the court deems just.

____
Attorney for Plaintiff

CAPTION) Case No.__________

COMPLAINT-ACCOUNT STATED

Plaintiff complains:

1. At all times herein mentioned, defendant was, and now is, a resident of the County of_________, State of California.

2. Within two years last past, an account was stated in writing by and between plaintiff and defendant, wherein and whereby it was agreed that defendant was indebted to plaintiff in the sum of $____________.

3. No part of the above sum has been paid except $______________, although demand has been made thereof and there is now due, owing and unpaid, the sum of $____________, with interest thereon at the rate of _____________% per annum from____________, 19______.

WHEREFORE plaintiff prays:

1. For judgment in the amount of $___________plus interest thereon at the rate of _______________% per annum from ________________, 19____.

2. For costs of suit herein incurred and such other relief as the court deems just.

____
Attorney for Plaintiff

CAPTION) Case No.__________
)
) COMPLAINT FOR MONEY
) (PROMISSORY NOTE)
__________________________)

Plaintiff alleges:

1. On or about____, 19____, at ___________, California, defendant, for valuable consideration, paid, executed and delivered to plaintiff his promissory note, dated___________, 19____, in the amount of $________________, payable as follows, (describe payments) with interest at the rate of___% per annum until paid. A copy of the note is attached hereto, marked Exhibit "A" and made a part hereof.

2. Defendant has failed to make the payment on the note above-described and he is now in default. There is now due, owing and unpaid from defendant, to plaintiff, the sum of $_______________.

3. By the terms of the note, it is provided that in the event legal action is taken to enforce collection, the maker promises to pay such sum as the court may fix as reasonable attorney's fees. $_________________is a reasonable attorney's fee for the prosecution of this action.

WHEREFORE, plaintiff prays:

1. For judgment in the amount of $____________.

2. For interest on the principal sum at the rate of _______% per annum from ____________, 19____.

3. For reasonable attorney's fees in the sum of $__________.

4. For costs of suit herein incurred and for such other and further relief as the court deems just and proper.

DATED:_________________, 19____.

____
Attorney for Plaintiff

CAPTION) Case No.____________
)
) ANSWER TO COMPLAINT
)
______________________)

COMES NOW defendant and in answer to the complaint on file herein admits, denies and alleges as follows:

1. Defendant denies generally and specifically each and every allegation contained in paragraphs 1, 2, and 3 of plaintiff's complaint.

2. Defendant admits the allegations contained in paragraph 4 of plaintiff's complaint.

3. Defendant has no information or belief sufficient to answer the allegations of paragraphs 5 and 6 of plaintiff's complaint and for that reason, denies each and every allegation contained therein, and the whole thereof.

4. Defendant denies that he is indebted to plaintiff in the sum of $__________, or in any sum whatsoever.

For an affirmative defense, defendant alleges as follows:

5. At all times relevant, on or before the date of the events sued on herein, plaintiff knew the hazards involved and had full knowledge of the conditions existing and appreciated the danger thereof. Plaintiff voluntarily assumed the risks and his assumption thereon was the sole proximate cause of his injuries and damges, if any.

WHEREFORE, defendant prays:

1. That plaintiff take nothing by his complaint.

2. That defendant be awarded his costs of suit and such other relief as the court deems just.

DATED:________________, 19____

____
Attorney for Defendant

CAPTION) Case No._________
)
) ANSWER TO COMPLAINT
)
______________________)

COMES NOW the defendant______________and in answer to the complaint for breach of contract on file herein, admits, denies, and alleges as follows:

1. Defendant denies generally and specifically each and every allegation contained in plaintiff's complaint and the whole thereof. Defendant further denies that plaintiff was damaged in the sum of $____________or in any sum whatsoever.

FIRST AFFIRMATIVE DEFENSE

2. On or about______, 19____, at the time the contract was allegedly entered into, defendant was a minor at the age of 16 years and at no time thereafter was the contract affirmed.

SECOND AFFIRMATIVE DEFENSE

3. On or about_______, 19____, in the Superior Court of _____________, County, the case of In Re_______________, case no._________________, defendant was adjudicated and incompetent by order of that court and is still presently incompetent.

THIRD AFFIRMATIVE DEFENSE

4. Defendant further alleges that payment on the above claim has been paid on ____________, 19____. A copy of the receipt executed by plaintiff is attached hereto, marked Exhibit "A" and incorporated herein.

FOURTH AFFIRMATIVE DEFENSE

5. On or about _______, 19____, defendant tendered to plaintiff the sum of $____________in full satisfaction of the claim arising out of the contract sued on herein. Plaintiff refused and continues to refuse to accept the sum tendered. On or about ___________, 19___, defendant deposited, in the name of plaintiff, the sum of $___________________in____________bank in the City of____________California and gave notice thereof to plaintiff of the deposit.

FIFTH AFFIRMATIVE DEFENSE

6. Defendant has been prevented from performing the following required acts, (specify) for the reason that plaintiff has prevented performance in the following manner. (Describe) At all times herein mentioned, defendant was and is presently ready, willing and able to perform the aforementioned condition.

SIXTH AFFIRMATIVE DEFENSE

7. On or about _______, 19____, a date subsequent to the execution of the contract, marked plaintiff's Exhibit "A", plaintiff and defendant made and entered into a new contract which by its terms extinguishes Exhibit "A".

SEVENTH AFFIRMATIVE DEFENSE

8. On or about_________, 19___, the plaintiff, with the intent to induce defendant to enter into the contract set for in plaintiff's Exhibit "A", made the following representations to defendant. (Describe) Said representations were untrue and were known to plaintiff to be untrue at the time they were made. Defendant relied on the statements as being true and had he known the untruth of the statements would not have entered into the contract hereinabove described.

9. In truth and in fact, the statements were false for the following reasons. On learning of the falsity, defendant notified plaintiff of defendant's intent to rescind and offered to restore to plaintiff the following benefits theretofor received. (Describe)

EIGHTH AFFIRMATIVE DEFENSE

10. At the time of entering into the contract, defendant was under amistake of fact in that, (describe). Defendant's mistake was due to the following, (describe) and was not caused by his defect.

Defendant signed the contract within with the above facts in mind when the true facts were as follows:(describe). Had defendant known the true facts he would not have signed the contract.

NINTH AFFIRMATIVE DEFENSE

11. Defendant entered into the contract under a misapprehension of law in that, (describe). Plaintiff was aware that defendant was under the misapprehension at the time of the contracting and did not inform defendant of the mistake, or otherwise rectify it. Defendant would not have entered into the contract had the true state of law been known to him.

TENTH AFFIRMATIVE DEFENSE

12. Defendant herein admits he failed to perform the obligation described in the complaint, but alleges that such failure was justified for the reason that plaintiff failed to perform as follows: (describe). Plaintiff's performance was a condition precedent to the performance of defendant's obligation.

WHEREFORE, defendant prays:

1. That plaintiff take nothing by his complaint.

2. That defendant be awarded costs of suit and such other relief as the court deems just.

____
Attorney for Defendant

FREQUENTLY USED REQUIRED ALLEGATIONS IN COMPLAINTS AND ANSWERS

RESIDENCE:

At all times mentioned, defendant was and now is a resident of the City of Los Angeles, County of Los Angeles, State of California.

FICTITIOUSLY NAMED DEFENDANTS:

The true names or capacities of defendants sued herein as doe 1 through 10, inclusive, are unknown to plaintiff who thereby sues said defendants by such fictitious names. Each of the defendants named herein as doe is negligently responsible in some manner for the events sued upon. Plaintiff will amend this complaint to insert the true names and capacities of the defendants named herein as doe, when said names and capacities have been ascertained.

FICTITIOUS BUSINESS NAME:

At all times herein mentioned, plaintiff___________ was and now is an individual, doing business under the fictitious firm name of_______________, and has filed a statement and published a notice, as required by Business and Professions' Code §17910 through 17917.

ALLEGATION OF CORPORATE STATUS:

At all times herein mentioned, plaintiff was and now is a corporation, organized and existing under the laws of California with its principal place of business at _________ (Describe).

PARTNERSHIP CAPACITY:

At all times herein mentioned, the plaintiff was and now is a partnership, doing business under the partnership name of _________________________, with its principal offices in___________, County, California.

MUNICIPAL CORPORATION:

At all times herein mentioned, defendant____________, was and now is a municipal corporation, organized and existing under and by virtue of the laws of the State of California.

MINOR APPEARING BY GUARDIAN AD LITEM:

Plaintiff___________is a minor of the age of_______, whose date of birth is________. On ________, 19___, _____________ was, by an order duly made and entered by the above entitled court, appointed guardian ad litem of plaintiff _______________.

PERSONAL REPRESENTATIVE OF ESTATE:

On _______, 19____, plaintiff_____________was issued letters testamentary by the _______court of_________. A certified copy of said letters is attached hereto, marked Exhibit "A" and made a part hereof. Plaintiff__________is presently the duly appointed, qualified and acting administrator of the estate of___________, deceased.

CONTRACTOR'S LICENSE:

At all times mentioned herein, plaintiff was and now is, a contractor with a license duly issued by the State of California bearing number____________.

PROFESSIONAL LICENSE:

At all times mentioned herein, plaintiff was and now is, an attorney at law, duly licensed to practice in all the courts of the State of California.

AGENCY:

Plaintiff is informed and believes and thereon alleges that at all times mentioned herein, each of the defendants was the agent and employee of each of the remaining defendants and in doing the things hereinafter alleged, was acting within the scope of said agency.

OWNERSHIP:

At all times herein mentioned, defendant was and now is, the owner of that certain motor vehicle described as follows: (Set forth description and license number.)

REALLEGATION OF PREVIOUS PARAGRAPHS

Plaintiff realleges paragraphs ____ through ______, and incorporates them herein as though fully set forth.

CAPTION) Case No.____________________
)
) OFFER TO COMPROMISE
) (C.C.P. §997)
__________________)

TO PLAINTIFF (OR DEFENDANT) AND TO________________
HIS ATTORNEY:

Defendant_____________offers to allow judgment to be taken against him in the above-entitled cause for the sum of $_________________, plus taxable costs incurred to the date of judgment.

If this offer to compromise is not accepted and notice given by plaintiff within the time provided by C.C.P. §997, defendant expressly denies, and shall deny that this sum, or any other sum is, or shall be due and owing from defendant to plaintiff.

Dated:_____________, 19____.

____
Attorney for Defendant

****

Not less than ten days prior to trial, any party may serve an offer to compromise on the other. If the offer is accepted, the offer, plus proof of acceptance, must be filed with the clerk. C.C.P. §998.

See C.C.P. §1025 on offers of defendant prior to commencement of action.

CAPTION) Case No.
)
) NOTICE OF MOTION TO TAX COSTS
______________________)

Date: ______________
Time: ______________
Department: ______________

TO THE ____________________ AND TO HIS ATTORNEY ____________________.

PLEASE TAKE NOTICE that on __________, 19_____, at the hour of 9:00 A.M. in Department _________ of the above-entitled court, ____________________ will move the Court for an order taxing the costs of this action to strike out of the memorandum of costs and disbursements previously filed herein the following items: (Set forth items and reasons for striking them out).

The motion will be made on the ground that the above mentioned items are not properly chargeable costs.

The motion will be based upon the provisions of C.C.P., §1033 this notice of motion, points and authorities and declarations attached hereto, the papers and records on file in this action and such other evidence, oral and documentary as may be presented at the hearing.

DATED: ____________________ 19_____.

____
Attorney for

****

This motion must be filed and served within ten days after service of the Memorandum of Costs. C.C.P., §1033.

A motion may also be made striking a Memorandum of Costs if the memorandum is filed more than ten days after entry of judgment. C.C.P., §1033.

CAPTION) Case No.______________
)
) COMPLAINT NEGLIGENT BUILDING
) CONSTRUCTION
____________________)

Plaintiff alleges:

1. That at all times herein mentioned, plaintiff was and now is the owner of that certain real property described as follows: (Set forth description.)

2. On or about ________, 19___, plaintiff and defendant entered into a written contract wherein defendant agreed to construct for plaintiff the above-mentioned property, a 3,000 sq. ft. office building, for which plaintiff was to pay the defendant the total sum of $____________. A copy of the construction contract is attached hereto, marked Exhibit "A" and made a part hereof. Defendant represented to plaintiff that he, the defendant would construct the building in a workmanlike manner.

3. Defendant commenced the construction project and completed on ___________, 19____.

4. Defendant constructed the project in such a negligent manner, the following defects appeared: (Describe defects.)

5. Plaintiff has demanded that defendant correct the defects, but defendant has failed and refused, and continues to fail and refuse to make the corrections.

6. By reason of the defective construction and defendant's refusal to correct the defects, plaintiff has been damaged by the failure of defendant to perform and complete the contract in accordance with the terms and with the plans and specifications in the sum of $______________, the amount required to pay another contractor to correct defendant's work.

FOR A SECOND CAUSE OF ACTION, PLAINTIFF ALLEGES:

7. Plaintiff incorporates each and every allegation of the first cause of action, realleges them as though set out in full.

8. Defendant carelessly and negligently constructed the building and as a proximate cause of defendant's negligence, plaintiff was obliged to expend additional sums to correct the work in the amount of $_______________.

9. The defects were of such a nature that the structure was uninhabitable and as a further proximate result of defendant's negligence, plaintiff was obliged to seek another location to operate his business at the additional expense of $____________.

WHEREFORE, plaintiff prays:

1. For damages in the sum of $______________.

2. For reimbursement for expenses in connection with occupying another office in the amount of $_____________.

3. For costs of suit herein and for such other relief as the court deems just.

DATED:_____________________, 19_____.

____
Attorney for Plaintiff

****

A failure to construct a building in a workmanlike manner is both a breach of contract and a tort. Zurich vs. Kings, 255 C.A. 2d, 919.

CAPTION)
)
)
)
________________________)

Case No.____________

COMPLAINT FOR NEGLIGENT SUPERVISION OF CONSTRUCTION BY ARCHITECT

Plaintiff complains:

1. At all times herein mentioned, defendant was and now is an architect duly licensed to practice as such in the State of California.

2. At all times herein mentioned, plaintiff was and now is the owner of the following described property: (Set forth description.)

3. On or about __________, 19___, plaintiff retained defendant to draft plans and specifications for the following described building, (Set forth description) to be constructed upon plaintiff's property. Defendant, in addition, contracted to superintend and supervise the construction of the above-described building.

4. Defendant drafted the plans and specifications and commenced to supervise the construction as it progressed.

5. Defendant so carelessly and negligently superintended and supervised the construction work that the work was not done in a good and workmanlike manner, to the extent that the building was declared unsafe by the Department of Building and Safety and plaintiff was refused a certificate of occupancy.

6. As a proximate result of the negligence of defendant, the plaintiff was obliged to make extensive repairs and modifications and was further obliged to tear down a portion of the building in order to make the repairs and modifications, all to plaintiff's damage in the sum of $_______________.

WHEREFORE, plaintiff prays:

1. For damages in the sum of $______________for the necessary repairs and modifications.

2. For costs of suit herein and such other relief as the court deems just.

DATED:____________________, 19___.

____
Attorney for Plaintiff

CAPTION) Case No.__________________
)
) COMPLAINT TO IMPOSE CONSTRUCTIVE
) TRUST
____________________)

Plaintiff complains:

1. At all times herein mentioned, defendant was and now is a resident of_______________.

2. At all times herein mentioned, a confidential and fiduciary relationship existed between plaintiff and defendant that (describe).

3. At all times herein mentioned, plaintiff was and still is the owner of that certain property situated in the City of_____________, County of_______________the legal description of which is (describe).

4. On or about__________, 19____, defendant represented to plaintiff that if plaintiff would transfer the property to defendant, defendant would manage the property and do the following, (describe).

5. The representations made by defendant to plaintiff were, in fact, false and when plaintiff made said representations, he knew them to be false and made them with the intent to deceive and defraud plaintiff and to induce plaintiff to transfer title to the property and to deprive plaintiff of ownership thereof.

6. At the time the representations were made, plaintiff was ignorant of the falsity of the representations and ignorant of the false intent of defendant but instead believed the representations to be true and the intent to be honest. In reliance upon said representations, plaintiff was induced to and did transfer legal title to the property to defendant, by grant deed. Said grant deed was recorded in the office of the county recorder, in book_____, page______, of the official records on___________, 19____. Had plaintiff known the true facts, he would not have transferred title to defendant.

7. Plaintiff received no consideration for transferring the title to the property to defendant.

8. On or about________, 19____, plaintiff demanded of defendant that he retransfer legal title to plaintiff, but defendant refused and continues to refuse, to retransfer title of the property to plaintiff.

9. During the period during which defendant has held legal title, defendant has received rents and profits in an estimated sum of $___________. Said rents and profits belong to plaintiff.

10. By reason of the fraudulent manner in which defendant obtained legal title, defendant is an involuntary trustee, holding the property and profits therefrom, in constructive trust for plaintiff, with the duty to reconvey to plaintiff forthwith.

11. As a proximate result of the wrongful acts of defendant, plaintiff has been damaged in the sum of $___________ and in additional sums, the extent of which is presently unknown to plaintiff who will seek leave to amend the complaint when the exact amounts have been ascertained.

WHEREFORE, plaintiff prays:

1. For judgment declaring that defendant holds title in trust for plaintiff.

2. For an order requiring defendant to retransfer title and possession of the property to plaintiff.

3. For an accounting of the rents and profits received by defendant and for judgment in the amount of the rents and profits so received.

4. For damages in the sum of $____________.

5. For costs of suit and such other relief as the court deems just.

____
Attorney for Plaintiff

****

American Trust vs. Fitzmaurice, 131, C.A. 2d, 382.

Civil Code §2224. Civil Code §3367.

CAPTION	)	Case No.____________
	)	
	)	COMPLAINT FOR DAMAGES UNDER
	)	DISCOUNT BUYING SERVICE
________________________	)	

Plaintiff complains:

1. At all times herein mentioned, defendant was and now is a corporation, organized and existing by virtue of the laws of the State of California and has its principal place of business in ______________, California.

2. At all times herein mentioned, defendant was and now is, operating a business as a discount buying organization as defined by Civil Code §1812.101.

3. On or about __________, 19___, plaintiff became a member of said discount buying organization by paying an initiation fee of $250.00, together with an agreement to pay yearly fees of $100.00, in exchange for which it was represented to plaintiff that he, plaintiff, would receive discount prices on goods.

4. On or about _________, 19___, plaintiff purchased through defendant, the following described property, (Describe property) and paid $____________therefor. Plaintiff was told by defendant that the goods would be delivered to his residence within two weeks thereafter. More than 6 weeks have elapsed and the goods have not been delivered nor has plaintiff been informed that they are available for pickup.

5. Plaintiff has demanded the refund of the sum of $_______________, but defendant has failed and refused and still fails and refuses to refund said sum, all to plaintiff's damage in the sum of $_________________.

6. More than 30 days has elapsed since the expiration of the 6 week period and the goods have not been delivered or made available and the refund has not been made, and there now remains due, owing and unpaid, the sum of $____________.

7. Plaintiff has incurred attorney's fees in connection with the maintenance of this action, the reasonable amount of which is $_____________.

WHEREFORE, plaintiff prays:

1. For judgment in the amount of $___________which is three times actual damages.

2. For attorney's fees in the sum of $__________.

3. For costs of suit and such other relief as the court deems just.

____
Attorney for Plaintiff

****

This complaint is brought under the provisions of the Discount Buying Act, Civil Code §1812.100. Civil Code §1812.116 requires that delivery of goods be made within 6 weeks. Civil Code §1812.123 provides for treble damages.

CAPTION	)	Case No.______________
	)	
	)	COMPLAINT FOR DAMAGES FOR VIOLATION
	)	OF HEALTH STUDIO ACT
________________________	)	

Plaintiff alleges:

1. Defendant, Muscle, at all times mentioned herein, was and now is, a corporation organized and existing by virtue of the laws of California, with its principal place of business in _________________County, State of California, and is licensed to transact business as a health studio.

2. On or about_________, 19____, plaintiff and defendant entered into a written contract which provided that plaintiff would receive the following described services from defendant, (describe) for which plaintiff would pay the defendant the sum of $________________. A copy of the contract is attached hereto, mared Exhibit "A" and incorporated herein. Pursuant to the contract, plaintiff on ____________, 19______, paid defendant the whole sum of $_______________.

3. The amount paid by plaintiff was in excess permitted by Civil Code §1812.86, to wit; $500.00. On or about ______________, 19_____, a time being more than 30 days after plaintiff executed the contract and paid the sum, plaintiff demanded of defendant a refund of $____________ which is the amount in excess of the $500.00, but defendant has failed and refused to refund the money and still fails and refuses to do so, all to plaintiff's damage in the sum of $__________________.

4. By reason of the foregoing, plaintiff has been damaged in the amount of $__________________.

5. In addition, plaintiff has retained attorney ______________________to represent him in this action and has incurred attorney's fees, the reasonable amount of which is$________.

WHEREFORE, plaintiff prays:

1. For judgment in the amount of $______________ which is three times the amount of actual damages.

2. For reasonable attorney's fees in the sum of $______________.

3. For costs of suit herein and such other relief as the court deems just.

____
Attorney for Plaintiff

****

The above cause of action is authorized by the Health Studio Act which is contained in Civil Code §§ 1812.80 through 1812.95. Similar rights are available under the Dance Studio Act which is found in Civil Code §§ 1812.50 through 1812.68.

CAPTION) Case No.____________
)
) COMPLAINT FOR DAMAGES FOR REPORTING
) UNTRUE CREDIT INFORMATION
______________________)

Plaintiff alleges:

1. That at all times herein mentioned, defendant was and now is, a corporation organized under the laws of the State of California, with its principal place of business at ____________, California.

2. That at all times herein mentioned, defendant was and now is engaged in the business, among other things, of issuing credit cards to consumers.

3. At all times herein mentioned, plaintiff was the holder of a credit card issued by defendant company.

4. On or about_______, 19____, defendant reported to ________________________, the following credit information with respect to plaintiff: (Describe information.) Said information was and is untrue and defendant at the time of giving it, knew that it was untrue for the following reasons: (Describe)

5. Prior to the communication of the unfavorable credit information, to wit; on or about ____________, 19______, plaintiff had inquired of defendant of a billing error and defendant failed and refused, and still fails and refuses to correct the billing error in conformity with Civil Code, §1747.50. Plaintiff is informed and believes and upon such information and belief, alleges that defendant made the aforesaid communication to____________ solely because of plaintiff's failure to pay the amount which was in dispute.

6. On or about __________, 19_____, defendant cancelled plaintiff's credit card. Plaintiff is informed and believes and upon such information and belief, alleges that the credit card was cancelled for the reason that plaintiff had not paid the disputed amount.

7. As a result of the reporting of the aforementioned information, plaintiff has been injured in the following respects, (Describe) all to his damage in the sum of $________________.

8. Plaintiff was obliged to retain attorney ____________________to represent him in this matter and has incurred attorney's fees, the reasonable value of which is$_________.

WHEREFORE, plaintiff prays:

1. For judgment in the amount of $________________.

2. For attorney's fees in the amount of $__________.

3. For costs of suit and such other relief as the court deems just.

____
Attorney for Plaintiff

****

This cause of action is authorized under the Song-Deverly Credit Card Act, Civil Code §§ 1747 through 1747.90.

CAPTION)
) Case No.___________
)
) COMPLAINT BY A CREDIT CARD HOLDER
) AGAINST CARD ISSUER
________________________)

Plaintiff complains:

1. At all times mentioned herein, defendant was and now is, a corporation organized and existing under the laws of the State of California, with its principal place of business in _________County, California. In connection with its business, defendant issues credit cards to consumers.

2. On or about ___________, 19____, plaintiff received a statement from defendant demand payment of the sum of $_________ which defendant asserted was the outstanding balance owing and unpaid on plaintiff's account.

3. On or about_____, 19____, plaintiff mailed to defendant at the address indicated in the billing statement, a letter which set forth that the signature on the voucher was not that of plaintiff's and that plaintiff had not incurred the obligation for which the sum was demanded. Plaintiff further requested defendant to delete the charge and defendant has failed and refused and still fails and refuses to do so. A copy of plaintiff's letter is attached hereto, marked Exhibit "A" and incorporated herein.

4. On or about _____, 19_____, a time more than 6 months after the date upon which Exhibit "A" was mailed to defendant, defendant again billed the plaintiff for the sum of $___________. The sum included the amount that was in dispute.

5. As a consequence of defendant's failure and refusal to correct the above-mentioned billing error, plaintiff has been injured in that his credit has been impaired. Plaintiff has been damaged in the sum of $______________.

6. It is necessary for plaintiff to retain the services of an attorney and he has done so by retaining Attorney ________________to prosecute this action. A reasonable amount for attorney's fees is $________________.

WHEREFORE, plaintiff prays judgment against defendant as follows:

1. For the sum of $_____________.

2. For attorney's fees in the amount of $__________.

3. For costs of suit and such other relief as the court deems just.

____
Attorney for Plaintiff

****

Civil Code §1747.50 permits the recovery of 3 times the amount of actual damages.

A similar action may be brought against a retailer under Civil Code §1747.60. The retailer shall be libel in the amount by which the outstanding balance of the card holder's account is greater than the correct balance, plus interest, finance charges and other charges.

CAPTION) Case No.____________
)
) COMPLAINT FOR DAMAGES FOR UNLAWFUL
) HOME SOLICITATION
______________________________)

Plaintiff complains:

1. At all times herein mentioned, defendant company was a corporation organized and existing under the laws of California with its principal place of business at __________, California.

2. On or about_______, 19____, defendant salesman presented himself at plaintiff's residence at______________street, _______________, California, for the purpose of soliciting from plaintiff the sale of the following described good: (Describe goods.) Plaintiff purchased the goods for the price of $__________.

3. Prior to starting the solicitation, defendant misstated his purpose for presenting himself and failed to present identification showing his true name, the name of the company, the address of the place of business of defendant or his agent. Plaintiff is informed and believes and upon such information and belief alleges that the misstatements were made intentionally with the purpose to induce plaintiff into making a purchase which he, the plaintiff, under other circumstances would not have made.

4. On or about________, 19____, plaintiff, in writing, contacted defendant company with the demand that they terminate the contract and return all payments thereunder in return for plaintiff's returning the goods. The tender was refused by defendant and 20 days has elapsed since the written demand was made.

5. As a proximate cause of the intentional violation under Business and Professions Code, §17500.3 a and b, plaintiff has been damaged in the sum of $____________which sum was arrived at by computing the following figures: (See below)

WHEREFORE, plaintiff prays for judgment as follows:

1. For damages in the sum of $____________.

2. For costs of suit herein and such other relief as the court deems just.

____
Attorney for Plaintiff

****

Damages are equal to 2 times the amount of the sale price or $250.00 whichever is greater, but not less than $50.00. B & P %17500.3 (c)

CAPTION)
)
)
)
)
________________________)

Case No.__________

COMPLAINT FOR DAMAGES UNDER CALIFORNIA CONSUMER REPORTING CREDIT ACT

Plaintiff alleges:

1. At all times herein mentioned, defendant was and now is, a corporation, organized and existing under the laws of the State of California, with its principal place of business in ______________County, California.

2. At all times herein mentioned, defendant was, and now is, engaging in the business of reporting credit to retail and other institutions.

3. On or about________, 19____, defendant furnished to__________, a consumer credit report, on the credit worthiness of plaintiff. Furnishing the consumer credit report, defendant knew or should have know that the user of the report would use the report to do other than what is allowed under Civil Code §1785.11. (Set forth unauthorized use.)

4. Defendant's conduct in furnishing said report was done willfully and negligently.

5. As a proximate cause of the negligent conduct of defendant, plaintiff has been damaged in the following respects: (Describe) to his total detriment, in the sum of $______________ (In an absence of actual damages, plaintiff is entitled to the sum of $300.00 under Civil Code §1785.30(a)1.)

6. Plaintiff has retained__________attorney to prosecute this action on his behalf and plaintiff will incur attorney's fees in connection with said prosecution.

WHEREFORE, plaintiff prays:

1. For damages in the sum of $_____________.

2. For punitive damages in the sum of $_________.

3. For reasonable attorney's fees.

4. For costs of suit herein and such other relief as the court deems just.

____
Attorney for Plaintiff

****

The basis for the above cause of action is found in Civil Code §§ 1785.1 through 1785.34. Plaintiff may also have a cause of action in the Federal Court under 15 U.S.C. §§ 681n through 681o, however an action in the Federal Court will include a state court action.

The statute of limitations in the state court action is two years from the date on which the liability arises with certain exceptions where disclosure is involved.

There are numerous causes of action available under the California Act, for example, with respect to failing to delete inaccurate information, failing to notify of a disputed credit transaction or failure to disclose information to a consumer.

CAPTION)
)
) NOTICE OF MOTION FOR CONTINUANCE
)
)
_________________________)

Case No.____________

TO THE DEFENDANT__________________AND TO HIS ATTORNEY:

YOU, AND EACH OF YOU, WILL PLEASE TAKE NOTICE that on____________, 19____, or as soon thereafter as the matter may be heard in Department______, of the above-entitled court, defendant will move the court for an order continuing the trial, heretofore set for _________, 19___, to the date of________, 19____.

The motion will be made on the grounds that the attorney designated to try the matter on behalf of plaintiff has suffered a heart attack and will be confined to the hospital to a date beyond the original trial date.

The motion will be based upon this notice of motion, the declaration of Dr.____________and the memorandum of points and authorities attached hereto, the papers and records on file herein and such other evidence, oral and documentary, to be presented at the hearing.

DATED:______________________, 19____.

____
Attorney for

****

An illness may constitute grounds for continuance. Williams vs. Elliot , 127. C.A. 2d, 357.

Absence of evidence may constitute a ground. C.C.P. §595.4.

Other cases: Beck vs. Reinholtz, 138 C.A. 2d, 719. Cohen vs. Herbert, 186 C.A. 2d, 488.

Denial of a continuance will be considered an abuse of discretion only where the ruling is arbitrary. Vann vs. Shilleh, 54 C.A. 3d, 192. Young vs. Redman, 55 C.A. 3d, 827.

CAPTION)   Case No.____________
)
)   EX PARTE MOTION FOR CONTINUANCE
)
________________________)

COMES NOW the_____________and hereby applies to the court for an order ex parte continuing the trial, heretofore set for ___________, 19____, until ___________, 19____. In support of this ex parte application, applicant states that the reason for making this order without filing a notice of motion is as follows: (Set for good cause).

I declare under penalty of perjury that the foregoing is true and correct.

Executed at _______________, California on ___________________, 19_____.

____

****

A motion for continuance may be made ex parte only where good cause is shown for not giving written notice. Rules of Court 224 and 512.

CAPTION)
)
) STIPULATION TO DROP CASE FROM
) CALENDAR AND AGREEMENT TO EXTEND
______________________________) TIME OF TRIAL

Case No.____________

COME NOW the plaintiff and defendant and by their respective counsel stipulate that the trial of this cause, heretofore set for __________, 19____, be dropped from the calendar to be restored according to law.

IT IS FURTHER STIPULATED that the defendant waives the provisions of C.C.P. §583 and that this action shall not be dismissed for failure to prosecute within a period of ________years from date.

DATED:____________________, 19____.

____
Attorney for Plaintiff

____
Attorney for Defendant

IT IS SO ORDERED:

DATED:____________________, 19____.

____
Judge of the Superior Court

CAPTION)   Case No.____________
)
) STIPULATION FOR CONTINUANCE
)
______________________________)

IT IS HEREBY STIPULATED BY AND BETWEEN ________________ and _________________________, ATTORNEYS OF RECORD FOR THE PARTIES WITHIN, that the trial in the above-entitled cause, heretofore set on ________________, may be continued to ____________, 19____.

DATED: __________________, 19____.

____
Attorney for Plaintiff

DATED: __________________, 19____.

____
Attorney for Defendant

IT IS SO ORDERED:

DATED: ___________________, 19____.

____
Judge of the Superior Court

****

The court shall postpone a trial for hearing on any motion for a period not to exceed 30 days when the appearing parties have stipulated. C.C.P. §595.2.

CAPTION)
)
)
)
______________________)

Case No.__________

COMPLAINT FOR DAMAGES ARISING FROM BREACH OF CONTRACT

Plaintiff complains:

1. On or about _______, 19______, in the City of ________________, California, plaintiff and defendant entered into a written (or oral) agreement. (If a written agreement), a copy of the agreement is attached hereto, marked Exhibit "A" and incorporated herein as though set out in full.

2. By the terms of the contract it was to be performed in the City of________________, County of __________, State of California.

3. (This paragraph is to be used when pleading offer and acceptance.) On or about ______, 19____, plaintiff made the following offer to defendant. (Set forth offer, such as an offer for services or an offer to sell an object.) Thereafter, on __________, 19____, defendant accepted plaintiff's offer by letter stating that he, defendant, would do the following: (Describe, such as alleging that defendant would pay for and pick up the object.)

4. Plaintiff has performed all conditions, covenants and promises under the contract which he was obliged to perform except for ________________, the performance of which was excused for the following reason: (Specify)

5. On or about_______, 19____, defendant breached the contract by the following acts. (Describe)

6. (Anticipatory breach) On or about___________, 19_______, defendant informed plaintiff that he would no longer sell and deliver to plaintiff the _____________on ____________, 19____, and on the same day, defendant sold ________________to a third party.

7. (Alternate anticipatory breach allegation) On or about__________, 19_____, the defendant mailed a letter to plaintiff which was received by plaintiff. The letter informed plaintiff that defendant intended not to comply with the terms and conditions of the contract marked Exhibit "A". A copy of the letter is attached hereto, marked Exhibit "B" and made a part hereof.

8. As a result of the defendant's breach of the contract, plaintiff has suffered damage in the following respects, (describe) in the sum of $_____________ .

WHEREFORE, plaintiff prays judgment as follows:

1. For damages in the sum of $___________.

2. For interest in the sum of $___________.

3. For costs of suit and such other relief as the court deems just.

____
Attorney for Plaintiff

****

Breach of contract allegations are discussed in Reichert vs. General Insurance 68 Cal. 2d, 822.

CAPTION)   Case No.___________
)
)   COMPLAINT FOR RESCISSION
)   AND RESTITUTION
__________________)

Plaintiff complains:

1. At all times herein mentioned, defendant was and now is a resident of the County of__________, State of California.

2. On or about________, 19____, plaintiff and defendant entered into a written contract, wherein and whereby it was agreed that plaintiff was to pay to defendant the sum of $______________for delivery of the following described items, (describe) which defendant was to deliver to plaintiff, on or before________, 19____. A copy of the agreement is attached hereto, marked Exhibit "A" and made a part hereof.

3. On or about________, 19____, plaintiff paid defendant a portion of the contract price, to wit; $__________ and thereby performed everything required by the contract to be performed by him.

4. Despite numerous demands by plaintiff to do so, defendant has failed and refused to perform the conditions of the contract with plaintiff in that he has not delivered, or caused to be delivered to plaintiff, the items as above-described.

5. On or about__________, 19____, by written notice to defendant, plaintiff rescinded the contract for failure of the consideration and demanded restitution of the money plaintiff paid. A copy of the notice of rescission is attached hereto and marked Exhibit "B" and made a part hereof.

6. Defendant has failed and refused, and continues to fail and refuse to restore to plaintiff the consideration heretofore paid by him.

9. By reason of defendant's failure to restore consideration, plaintiff has been damaged in the sum of $_________.

10. By reason of defendant's failure to restore the consideration, plaintiff has been further damaged in that he has been obliged to purchase identical items, after waiting a reasonable time, at a cost of $___________, an amount in excess of the contract price, in the amount of $______________.

WHEREFORE, plaintiff prays:

1. For judgment in the amount of $___________ with interest thereon at the rate of ______% from _________, 19____.

2. For the sum of $__________, which is the difference between the contract price and the price which plaintiff had to pay for the identical item.

3. For costs of suit and such other relief as the court deems just.

____
Attorney for Plaintiff

****

The prerequisite to filing suit; the rescinding party must promptly give notice of rescission, Civil Code §1691. Notice of a pleading is deemed notice of rescission and an offer of the restoration of the consideration advanced. Civil Code §1691.

See also Civil Code §§ 1688 through 1693.

CAPTION)
)
) COMPLAINT FOR CONTRIBUTION
)
______________)

Case No.__________

Plaintiff complains:

1. Defendant at all times herein mentioned was a resident of the County of_________, California.

2. On or about _______, 19____, plaintiff and defendant executed and delivered to_____________their joint and several promissory note in writing, in the sum of $1,000.00, payable on demand.

3. On ________, 19____, plaintiff paid the total $1,000.00 to ______________, pursuant to ____________'s demand.

4. Defendant paid no part of the note to __________________and although plaintiff has demanded that defendant contribute, defendant has failed and refused and still fails and refuses to contribute to plaintiff, his share of the obligation in the amount of $500.00, or any part thereof.

WHEREFORE, plaintiff prays:

1. For contribution in the amount of $___________

2. For interest on the foregoing sum at the rate of_____% per annum from ________, 19____.

3. For costs of suit herein and such other relief as the court deems just.

____
Attorney for Plaintiff

****

Contribution is available on a joint or jointer's several obligation. Civil Code §1432. See also Civil Code §2848. Contribution is not available on several obligations. Garcia vs. Superior Court, 45 C.A. 2d, 31.

There is no necessity that there be an expressed contract for contribution among joint obligors. Pacific Freight Line vs. Pioneer, 39 C.A. 2d, 609.

CAPTION)
)
)
)
____________________)

Case No.____________

COMPLAINT FOR CONVERSION

Plaintiff complains:

1. At all times herein mentioned, plaintiff was and still is the owner and was and is presently entitled to possession of the following personal property, (describe property).

2. On or about ______, 19____, the value of the above-described property was $_____________ and on that date was in the possession of plaintiff at ____________, California.

3. On or about ________, 19____, defendant took the property from the possession of plaintiff and converted it to his own use, all to plaintiff's damage in the sum of $__________.

4. In addition to the above damages, plaintiff has expended $______________ in pursuit of the converted property.

WHEREFORE, plaintiff prays:

1. For the value of the property, in the sum of $__________________.

2. For interest at the rate of _____% per annum from and after ___________, 19____.

3. For the recovery of expenses in the sum of $__________________.

4. For costs of suit and such other relief as the court deems just.

____
Attorney for Plaintiff

****

One must be the owner and have the right to possession of personal property in order to maintain the action. Eistrat vs. Western Hardwood, 164 C.A. 2d, 374. Devries vs. Brundack, 53 Cal. 2d , 643.

Damages allowed are the value of the property at the time of conversion plus interest from that time, or an amount sufficient to indemnify the injured party for the loss which is the proximate result of the wrongful act. In addition, a fair compensation for the time expended in pursuit of the property, Civil Code §3336.

CAPTION)
)
) COMPLAINT FOR DAMAGES
) (CONVERSION)
______________________)

Case No.__________

Plaintiff alleges:

1. At all times herein mentioned, plaintiff was and now is the owner of the following-described personal property, (set forth description) and entitled to possession thereto. The reasonable value of the above-described property is:________________.

2. At all times herein mentioned, defendant was and now is engaged in the business of repairing______________and holds himself out to the general public as one who is engaged in such business. On or about___________, 19___, plaintiff delivered the above-described object to the custody and possession of defendant for the purpose of having the above-described personal property repaired.

3. Defendant took possession of the property and agreed orally to make the necessary repairs and redeliver it to plaintiff when the repairs were completed.

4. Although plaintiff has made demand and has tendered to defendant the agreed amount for the repair work, defendant has failed and refused to redeliver the above-mentioned item and has converted the same to his own use, all to the plaintiff's damage in the sum of $_______________.

5. Plaintiff has heretofore made demand for payment of the damages from defendant, but no part thereof has been paid.

6. Since the defendant's refusal and prior to the filing of this action, plaintiff has made the following efforts to recover the property: (Describe efforts and expenses incurred.)

WHEREFORE, plaintiff prays judgment against defendant as follows:

1. For the value of the property at the time converted in the sum of $___________________.

2. For interest at______% on the foregoing sum from and after ______________, 19____.

3. For the sum of $______________for sums actually spent in pursuit of the converted property.

4. For such other relief as the court deems just and proper.

DATED:_____________________, 19____

____
Attorney for Plaintiff

****

A plaintiff may recover in a conversion action, the value of the property at the time of the conversion, with interest from that time, or an amount sufficient to compensate the party injured for the loss, which is the natural and proximate result of the conversion. Plaintiff may also recover a fair compensation for the time and money properly spent in pursuit of the property. Civil Code §3336. Chatterton vs. Boone, 31 C.A., 2d 943.

Where defendant has put it out of his power to redeliver the property, demand is unnecessary. Downey vs. Martin, 96 C.A., 2d 94.

CAPTION	)	Case No._______________
	)	
	)	COMPLAINT FOR CONVERSION AGAINST TENANT
	)	
____________________	)	

Plaintiff complains:

1. At all times herein mentioned, plaintiff was and still is the owner of that certain parcel of real property, commonly known as __________Street,___________California. Said real property is improved with a building constructed primarily for the use as a store.

2. From the date of_____________, 19___, to ____________, 19____, defendant was in possession of the building under a lease for a period of a year. The property was leased to defendant with the agreement that defendant would be allowed to use the following fixtures, (describe) and return the building and the fixtures to plaintiff in good condition at the termination of the lease. A copy of the lease is attached hereto, marked Exhibit "A" and incorporated herein as though set out in full.

3. On or about_________, 19____, defendant vacated the above premises and surrendered possession thereof to plaintiff. When defendant vacated the premises, he moved certain parts thereof, which theretofore had been attached, (describe shelves, showcases, etc.,) and in so doing defendant damaged the premises in the following respects, (describe damage).

4. At the time of defendant's removal of the fixtures the fixtures had a value of $______________ and by his acts, defendant converted the fixtures to his own use to plaintiff's damage in the sum of $________________.

WHEREFORE, plaintiff prays:

1. For judgment in the amount of $_____________. with interest at the rate of_____% per annum from_________, 19____.

2. For costs of suit herein and such other relief as the court deems just.

____
Attorney for Plaintiff

****

Fixtures, although part of the real property, may be the subject of a conversion once they are severed. California vs. Boothe, 220 Cal. 279. McNally vs. Connolly, 70 Cal. 3.

CAPTION)
)
)
)
________________________)

Case No.____________

COMPLAINT FOR CONVERSION FOR REFUSING TO PAY OVER MONEY FOR SECURITIES

Plaintiff complains:

1. On or about______, 19____, plaintiff employed defendant as his agent to collect and receive from__________, money (or securities) for the purpose of remitting and paying the same to plaintiff. Plaintiff agreed to allow defendant to retain the sum of $_________from the money collected,(or from the proceeds of the sale of other securities for which the new securities were received.

2. Defendant collected the various sums (or securities) but has failed and refused and still fails and refuses to turn same over to plaintiff.

3. After deducting from the above amount, the commission to which defendant is entitled, plaintiff is entitled to the possession of _____________and there remains due, owing and unpaid from defendant, the sum of $_________________(or defendant is obliged to turn over the securities).

4. Plaintiff has duly demanded payment of the above sum (or securities) but defendant has refused and neglected to pay the same to plaintiff or to turn over the securities, but has converted the money (or securities) to his own use. The value of the securities, at the time of the conversion was $___________________.

WHEREFORE, plaintiff prays:

1. For judgment in the amount of $_____________, with interest at the rate of_______% per annum from_________, 19______.

2. For costs of suit herein and such other relief as the court deems just.

____
Attorney for Plaintiff

****

See Shahood vs. Cabin, 154 C.A. 2d, 745.

See also Pugh vs. Porter, 118 Cal, 628.

The selling of securities or goods, contrary to instructions, constitutes conversion.

In re Treadwell, 67 Cal 353.

CAPTION)
)
)
)
________________)

Case No.__________

COMPLAINT FOR CONVERSION AGAINST BAILEE

Plaintiff complains:

1. At all times herein mentioned, plaintiff was and still is the owner of, and entitled to the possession of, that following item of personal property, (describe item).

2. On or about ________, 19___, plaintiff delivered the above-mentioned personal property to defendant, under an agreement wherein defendant would use the property for a period of__________months and thereafter return the property to plaintiff, either on demand, or on or before __________, 19____.

3. On or about__________, 19____, plaintiff demanded of defendant that the defendant return to him the above-described property. Defendant refuses and still refuses to return the property and has converted it to his own use.

4. At all times herein mentioned, the property was valued at the sum of $______________.

WHEREFORE, plaintiff prays:

1. For judgment for the market value of the property at the time of conversion in the amount of $______________with interest from that date at the rate of ______% per annum.

2. For costs of suit herein and such other relief as the court deems just.

____
Attorney for Plaintiff

CAPTION	APPLICATION FOR SUMMARY ORDER FOR SHAREHOLDERS MEETING (Corp. C. §600(c))

To the Superior Court of Los Angeles County:

1. The applicant herein is a shareholder of record of __________ common shares of Raphe Corporation.

2. Raphe Corporation is a California Corporation organized and existing by virtue of the laws of California.

3. The by-laws of Raphe Corporation provide that an annual meeting of shareholders shall be held at 100 Wilshire Boulevard, Los Angeles, California on the 4th day of March of each year at 10:00 A.M., unless the 4th day of March falls on a Saturday, in which event the annual meeting shall be held at the same place and hour on the 7th day of March.

4. More than 60 days has elapsed since the 4th day of March, 1977, the date at which the meeting should be held. No meeting was called, noticed or held.

5. The County of Los Angeles is the proper county in which to institute this action by virtue of the fact that Raphe Corporation has its principal executive offices in said county.

WHEREFORE the undersigned applicant prays that the court order a meeting to be held and further prays that the court designate the time and place of such meeting.

____
Applicant

CAPTION)
________________)

APPLICATION FOR SUMMARY ORDER FOR A SPECIAL MEETING
(Corp. C. §305(c)

To the Superior Court of Los Angeles County.

1. This application is filed by ______________ pursuant to the provisions of Corp. C. §305(c).

2. Raphe Corporation, the respondent herein, is a corporation organized and existing by virtue of the laws of the State of California.

3. The County of Los Angeles is the proper county in which to institute this application by virtue of the fact that Raphe Corporation has its principal executive offices located in said county.

4. Raphe Corporation has a board of directors which consist of 3 directors. On or about ______________, 19__ two of the offices of the board of directors became vacant by virtue of the resignation of said members. Pursuant to the provisions of Corp. C. §305(a), the remaining director filled said vacancies by the appointment of ___________ and ______________ to the board.

5. The present configuration of the board of directors is such that less than a majority of directors that have been elected by the shareholders. This is in contravention to the provisions of Corp. C. §305(c).

6. The configuration of the board of directors is presently constituted as set forth in Paragraph 5 and at this time your applicant holds more than 5% of the total number of shares outstanding which have voting rights for directors.

7. It is the desire of your applicant that a special meeting of shareholders be called to elect an entire board.

WHEREFORE your applicant prays that this Honorable Court order that a meeting be held and grant such other relief as may be equitable.

____
Attorney for Applicant

(The hearing on an application shall be held on not less then 10 business days notice to the corporation. If the corporation intends to oppose the application it shall file with the court a Notice of Opposition not less than 5 days prior to the hearing date. All moving and opposing papers shall be supported by affidavits. The hearing takes precedence over other matters on the calendar)

CAPTION	ORDER TO SHOW CAUSE WHY MEETING SHOULD NOT BE HELD

To Groucho, Harpo, Chico and Zeppo, Directors of the Board of Raphe Corporation:

You and each of you are ordered to appear before the above-entitled court in Department ____, located in Room _____, at 111 Hill Street, Los Angeles, California at the hour of 9:00 A.M. on June 12, 1977, then and there to show cause, if any you have, why an annual meeting of the shareholders should not be called at a designated time and place.

Dated: ______________

____
Judge

CAPTION	ORDER DESIGNATING TIME AND PLACE OF MEETING

This case came on regularly before the court on ______________, 19__ in Department ______ for the purpose of ordering a meeting and the time and place thereof of the shareholders of Raphe Corporation.

Good cause of hearing, it is ordered that an annual meeting of the shareholders of Raphe Corporation be held at 100 Wilshire Boulevard, Los Angeles, California on July 1, 1977 at the hour of 10:00 A.M.

Dated: _________

____
Judge

CAPTION	COMPLAINT FOR DAMAGES; DERIVATIVE ACTION (Corp. C.§800)

1. Defendant _______________ Corporation hereinafter referred to as "Corporation" is and at all times herein mentioned was a corporation duly organized and existing under and by virtue of the laws of California. Said corporation has it's principal executive office in Los Angeles County California.

2. At the time of the occurrence of the transaction which is the basis of this suit and at the present time plaintiff was and now is a shareholder of record of shares of the corporation. (If plaintiff was a beneficial holder of shares or a holding of voting trust certificates at the time of the transaction sued upon or if the shares or voting trust certificates thereafter devolved upon plaintiff by operation of law from a person who was at the time of the transaction a holder of said shares, such facts should be alleged).

3. Allege in this paragraph facts which constitute cause of action against defendants other than the corporation, would show injury to corporation.

4. On or about ___________, 19_ and on five occasions thereafter plaintiff made the following efforts to secure action by the board of directors of the corporation to pursue the above claim against the aforementioned defendants: (set forth here with particularity the efforts made to secure action by the board or set forth the reasons for not making such effort.)

5. Plaintiff has informed the corporation in writing of the ultimate facts of each cause of action against the defendants by delivering to the corporation a true copy of the complaint which is filed herein.

6. The board of directors and the corporation refused and continued to refuse to prosecute this action and plaintiff's efforts to obtain such action have failed for the following reasons: (Set forth the reasons.) In so refusing to prosecute this action the board of directors did not act in good faith or in any reasonable belief that its refusal to commence this action was in the best interest of the corporation. The refusal by the board of directors was an exercise of bad faith and a breach of its fudiciary duty to maintain and defend the interest of the corporation.

7. If plaintiff is successful in this action a substantial benefit will result to defendant corporation on whose behalf this action is being commenced and plaintiff is entitled to his attorney's fees incurred herein in the sum of _____________ against the corporation.

(Prayer)

____

Attorney for Plaintiff

CAPTION	)))))	NOTICE OF MOTION FOR AN ORDER ALLOWING PLAINTIFF TO MAINTAIN DERIVATIVE ACTION (Corp. C. §800(a)(1)

To ___________________ Corporation and to ___________________, members of the Board of Directors of said corporation.

NOTICE IS HEREBY GIVEN that on ________________, 19__ at __M. or as soon thereafter as the matter may be heard in Department _________ of the above-entitled court plaintiff will move the court for an order allowing plaintiff to prosecute the derivative action. A copy of the complaint in said action is attached hereto, marked Exhibit "A" and incorporated herein.

This motion is based upon the fact that there is a strong prima facie case in favor of the claim inserted on behalf of the corporation and that no other similar action has been or is likely to be instituted.

Plaintiff acquired the shares before there was disclosure to the public or to the plaintiff of the wrong-doing of which plaintiff complains.

Unless the action can be maintained, the defendant may retain a gain derived from defendant's willful breach of a fiduciary duty.

The requested relief will not result on unjust enrichment of the corporation or any shareholder of the corporation.

This motion is based upon the affidavit of ___________________, a copy of which is attached hereto, marked Exhibit "B". This motion will further be based upon other evidence or and documentary which may be aduced at the hearing.

____
Attorney for Plaintiff

(This motion must be supported by evidence either in the form of an affidavit or testimony as the court will determine. Although the code does not specify, the hearing should probably be upon 10 days notice.)

CAPTION	NOTICE OF MOTION FOR ORDER REQUIRING PLAINTIFF TO FURNISH SECURITY (Corp. C. §800(c)

To the plaintiff and his attorney of record:

NOTICE IS HEREBY GIVEN that on ________________, 19__ at __M. or as soon thereafter as the matter may be heard in Department ___ of the above-entitled court defendant ___________ will move for an order requiring plaintiff to furnish security as provided in Corp. C. §800(c). in the amount of ___________.

The motion will be based upon the following grounds:

1. That there is no reasonable possibility that the prosecution of the cause of action alleged in the complaint against the moving party will benefit the corporation or its shareholders.

2. The moving party did not participate in the transaction complained of in any capacity.

3. The motion will be based upon this notice of motion and on the declaration of _____________ and a Memorandum of Points and Authorities served and filed herewith. And on such other evidence, oral and documentary as may be presented at the hearing.

____
Attorney for defendant

(This motion must be made within 30 days after service of summons on the corporation or any defendant officer. The court may extend the period up to 60 days. Maximum allowable security for all plaintiffs is $50,000.)

CAPTION

COMPLAINT TO RECOVER IMPROPERLY PAID DISTRIBUTIONS (Corp. C. §2009(a))

Plaintiff complains:

1. Plaintiff is a California Corporation organized and existing by virtue of the laws of the State of California.

2. Plaintiff corporation is in the process of dissolving and winding up its affairs and pursuant thereto has filed a Certificate of Election to Dissolve on ________, 19__, a copy of which is attached hereto, marked Exhibit "A" and incorporated herein as though set out in full.

3. Defendants Mutt and Jeff are shareholders of said plaintiff corporation and as such have received certain distributions that will be described below. Said shareholders are being joined as defendants pursuant to the provisions of Corp. C. §2009(a).

4. Herman and Sherman are creditors of the corporation in that they are joint payees of a promissory note in the sum of $10,000. A copy of said note is attached hereto, marked Exhibit "B" and incorporated herein as though set our in full. No sum on said note has been paid, although demand has been made thereof and the entire balance remains due, owing and unpaid.

5. Suit is being instituted in the name of the corporation by Herman and Sherman pursuant to the provisions of Corp. C. §2009(b).

6. On or about _____________, 19__, the only asset of the corporation, a checking account with a balance of $10,000, was distributed equally among the above-named shareholders. At the time of distribution, the above-mentioned debt was neither paid nor had any provision for the payment of said debt been made.

WHEREFORE, plaintiff prays:

1. For an order requiring the shareholders above-mentioned to return the sum of $10,000 to the corporation;

2. For an order impounding the funds until adequate provision for payment to Herman and Sherman can be made;

3. For costs of suit and such other relief as the court deems just.

____
Attorney for Plaintiff

(There is no restriction in §2009 with respect to the county in which suit may be brought. Thus, suit may be instituted wherever venue would be proper under the Code of Civil Procedure).

(Suit shall be instituted with the corporation named as plaintiff.Any shareholders not joined as defendants may be brought in on motion of any other defendant).

(See §2009(c) for the manner in which a shareholder can recover from other shareholders)

CAPTION

COMPLAINT FOR INVOLUNTARY DISSOLUTION
(Corp. C. 1800)

Plaintiffs complain:

1. The county of Los Angeles is the proper county in which to bring and maintain this action by virtue of the fact that defendant Raphe Corporation has its principal executive office located therein.

2. That at all times herein mentioned defendant Raphe Corporation was and now is a California Corporation organized and existing by virtue of the laws of California.

3. At the time of the commencement of this action, and at the present time, the corporation, Raphe Corporation, had a board of directors with 4 directors in office, Harpo, Groucho, Chico and Zeppo. Harpo, Groucho and Zeppo, the plaintiffs in this action, are presently directors in office and constitute more than one-half of the directors of Raphe Corporation.

(Shareholders holding shares representing not less than 1/3 the total number of outstanding shares or any shareholders of closed corporations or any shareholder if the ground for dissolution is that the period of the corporation has expired or any other person expressly authorized in the articles may also be parties plaintiff.)

4. The corporation has an even number of directors who are equally divided and cannot agree as to the management of the affairs of the corporation. Such inability to agree has resulted in the fact that the business of the corporation can no longer be conducted to advantage and there is danger that the property and business of the corporation will be impaired.

5. The holders of voting shares of the corporation are so divided into factions that they cannot elect a board consisting of an uneven number.

(For other grounds for involuntary dissolution, see Corp. C. Sec. 1800b)

6. Urgent corporate business of a nature that requires immediate attention is pending. The board of directors as constituted has been unable to decide on the method by which this business should be administered. Plaintiffs are informed and believe and thus allege that unless a provisional director is appointed pending the outcome of this action, irreparable damage will be visited upon the corporation.

WHEREFORE, plaintiffs pray:

1. That Raphe Corporation be dissolved and its business wound up.

2. That a provisional director be appointed pending the action.

3. That the court grant such other relief as it deems just.

____
Attorneys for Plaintiffs

(A Complaint for Involuntary Dissolution must be verified)

CAPTION	COMPLAINT TO COMPEL RIGHT OF INSPECTION (Corp. C. §1603)

Plaintiff complains:

1. Plaintiff was and now is a shareholder of 1000 shares of common stock of Raphe Corporation.

2. Raphe Corporation is a California Corporation organized and existing by virtue of the laws of the State of California.

3. The County of Los Angeles is the proper county in which to bring and maintain this action by virtue of the fact that defendant Raphe Corporation has its principal executive offices located therein.

4. The accounting books and records of said corporation are prepared, kept and maintained at the principal executive office.

5. Plaintiff is informed and believes and upon such information and belief alleges that the accounting books and records will reveal that the corporation does not possess retained earnings or other assets from which it can lawfully make a distribution to shareholders. By an announcement on January 2, 1977 the board of directors stated that it would make a distribution to shareholders in the amount of ________ per share. The accounting books and records are reasonably related to the shareholders' interests in that they will review the absence of assets from which a distribution can be made.

6. On or about _______ 1977 plaintiff personally served upon ___________ the person having custody and control of said accounting books and records, a written demand to inspect said books. A copy of said written demand is attached hereto, incorporated herein and marked Exhibit "A".

7. Said __________ has refused and failed to make the accounting books and records available to the plaintiff during usual business hours or during any other time. Plaintiff has sent two additional demands, one to _____________ and the other to each member of the board of directors in which the plaintiff has expressed a willingness to present himself during usual business hours to inspect the records. None of the demands has been responded to.

8. The failure of the corporation to comply with plaintiff's demand is without justification.

WHEREFORE, plaintiff prays:

1. For an order permitting plaintiff to inspect the books and records.

2. In the alternative for an order appointing an accountant to audit the books and records kept in this state.

3. For reasonable expenses incurred by plaintiff, including attorney's fees in connection with this action pursuant to Corp. C. §1604.

4. For costs of suit and such other relief as the court deems just.

____
Attorney for Plaintiff

CAPTION	ORDER TO SHOW CAUSE TO PRODUCE ACCOUNTING BOOKS AND RECORDS

To _____________, Custodian of the accounting books and records of Raphe Corporation:

Good cause appearing it is ordered that you produce to _____________ the accountants appointed by this court, the following books and documents in your custody:

(set forth description of books and documents)

Failure to comply with this order shall render you, _______________ liable for punishment for contempt of court.

____
Judge

CAPTION

COMPLAINT TO DETERMINE VALUE OF DISSENTING SHARES

(Corp. C. §1304)

Plaintiff complains:

1. Raphe Corporation is a California Corporation existing and organized by virtue of the laws of the State of California.

2. Plaintiff herein is a dissenting shareholder of 100 shares of common stock in Raphe Corporation.

3. The County of Los Angeles is the proper county in which to institute this action by virtue of the fact that defendant corporation has its principal office in said county.

4. On or about ____________, 19__ defendant Raphe Corporation entered into a merger agreement with Homer Corporation. A copy of said merger agreement is attached hereto, marked Exhibit A, and incorporated herein.

5. On or about ____________, 19__ defendant mailed to plaintiff a copy of a Notice of Approval of the reorganization by the outstanding shareholders of Raphe Corporation. A copy of said notice is attached hereto marked Exhibit "B" and incorporated herein.

6. On or about ____________, 19__ (within 30 days after the date on which the Notice of Approval was mailed), plaintiff served on defendant a written demand for the purchase of plaintiff's shares and for the payment to plaintiff in cash of the fair market value of such shares. A copy of the demand is attached hereto marked Exhibit "C" and incorporated herein.

7. On the same date as plaintiff submitted the demand above mentioned, plaintiff submitted to the corporation at its principal office the shareholder certificates representing the shares held by plaintiff, the shares for which plaintiff demanded purchase by the corporation.

8. Defendant corporation offered plaintiff for the purchase of his shares the amount of $10 per share. Plaintiff alleges that the fair market value of the shares on the day prior to the announcement of the proposed reorganization was $15 per share.

9. Defendant has refused to pay plaintiff the amount of $15 per share or any amount and to date no sums have been paid.

10. There is no dispute that the shares are in fact dissenting shares. (If there is a dispute the fact of this dispute must be alleged).

WHEREFORE plaintiff prays:

1. For a judgement declaring the shares to be worth $15 per share and an order to the corporation that the corporation pay to plaintiff an amount equal to $15 per share times the number of shares held by plaintiff;

2. For costs of suit and such other relief as the court deems just.

(Attorney for Plaintiff)

(This action must be filed within 6 months after the date on which notice of approval by the outstanding shares was mailed to shareholder).

CAPTION	COMPLAINT TO RECOVER UNLAWFUL DISTRIBUTION (Corp. C. §506)

Plaintiff complains:

1. Plaintiff corporation, Raphe Corporation, is a California Corporation organized under and existing by virtue of the laws of that State.

2. John Herman is a creditor of the corporation. The corporation became indebted to John Herman as a result of failing to pay the sum due on a promissory note in the principal amount of $1,000. A true copy of said note is attached hereto, marked Exhibit "A" and incorporated herein. There remains due, owing and unpaid on said note the sum of $1,000.

3. This suit is being instituted in the name of Raphe Corporation pursuant to the provisions of Corp. C. §506(b).

4. Defendants Groucho, Harpo and Chico are shareholders of Raphe Corporation who, on January 2, 1977, received a distribution of assets in the form of a dividend.

5. At the time the distribution was made the amount of the retained earnings of the corporation immediately prior to the distribution were less than the amount of the distribution. In addition, at the time the distribution was made and immediately thereafter, the sum of the assets of the corporation were less then the sum of its liabities and the sum of the current assets of the corporation were less then the sum of the current liabilities. And, in addition, the average earnings of the corporation before taxes and income and interest for the two preceding fiscal years was greater than the average of the interest expense of the corporation for such fiscal years.

6. The amount of the dividend distributed was $1,200. Plaintiff remits all sums in excess of the liabilities owed to the creditors named herein.

7. At the time the distribution was made the named creditors neither knew or consented to the distribution. At the time the liability was incurred in favor of the named creditors against plaintiff corporation, the distribution had not yet been made.

WHEREFORE, plaintiff prays:

1. For judgment in the amount of $1,000 with interest thereon at the legal rate until the judgment is paid;

2. For costs of suit herein and such other relief as the court deems just;

____
Attorney for Plaintiff

(Depending upon the amount in question, this action may be instituted in either the Municipal or Superior Court. Venue shall be in accordance with the rules of the Code of Civil Procedure)

(Suit is brought in the name of the corporation and may be instituted either by a creditor or a non-consenting shareholder. Any shareholder sued under this section may implead all other shareholders liable under this section and may compel contribution either in the main action or an independent action. Corp. C. §506(c)

Caption

COMPLAINT FOR REPLACEMENT OF LOST SHARE CERTIFICATE
(Corp. C. §419(b)

Plaintiff complains:

1. Raphe Corporation is a California Corporation duly organized and existing by virtue of the laws of that State.

2. The County of Los Angeles is the proper county in which to commence this action by virtue of the fact that Raphe Corporation has its principal executive offices in said county.

3. On or about January 1, 1974 plaintiff purchased 100 shares of common stock of Raphe Corporation and had issued to him a share certificate which stated that plaintiff was the record owner of said number of shares.

4. On or about June 1, 1976 plaintiff's office building, where the certificate was kept, was destroyed by a fire and with it was destroyed the stock certificate referred to above.

5. Plaintiff has made demand on Raphe Corporation that Raphe Corporation issue to plaintiff a new share certificate. Defendant Raphe Corporation has failed, refused and neglected to issue a new share certificate although repeated demands have been made thereof.

WHEREFORE plaintiff prays:

1. For an order requiring the corporation to issue and deliver to plaintiff a new certificate for the above-mentioned shares;

2. For costs of suit and for such other relief as the court deems just.

____
Attorney for Plaintiff

CAPTION

ORDER FOR ISSUANCE OF NEW SHARE CERTIFICATE
(Corp. C. §419(c)

This cause came before the Honorable __________________, Judge of the Superior Court, in Department A of the above-entitled court on ______________, 19__, and after hearing evidence, oral and documentary, the court is satisfied that plaintiff is the lawful owner of 100 shares of common stock of Raphe Corporation and that the certificate has been destroyed and there is no sufficient cause why a new certificate should not be issued in place thereof.

Therefore, it is ordered that Raphe Corporation, immediately upon the posting of a bond by plaintiff in the sum of $______________ to indemnify said corporation against any claim that may be made against it on account of the destruction of the certificate, shall issue to the plaintiff a new certificate in which plaintiff shall be designated as record owner of 100 shares.

____
Judge

CAPTION) Case No.____________
)
) COMPLAINT FOR DECLARATORY RELIEF
)
___________________________)

Plaintiff complains and for cause of action alleges:

1. At all times herein mentioned, defendant was and now is a resident of __________County, California.

2. On or about______, 19___, in the City of________, California, plaintiff and defendant entered into a written agreement. A copy of the agreement is attached hereto, made a part hereof and incorporated herein.

3. An actual controversy has arisen and now exists between plaintiff and defendant concerning their respective rights and duties under said contract in that plaintiff contends paragraph 12 of said contract creates the following duties in defendant. (Set forth contentions), and defendant disputes this contention and contends the following: (Set forth defendant's contentions).

4. Plaintiff, by this action, seeks a judicial determination of his rights and duties under paragraph 12 of the abovementioned contract. Such a declaration is necessary to enable plaintiff to ascertain his rights and obligations under said agreement.

WHEREFORE, plaintiff prays judgment against defendant as follows:

1. For a declaration as follows: (Set forth requested judgment of the court).

2. For costs of suit herein and for such other relief as the court deems just.

DATED:_________________, 19_____.

____
Attorney for Plaintiff

****

C.C.P. §1060 permits a person affected by a deed,will, contract, or other legal instrument to seek a declaration of his rights and duties under the instrument. In addition declaratory relief may be used to test the validity of a statute. Abbott vs. City of Los Angeles 53 C.A. 2d, 674.

An action for declaratory relief may be joined with another action.

If declaratory relief is appropriate, the court must assume jurisdiction. Columbia Pictures vs. Detoth, 26 Cal 2d, 753.

CAPTION) Case No.______________
)
) COMPLAINT FOR DAMAGES FOR LIBEL
)
__________________)

Plaintiff complains:

1. At all times herein mentioned, defendant was and now is, a resident of the City of___________, County of ____________, State of California.

2. At all times mentioned herein, plaintiff was and now is engaged in the occupation of__________and resides in the City of_________, County of_________, State of California. Plaintiff has resided in said city for a period of___years and during that time has enjoyed an excellent reputation in both the community where he lives and the community where he works.

3. On or about______, 19___, defendant published a letter which stated the following defamatory material about plaintiff, (either set forth precise language or attach defamatory material as an exhibit).

4. The publication contains the name of the plaintiff as the object of the defamatory material, (or was made concerning the plaintiff and was so understood by those who read the publication).

5. The entire material is false as it applies to the plaintiff.

6. The entire material constitutes liabel per se in that it clearly exposes plaintiff to hatred, contempt, ridicule and obloque, for the following reasons, (specify reasons). (If the material is ambiguous, it must be alleged that the material is defamatory because the language sets forth facts which indicate why the words carry a defamatory meaning to those who read it, rather than an innocent meaning.)

7. The material was seen and read by the following persons, who read and saw the material in_________, California.

8. As a proximate result of the above described publication, plaintiff has suffered loss of his reputation, shame, mortification and hurt feelings, all to his damage in the sum of $________________.

9. As a further proximate result of the above-described publication, plaintiff has suffered the following special damages, (specify, such as injury to business or occupation), all to his injury in the sum of $___________. (If the publication is libel per se, an allegation of special damages is not necessary.)

10. The above-described publication was published by defendant of feelings of hatred and ill-will toward the plaintiff and with the desire to oppress plaintiff, therefore, plaintiff seeks an award of punitive damages in the sum of $____________.

WHEREFORE, plaintiff prays:

1. For general damages in the sum of $_________.

2. For special damages in the sum of $_________.

3. For punitive damages in the sum of $_______.

4. For costs of suit and such other relief as the court deems just.

____
Attorney for Plaintiff

****

Special damages need not be pleaded if the publication is clearly libelous on its face, Gautier vs. General Telephone, 234 C.A. 2d, 302.

Venue is proper in the county where defendant resides. C.C.P. §395a.

Complaint must specify with particularity the alleged defamatory material.

C.C.P. §460 provides that it may be pleaded generally that the matter was published or spoken concerning the plaintiff.

Innuendo must be pleaded where the words are susceptible of two interpretations, Washer vs. Bank of America 21 Cal 2d, 822.

Publication must be pleaded. Draper vs. Hellman, 203 Cal 26.

Special Damages when required must be alleged with particularity, Smith vs. Los Angeles Book Binders, 133, C.A. 2d, 486.

See Civil Code §§ 45 and 45a for definitions of libel and libel per se

CAPTION)
)
) COMPLAINT FOR TRADE LIBEL
)
______________________)

Case No.________________

Plaintiff complains:

1. At all times herein mentioned, defendant was and now is a resident of the City of__________, County of___________, State of California.

2. At all times herein mentioned, plaintiff was the owner of that certain business and business goods associated therewith, in the City of__________, County of__________, State of California. The business goods consisted of the following, (describe).

3. On or about______, 19____, defendants willfully, unlawfully, and without justification or privilege communicated to other persons statements which degraded, criticized, and cast aspersion on plaintiff's business goods. Such statements were false.

4. The statements made by the defendant resulted in a reduction of the value of the goods in the sum of $__________.

WHEREFORE, plaintiff prays:

1. For damages in the sum of $___________.

2. For costs of suit herein and such other relief as the court deems just.

____
Attorney for Plaintiff

****

Rosenberg vs. J.C. Penny, 31 C.A. 2d, 609.

Erlich vs. Etner, 224, C.A. 2d, 69.

CAPTION)
) COMPLAINT FOR SLANDER
)
)
________________)

Case No.__________

Plaintiff complains:

1. At all times herein mentioned, defendant was and now is a resident of the City of__________, County of__________, State of California.

2. At all times herein mentioned, plaintiff was and now is a resident of the City of__________, County of________, State of California and has, for the past ten years, enjoyed an excellent reputation both in the community where he lives and where he works as a_______________.

3. On or about_________, 19____, defendant stated at a meeting of the___________union, to a gathering of 50 people, the following words, "plaintiff has been convicted of child molestation."

4. The words were heard by ________and____________ and several other persons, whose names are not known to plaintiff.

5. The words were slanderous per se because they accused plaintiff of committing the crime of child molestation.

6. (If the words are not slanderous per se, or if there is doubt whether they applied to plaintiff, facts must be alleged to show why they are slanderous and why they applied to plaintiff.)

7. As a result of the defamatory remarks of defendant, plaintiff has suffered general damages to his reputation in the sum of $___________.

8. As a further proximate result of the above-described defamatory statements of defendant, plaintiff has suffered the following special damages, loss of position in the union, decrease in business, etc., all to his injury in the sum of $_____.

9. The above-described words were spoken by the defendant because of his feelings of hatred and ill will toward the plaintiff and such statements were made willfully and maliciously and thus plaintiff is entitled to punitive damages in the amount of $_______________.

WHEREFORE, plaintiff prays:

1. For judgment in the amount of $________for general damages.

2. For judgment in the amount of $________for special damages.

3. For judgment in the amount of $________for punitive damages.

4. For costs of suit and such other relief as the court deems just.

____
Attorney for Plaintiff

****

Plaintiff need not specify the exact words alleged to be slanderous, however, pleading of innuendo is required where words are ambiguous. Washer vs. Bank of America, 21 Cal. 2d, 822.

Pleading of inducement is required to set forth extrinsic circumstances where the language is ambiguous. White vs. Valenta, 234 C.A. 2d, 243.

See Civil Code §46.

Accusing one of conviction of a crime is slander per se, Clay vs. Lagiss, 143 C.A. 2d, 441.

CAPTION	)	Case No.__________
	)	
	)	COMPLAINT FOR SLANDER OF TITLE
	)	
____________________	)	

Plaintiff complains:

1. At all times herein mentioned, defendant was and now is, a resident of the City of________, State of California.

2. At all times herein mentioned, plaintiff was the owner of, and in possession to the following described real property situated in the County of___________, (describe).

3. On or about______, 19___, defendant willfully and unlawfully, and without justification or privilege stated the following words in the presence of plaintiff and his property, (describe).

4. The words were false and cast doubt on plaintiff's title to the property.

5. The words uttered by defendant directly impaired the immediately saleability of the property to____________, a potential purchaser who was present when the statements were made.

WHEREFORE, plaintiff prays:

1. For damages in the sum of $______________.

2. For costs of suit herein and such other relief as the court deems just.

____
Attorney for Plaintiff

****

Hill vs. Allan, 249 C.A. 2d, 470.

CAPTION	)	Case No.______________
	)	
	)	ANSWER TO COMPLAINT FOR
	)	DEFAMATION
____________________	)	(With Optional Affirmative Defenses)

COMES NOW defendant__________, and in answer to the complaint on file herein, admits, denies and alleges as follows:

1. Under the provisions of C.C.P. §431.30, this answering defendant denies generally and specifically each and every allegation contained in plaintiff's complaint and the whole thereof and further denies that plaintiff was damaged in the sum of $__________or in any sum whatsoever.

FIRST AFFIRMATIVE DEFENSE

2. At no time was a notice and demand for retraction served on defendant and thus defendant was unable to make the required correction or retraction.

SECOND AFFIRMATIVE DEFENSE

3. Plaintiff's complaint fails to allege any special damages, thus plaintiff cannot recover such damages.

THIRD AFFIRMATIVE DEFENSE

4. This answering defendant is not liable for the alleged defamatory statement made by ______________for the reason that ___________is not the agent or employee of defendant and this answering defendant exercised due care to prevent the publication.

FOURTH AFFIRMATIVE DEFENSE

5. The statements alleged to be defamatory, were in fact, truthful for the following reasons, (describe).

FIFTH AFFIRMATIVE DEFENSE

6. The statements alleged to be defamatory were made by defendant in good faith honestly and not with malice, for the following reason, (describe).

SIXTH AFFIRMATIVE DEFENSE

7. The statements complained of in plaintiff's complaint were made by defendant in his official capacity as___________ and thus were privileged under Civil Code §47(1) for the following reasons, (describe).

SEVENTH AFFIRMATIVE DEFENSE

8. The statements alleged to be defamatory were made by defendant during the legislative proceeding of___________legislative body and thus were absolutely privileged under Civil Code §47(2), (or were made in connection with a judicial proceeding).

EIGHTH AFFIRMATIVE DEFENSE

9. The alleged defamatory statements were made by defendant on_________, 19____, in a fair and true report contained in the following publication, (specify) and said report accurately described the proceedings of a public meeting held for the following lawful purpose, (describe).

NINTH AFFIRMATIVE DEFENSE

10. The statements complained of as being defamatory were made by defendant on_______, 19____, and such statements were consented to by plaintiff in the following manner, (describe).

TENTH AFFIRMATIVE DEFENSE

11. The cause of action of plaintiff is barred by the statute of limitations in that the complaint was filed on _________and the alleged statements were made on______________, greater than one year.

ELEVENTH AFFIRMATIVE DEFENSE

12. The alleged defamatory statements were made by defendant without any feelings by defendant of hatred or ill will toward plaintiff and did not carry any defamatory meaning to those who heard the remarks.

TWELFTH AFFIRMATIVE DEFENSE

13. The alleged defamatory statements were made by this answering defendant in his capacity as an employee of the City of___________.

WHEREFORE, defendant prays that plaintiff take nothing by his complaint and that defendant be awarded his costs of suit and other relief as the court deems just.

____
Attorney for Defendant

****

These defenses may be raised by demurrer where facts supporting the defenses appear on the face of the complaint.

Defenses:

Special Damages: Pridonoff vs. Balokovich, 36 Cal. 2d, 788

Retraction Statute: Notice and demand must be served within 20 days after the publication or broadcast. Civil Code §48a(1). Field Research vs. Superior Court, 71 Cal. 2d, 110. This applies only to newspapers and radio, and not to magazines.

Truth: Swaffield vs. Universal, 271 C.A. 2d, 147.

Privilege: Qualified, conditional and absolute, Saroyan vs. Burkett, 57 Cal. 2d, 706. King vs. Borges, 28 C.A. 3d, 27.

Governmental Immunity: Lipman vs. Brisbane School District, 55 Cal 2d, 224.

	)	Case No. ___________
	)	
	)	NOTICE OF MOTION TO VACATE
CAPTION	)	DEFAULT AND DEFAULT JUDGMENT
	)	DUE TO LACK OF PERSONAL SERVICE
	)	[C.C.P. §473.5]
	)	Date:_______________
	)	Time:_______________
______________________________	)	Dept:_______________

TO____________________PLAINTIFF AND TO HIS ATTORNEY:

YOU AND EACH OF YOU WILL PLEASE TAKE NOTICE that on ____________, 19___, at the hour of __________A.M., or as soon thereafter as counsel may be heard, in Department ____ of the above-entitled court, defendant will move the court for an order to vacate and set aside the default and default judgment entered in the above action and to allow defendant to defend the action by filing the answer, a copy of which is attached hereto.

The motion will be made on the ground that the defendant was not personally served with the summons and complaint, but was served by publication only, and had no actual notice in time to defend the action.

The motion will be supported by the notice of motion, the memorandum of points and authorities and declaration in support thereof attached hereto, the papers and records on file herein, and such other evidence oral and documentary as may be presented at the hearing on the motion.

DATED: ______________________, 19____.

____
Attorney for Plaintiff

****

This motion must be served and filed within a reasonable time. However, it cannot exceed the earlier of:

2 years after entry of a default judgment; or
180 days after service upon defendant of a written notice that the judgment has been entered. C.C.P. §473.5.

A supporting affidavit must allege that the party's lack of actual notice was not due to his avoidance of service or inexcusable neglect.

A copy of the answer, motion or other pleading proposed to be filed must be filed with this motion.

CAPTION) Case No. ____________
)
) NOTICE OF MOTION TO SET ASIDE AND
) VACATE DEFAULT AND DEFAULT JUDGMENT
) [C.C.P. §473]
) Date:________________
______________________) Time:________________
Dept:________________

TO____________________, PLAINTIFF AND TO HIS ATTORNEY:

PLEASE TAKE NOTICE that on______________, 19____, at the hour of ________A.M., or as soon thereafter as the matter may be heard, in Department ____of the above-entitled court, defendant will move for an order vacating the default and the default judgment entered in the above-entitled proceeding, on the ground that the default was taken as a result of the excusable neglect of the defendant.

The motion will be based upon this notice of motion, the memorandum of points and authorities attached hereto, the declaration of _______________ in support thereof, the papers and records on file herein, and such other evidence oral and documentary as may be presented at the hearing on the motion.

DATED: ____________________, 19____.

____
Attorney for Defendant

****

This motion must be accompanied by a copy of the answer or other pleading proposed to be filed.

The application must be filed within a reasonable time, but in no case exceeding 6 months after the judgment, order or other proceeding was taken. C.C.P. §473.

Excusable neglect may be found in a case where an attorney moves his office. Northridge vs. Hamblin, 48 C.A.3d 819.

Other cases:

Robinson vs. Hiles, 119 C.A.2d 666;
City of Ontario vs. Superior Court, 2 C.3d 335.

Failure of a secretary to note in a diary the date of a hearing might be excusable. Palmer vs. Moore, 266 C.A.2d 134.

Misplacing of papers or forgetfulness or the failure to recognize the significance of a pleading ordinarily are not good excuses. Price vs. Hibbs, 225 C.A.2d 209.

Generally, the "busy attorney" reason has not been considered a good one. Martin vs. Taylor, 267 C.A.2d 112.

CAPTION)
) Case No.__________
)
) DEMURRER TO COMPLAINT
)
________________________)

COMES NOW defendant____________, and demurs to count_____of the complaint on the following grounds: (Set forth appropriate statutory grounds which may be one or all of the following.)

1. The court has no jurisdiction of the subject matter of the cause of action.

2. The plaintiff does not have legal capacity to sue.

3. There is another action pending between the same parties on the same cause of action in the________court of __________County, case #________.

4. There is a defect or misjoinder of parties.

5. The complaint does not state facts sufficient to constitute a cause of action.

6. The pleading is uncertain in the following respects: (Uncertainty must be specifically pleaded. Demurrers for uncertainty are looked upon with disfavor.)

7. It cannot be ascertained from the complaint whether the contract sued upon is written or oral.

WHEREFORE, defendant prays that the demurrer be sustained, (with or without) leave to amend.

DATED:______________, 19____.

____
Attorney for Defendant

I hereby certify that this demurrer is filed in good faith and not for the purpose of delay and, in my opinion, the grounds are well taken.

____
Attorney for Defendant

****

The party filing a demurrer must serve and file therewith, a notice of hearing, shich shall specify a hearing date not less than 10 nor more than 15 days from the filing of the demurrer. Rules of Court 202(b).

A demurrer must be taken to each count that is vulnerable. A demurrer to the whole complaint will be overruled if any single count is invulnerable.

Points and authorities must be submitted in support of each ground. The absence of points and authorities may be construed by the court as an admission that the demurrer is not meritorious. Rule 202(a).

It is of utmost importance to consult local rules on demurrers.

The demurrer must be filed within the time allowed to answer. A demurrer to the complaint may be filed separately or with the answer. A notice of motion to strike may be filed with a demurrer. C.C.P. § 430, §431 and §435.

CAPTION)
)
) NOTICE OF HEARING ON DEMURRER
)
_____________________________)

Case No.__________

Date:_______________
Time:_______________
Department:_________

TO THE PLAINTIFF_________________AND TO HIS ATTORNEY:

YOU, AND EACH OF YOU, WILL PLEASE TAKE NOTICE that a demurrer to the complaint was filed on_____, 19____, and has been set for hearing on_________, 19____, at the hour of________ a.m. in Department______of the above entitled court.

DATED:____________, 19______.

____
Attorney for Defendant

CAPTION)   Case No.____________
)
) DEMURRER TO ANSWER
)
_________________________)

COMES NOW the plaintiff and demurs to the answer of defendant on the following grounds:

1. Defendant's first affirmative defense does not state facts sufficient to constitute a cause of action.

2. It cannot be ascertained from the first affirmative defense whether the contract on which the defense is based is written or oral.

3. Paragraph____of the answer is uncertain for the following reasons: (Set forth reasons.)

DATED:_______________, 19_____.

____
Attorney for Plaintiff

****

The grounds for an objection by demurrer to answer are found in C.C.P. §430.20.

A notice of hearing on a demurrer to an answer is required.

CAPTION)   Case No.____________
)
) NOTICE OF MOTION TO STRIKE
) COMPLAINT
____________________________)

Date:________________
Time:________________
Department:__________

TO THE PLAINTIFF________________AND TO HIS ATTORNEY:

PLEASE TAKE NOTICE that on___________, 19____, at the hour of_______a.m. or as soon thereafter as the matter may be heard in Department_____ of the above entitled court, defendant will move the court for an order striking the following portions of the complaint. (Set for portions under attack.)

The motion will be made upon the following grounds: (Specify grounds.)

The motion will be based upon the notice of motion, points and authorities, and the declarations attached hereto, the pleadings and records on file herein and such other evidence, oral and documentary as may be presented at the hearing.

DATED:____________________, 19_____.

____
Attorney for Defendant

****

A party may within the time allowed to answer serve and file a notice of motion to strike the whole or any part of the complaint. He may also demur at the same time. The notice of motion to strike shall specify a hearing date not more than 15 days from the filing of the notice plus any additional time that the party is otherwise required to give the other party. C.C.P. §435(e).

It is important to consult local rules in filing a motion to strike.

The function of the motion to strike is to eliminate irrelevant and redundant portions of the pleading.

A motion to strike has been used to strike an unverified complaint where verification was required. Greenfield vs. Steamer, 6 Cal 2d, 67.

A motion to strike may attack a sham pleading. Lincoln vs. Didak, 162 C.A. 2d, 625.

The motion may be used to attack a pleading untimely filed. Buck vs. Morrosis, 114 C.A. 2d, 161.

CAPTION)
)
)
__________)

NOTICE OF MOTION FOR DEPOSIT IN COURT OF RENTS HELD BY THE DEBTOR

TO THE DEFENDANT IN THE ACTION AND TO __________________ HIS ATTORNEY:

YOU AND EACH OF YOU WILL PLEASE TAKE NOTICE that on ___________, 19__, at the hour of ___________a.m. in Department ___________ of the above entitled court, plaintiff will move the court for an order requiring the defendant to deposit into court rentals as they are received from the property commonly known as 123 Elm Street, Los Angeles, California, the property which is the subject of this action.

Said motion will be made for the reason that the rents belong to the plaintiff in that the plaintiff has executed on the property presently perfecting the sale on that execution.

Said motion will be made upon the basis of the papers on file herein and such other evidence, oral and documentary, as may be produced at the hearing.

Dated:_______________

____
Attorney for Plaintiff

****

The authority for deposit in court is found in CCP §572.

Rentals from property allegedly conveyed by a judgment debtor in fraud of judgment creditor may be impounded by the court. Michael vs. Adair, 66 C.A. 2d 282.

CAPTION)
)
)
_________)

DECLARATION IN SUPPORT OF MOTION FOR DEPOSIT IN COURT

I, __________________declare:

I am the plaintiff in the within action and ______________ is the defendant herein against whom a judgment has been rendered.

On ______________, 19___, at my request, a writ of execution was levied on the property described as follows:

A public sale was duly held and I purchased the property at the execution sale and am awaiting perfection of that sale.

Immediately prior to the sale the defendant conveyed the property to _______________________ and it is contended that the coveyance was without consideration and was done with the intent to deprive plaintiff of his ability to effectively execute upon the property. Plaintiff is informed and believes and upon such information and belief alleges that ___________________ the tenant in said property has been and still is paying rent to the defendant.

I declare under penalty of perjury that the foregoing is true and correct.

Executed at ______________, California on ____________, 19___.

____
Plaintiff

CAPTION)
)
)
________)

ORDER FOR DEPOSIT

The motion for an order for deposit came on for hearing on ______________, 19_____, ____________________________ appeared as attorney for plaintiff and ____________________________________ appeared as attorney for defendant.

After considering the motion and points and authorities and declarations submitted therewith, on behalf of both sides, the court finds that the rentals which are held by defendant be retained by the court until final disposition of the matter.

Therefore, it is ordered that defendant deposit the sum of ________________ with the clerk of this court who is directed to deposit the funds with the County Treasurer until further order of the court.

Dated: ____________ ____________________________
Judge

****

CAPTION	)	Case No.____________
	)	
	)	PETITION TO PERPETUATE TESTIMONY
	)	PRIOR TO ACTION
______________________	)	

The petition of__________respectfully shows:

1. Petitioner expects to file an action in__________ court, of the State of California, for the County of__________, for personal injuries. Petitioner expects to be the plaintiff in the action.

2. Petitioner is presently unable to bring the action for the following reasons. (Set forth reasons.)

3. The facts which petitioner desires to establish by the proposed testimony are: (Set forth facts.)

4. Petitioner seeks to perpetuate the testimony for the following reasons, (Set forth reasons.) and to prevent a failure of justice by virtue of a delay.

5. The names and addresses of the persons whom petitioner believes will be the defendants in the action are as follows: (Set forth names and addresses.)

6. The names and addresses of the persons sought to be examined and the substance of their testimony expected to be elicited is as follows: (Set forth names, addresses and descriptions of testimony.)

WHEREFORE, petitioner prays that the court enter an order authorizing petitioner to take the deposition of__________ and ________________ for the purpose of perpetuating such testimony.

DATED:__________________, 19____.

____
Petitioner

****

A person may perpetuate his own testimony or that of another either before the filing of an action or pending an appeal by filing a verified petition. C.C.P. §2017(a).

A notice must be served upon each person named in the petition expected to be an adverse party. At least 20 days before the hearing on the notice, the application shall be served in a manner as a summons must be served.

The purpose of this section is to preserve testimony and not to accomplish discovery. Hunt-Wesson vs. Stanislaus County, 273 C.A. 2d, 982.

CAPTION) Case No.______________
)
) INTERROGATORIES PROPOUNDED TO
__________________) PLAINTIFF

TO: ________________________PLAINTIFF AND TO____________________
HIS ATTORNEY OF RECORD:

Defendants,________________________, pursuant to §'s 2030 and 2016, Code of Civil Procedure, request that plaintiff answer the following interrogatories under oath, separately and fully, within 30 days of service hereof.

INTERROGATORY NO. 1

Referring to paragraph 5 of your first cause of action:

A. Were the alleged representations by telephone or in person?

B. If the said representations were in person, at what place were they made and who was present?

C. Was the alleged computation made within your sight?

D. Was any written computation ever given to you?

E. If the answer to D is yes, what were the figures? (Attachment of a copy will be a sufficient answer).

F. Is there any written instrument of any kind or nature setting forth that you were to net the sum of $85,000.00?

G. If the answer to F is yes, what is the wording of such instrument? (Attachment of a copy will be a sufficient answer).

INTERROGATORY NO. 2

Referring to paragraph 6 of your first cause of action:

A. Were the alleged representations by telephone or in person?

B. If the said representations were in person, at what place were they made and who was present?

INTERROGATORY NO. 3

Referring to paragraph 8 of your first cause of action:

A. Were the alleged representations by telephone or in person?

B. If the said representations were in person, at what place were they made and who was present?

C. What is the maximum number of days embraced by your words "shortly after?"

D. Do you contend that your Exhibit 4 provides for withdrawal of $5,000.00?

E. If the answer to D is "yes," what are the facts upon which your contention is based?

INTERROGATORY NO. 4

Referring to paragraph 9 of your first cause of action:

A. With whom did______________make the alleged agreement?

B. Referring to your Exhibit 5, what "refinance charges of the buyers" appear thereon?

C. If in your answer to B, above you have included $6,212.34 prepayment charges to______________, what are the facts upon which you base your contention the payment of the obligation to______________________constituted a buyer's refinance charge?

INTERROGATORY NO. 5

Referring to paragraph 10 if your first cause of action you refer to a " the full sum of $335,000.00." In what way does this differ from the "gross sales price of $335,000.00" referred to on page 2, line 31, page 3, lines 3, 18-19 and page 4, line 4?

INTERROGATORY NO. 6

Referring to paragraph 11 of your first cause of action, you allege receipt of $75,356.64 and attached to your Complaint is Exhibit 5 which shows as the first of Charges, "By Second Trust Deed $35,000.00" and which further shows as the next to the last item "Balance due you for which check is enclosed $33,054.65." How is the $75,356.65 referred to in your paragraph XI arrived at?

INTERROGATORY N0. 7

Referring to your paragraph 12 of your first cause of action, what are the facts upon which you have based your contention that the alleged statements of____________were fraudulent?

INTERROGATORY NO. 8

Referring to paragraph 7 of your second cause of action what are the facts upon which you base your contention that the defendants conspired together?

INTERROGATORY NO. 9

Referring to paragraph 8 of your second cause of action:

A. Which defendant or defendants actually made the representations referred to in your subparagraph 1?

B. If your answer names any person or persons other than____________:

1) Were the representations by telephone or in person?

2) When were the representations made?

3) If the representations were in person, where were they made and who was present on each occasion?

INTERROGATORY NO. 10

Referring to paragraph 10 of your second cause of action:

A. Were the alleged representations by____________ written or oral?

B. Were the alleged representations by____________ in person or by the telephone?

C. If the answer is in person, where were the alleged representations made and who was present.

D. Were the alleged representations by____________ written or oral?

E. Were the alleged representations by____________ in person or by telephone?

F. If the answer is in person, where were the alleged representations made and who was present?

DATED: ____________________, 19____.

____
Attorney for

CAPTION) Case No.____________

) NOTICE OF MOTION TO REQUIRE ANSWERS TO INTERROGATORIES AND FOR SANCTIONS

Date:____________
Time:____________
Department:____________

TO________________AND TO________________, HIS ATTORNEY:

YOU AND EACH OF YOU, WILL PLEASE TAKE NOTICE that on ____________, 19____at the hour of_____a.m. in Department________of the above entitled court,__________will move the court for an order requiring__________to answer the following interrogatories heretofore submitted, (Set forth the number of interrogatories for which answers are desired.) and to pay____________ the reasonable expenses and attorney's fees incurred in bringing this motion and obtaining the answers requested.

The motion will be made on the grounds that____________ refused, without proper justification, to answer said interrogatories. The motion will further be based upon C.C.P. §2034(a), upon the declaration and points and authorities attached hereto, the papers and records on file herein and such other evidence, oral and documentary to be presented at the hearing on the motion.

DATED:________________, 19____.

____
Attorney for

****

This procedure is authorized by C.C.P. §2034.

The trial court may apply, if requested, the ultimate sanction of default against a litigant who persists in refusal to comply with his discovery obligations. <u>Petersen vs. City of Vallejo</u>, 259 C.A. 2d, 757.

CAPTION)   Case No.__________
)
) NOTICE OF DEPOSITION
)
____________________________) Date:________________
Time:________________
Place:_______________

TO ______________AND________________, HIS ATTORNEY:

YOU ARE HEREBY NOTIFIED, that on____________, 19____, at the hour of______a.m., the plaintiff in the above entitled cause will take the deposition of_____________whose address is ____________________________, ______________California.

The deposition will be taken at the office of__________ ____________which is located at_____________________. The deposition will be on oral examination before ________________ a notary public or any other notary public. The deposition will continue from day to day until completed.

DATED:_________________, 19_____.

____
Attorney for

CAPTION) Case No.__________
)
) REQUEST FOR ADMISSIONS
)
__________________________)

TO________________AND TO__________________, HIS ATTORNEY:

________________hereby requests that you admit within 20 days from the date of the service of this request, the genuineness of the following documents and the truth of the matters of fact herein listed.

1. The promissory note, a copy of which is attached hereto and marked Exhibit "A" is a genuine document.

2. That the signature on said document was in fact executed by_________________.

3. The amount of the note, to wit $10,000.00 remains due, owing and unpaid.

DATED__________________, 19_____.

____
Attorney for

****

After the service of summons or the appearance of a party, any other party who has appeared may serve upon such party, who has been served or who has appeared, a written request for admissions. Each of the matters of which an admission is requested shall be deemed admitted unless within the period designated in the request, or not less than 20 days after service, the matters are denied under oath. C.C.P. §2033.

CAPTION)
)
)
)
_______________________)

Case No.______________

NOTICE OF MOTION FOR DISMISSAL
(FAILURE TO SERVE SUMMONS AND
FILE RETURN)

Date:_______________
Time:_______________
Department:_________

TO____________________PLAINTIFF AND TO HIS ATTORNEY:

YOU AND EACH OF YOU SHALL PLEASE TAKE NOTICE that on _____________, 19____ at the hour of_____ A. M. in Department _____________ of the above entitled court, defendants will move the court for an order dismissing the within action.

Said motion will be made upon that the grounds that service and return of summons has not been made within three years of the commencement of the action. The motion will be further based upon the declaration and points and authorities attached hereto, all papers and records on file herein and upon such other evidence oral and documentary to be presented at the hearing on this motion.

DATED:_______________, 19______.

____
Attorney for Defendant

****

A motion to dismiss may be made for failure to serve a summons and file the return within three years from the commencement of the action. A motion may also be made in places where a summons is required on a cross complaint and a summons is not served and returned within three years. C.C.P., §581(a).

The above provisions are inapplicable where parties have filed a stipulation extending the time or where the party against whom the action is prosecuted has not made a general appearance.

A motion to dismiss shall not be construed as a general appearance.

A general appearance made after the three year period will not deprive a defendant of his right to a dismissal. Bushing vs. Superior Court 12 Cal. 3rd 44.

CAPTION	)	Case No.________________
	)	
	)	NOTICE OF MOTION TO DISMISS
_______________________	)	(FAILURE TO BRING ACTION TO TRIAL)

Date:__________________
Time:__________________
Department:____________

TO THE________________PLAINTIFF AND TO HIS ATTORNEY:

YOU AND EACH OF YOU PLEASE TAKE NOTICE that on __________, 19______, at the hour of_______ A. M., in Department _________ of the above entitled court, defendant will move the court for an order dismissing the above entitled action. The motion will be made upon the grounds that two years has elapsed since the filing of the summons and complaint and that plaintiff has failed to bring the action to trial. The motion will be further be based upon the declaration and points and authorities attached hereto and all papers and records on file herein and upon such evidence oral and documentary to be presented upon the hearing of this motion.

DATED:________________, 19________.

____
Attorney for Defendant

****

Court rules require forty-five days notice for the hearing on this motion.

It is discretionary for the court to dismiss an action where it is not brought to trial within two years after it was filed. It is mandatory that the action be dismissed where it is not brought to trial within five years after its commencement.

After the granting of a new trial, the action must be brought to trial within three years after the entry of the order granting a new trial. C.C.P., §583.

CAPTION	))))))))))	No. ____________ NOTICE OF MOTION FOR LIEN ON CAUSE OF ACTION Date: ____________ Time: ____________ Dept: ____________

TO ______________________ AND TO HIS ATTORNEY:

YOU AND EACH OF YOU are hereby notified that on __________ __________, 19_____, at the hour of ____________ A.M. in Department ________ of the above-entitled court, the judgment creditor ______________________ will move this court for a lien upon the cause of action and any subsequent judgment obtained by plaintiff and for leave to intervene in the action.

Said motion will be made upon the ground that such lien and intervention are necessary in order to realize upon the judgment entered into the action of the moving party against the plaintiff. The motion will further be based upon C.C.P. §688.1, and upon the declaration and points and authorities attached to the motion and all other papers, records and documents on file herein, and upon evidence oral and documentary as to be presented at the hearing on the motion.

DATED: ______________________________.

____
Attorney for ______________

CAPTION	No. ____________ NOTICE OF MOTION FOR ISSUANCE OF WRIT OF EXECUTION AFTER 10 YEARS Date:______________ Time:______________ Dept:______________

TO DEFENDANT____________________AND TO HIS ATTORNEY:

YOU AND EACH OF YOU WILL PLEASE TAKE NOTICE that on ______________, 19___, at the hour of ____________ A.M., in Department ____ of the above-entitled court, plaintiff will move the court for an order to issue execution on the judgment entered on ______________, 19___, and recorded in Judgment Book ______ at page______, in the Clerk's Office in ____________ County, California.

The motion will be made upon the grounds that plaintiff was unable to levy execution within the 10 years allowed although due diligence was exercised in efforts to do so and in efforts to locate the defendant.

The motion will be based upon the provisions of C.C.P. §685, this notice of motion and affidavit and points and authorities attached hereto, all the papers and records on file herein, and upon such other evidence, oral and documentary, as may be presented at the hearing on the motion.

DATED: ______________________.

____
Attorney for Plaintiff

****

C.C.P. §685.

Lesh vs. Lesh, 8 C.A.3d 883.

CAPTION	No. ______________________ DECLARATION IN SUPPORT OF MOTION FOR ISSUANCE OF WRIT OF EXECUTION

I, __________________, declare:

I am the plaintiff and judgment creditor in the above-entitled cause. On ________________, 19______, judgment was entered for plaintiff in the sum of $_________plus costs, and was recorded in Judgment Book ________ at page _______ in the Clerk's Office of ___________County, California.

Plaintiff has made the following efforts to locate property of the defendant upon which execution of judgment could have been made: (set forth efforts).

Plaintiff has made the following efforts to locate the defendant (set forth efforts), and has been unable to do so.

More than 10 years has elapsed since the entry of judgment and no party of the judgment has been paid. Recently plaintiff has discovered the whereabouts of the defendant, and has further discovered assets which are subject to execution.

WHEREFORE, it is prayed that an order be made for the issuance of a writ of execution in the amount of $_______ plus interest thereon at 7% per annum and costs.

I declare under penalty of perjury that the foregoing is true and correct.

EXECUTED at__________________, California, on____________, 19____.

____
Plaintiff

****

The motion, points and authorities and declaration must be served on the defendant.

CAPTION)
) No. ___________
)
) ORDER FOR ISSUANCE OF WRIT OF EXECUTION
)
)
_________________________)

The motion of plaintiff for an order allowing the issuance of a writ of execution upon the judgment entered on _____________, 19_____, and recorded in the Judgment Book No. ______ on page____ in the Clerk's Office of the County of _____________, California, came on regularly for hearing before the undersigned on ________ _____________, 19___. Notice was duly given, and defendant did not appear.

Evidence oral and documentary was presented, and the matter was submitted to the court. Good cause appearing therefor,

IT IS HEREBY ORDERED that the motion of plaintiff is granted, and the Clerk of the Court is ordered to issue the writ of execution.

DATED: _______________________.

____
Judge

CAPTION ______________________________	No. ____________ APPLICATION FOR WRIT OF EXECUTION AGAINST DWELLING HOUSE [C.C.P. §690.31]

The verified application respectfully shows:

Applicant is a judgment creditor of____________. A judgment was entered in Judgment Book ______, page_____, on ________________, 19____, in the Clerk's Office of the County of _______________, California, for the sum of $____________ plus costs.

The defendant resides in a dwelling house the common address of which is____, and the legal description of which is_____________________ ____.

The value of the dwelling house if $_________, and the total amount of the liens and encumbrances on said dwelling house are $_______________. Such amounts exceed the allowable exemption by $______________.

(Alternate paragraph). The dwelling house is not exempt for the reason that an abstract of judgment recorded with the County Recorder of ______________County, California on__________, 19____, and a declaration of homestead was recorded with the County Recorder of _______________County on _______________, 19___. A search of the records of the County Tax Assessor reveals that there is no home owner's exemption claim either by the debtor or the spouse of the debtor. (Or an allegation that the debtor or spouse are not entitled to the exemption.)

WHEREFORE, your applicant prays that the court set a time and place for a hearing and order the debtor to show cause why a writ of execution should not issue.

I declare under penalty of perjury that the foregoing is true and correct.

EXECUTED at Los Angeles, California, on _________, 19____.

____
Declarant

****

This application must be verified.

CAPTION	No. ______________
	ORDER TO SHOW CAUSE WHY WRIT OF EXECUTION AGAINST DWELLING HOUSE SHOULD NOT ISSUE
	Date: ______________ Time: ______________ Dept: ______________

TO THE DEFENDANT ______________________:

This court having on the _____ day of ______________, 19____, upon the verified application of the plaintiff above-named, considered whether a writ of execution should issue on your dwelling house, and having determined that there is good cause for the issuance of said writ,

IT IS HEREBY ORDERED that defendant ______________________ be and appear before this court on ______________________, 19___, at the hour of __________ A.M. in Department _____ of the Courthouse at ______________________________ Street, Los Angeles, California, then and there to show cause, if any he may have, why the aforementioned writ of execution should not issue.

DATED: ________________________.

____
Judge

****

The creditor's application, the order to show cause, and the notice to homeowner, which is the next form, must all be served on the homeowner.

If the hearing is held in the absence of the debtor or spouse, further notice must be served. If the debtor or spouse submits a declaration setting forth a valid excuse for their absence, the Clerk must set a hearing to determine whether the writ of execution should be recalled. C.C.P. §690.31(h).

"IMPORTANT NOTICE TO
HOMEOWNER AND RESIDENT

1. Your house is in danger of being sold to satisfy a judgment obtained in court. You may be able to protect the house and real property described in the accompanying application from execution and forced sale if you or your family now actually reside on the property and presently do not have a declared homestead on any other property in the State of California. YOU OR YOUR SPOUSE MUST COME TO THE HEARING TO SHOW THESE FACTS.

2. If you or your spouse want to contest the forced sale of this property, you or your spouse must appearing at ____
____________________ on ____________________
(location set forth on OSC) (date and time)
to answer questions concerning the statements made in the attached application. THE ONLY PURPOSE OF THE HEARING WILL BE TO DETERMINE WHETHER THE PROPERTY CAN BE SOLD, NOT WHETHER YOU OWE THE MONEY.

3. FOR YOUR OWN PROTECTION, YOU SHOULD PROMPTLY SEEK THE ADVICE OF AN ATTORNEY IN THIS MATTER."

* * * * *

REQUIRED NOTICE PRIOR TO HEARING - CCP § 690.31d

"IMPORTANT NOTICE TO
HOMEOWNER AND RESIDENT

1. You were recently served with a court order requiring your presence at a hearing to determine why the court should not issue a writ of execution for the forced sale of your home. YOU AND YOUR SPOUSE FAILED TO APPEAR AT THE HEARING AND THE COURT HAS ORDERED THAT YOUR HOME BE SOLD TO SATISFY A JUDGMENT AGAINST YOU."

2. Your absence at the hearing has contributed to the issuance of the accompanying writ of execution. If the absence of you or your attorney at the hearing was legally excusable and you believe in good faith that your home may be entitled to an exemption from execution, you should complete the form below the date, sign, and return the form below no later than ________________ (Insert date no later than five days prior to date of sale.)

3. FOR YOUR OWN PROTECTION YOU SHOULD IMMEDIATELY SEEK THE ADVICE OF AN ATTORNEY.

... (Cut Out and Return This Form to)...
____________________ (Name and Title of Levying Officer)
_______________________ (Street Address and City)
____________________ (Area Code and Telephone Number of Levying Officer)

I declare that my absence from the previous hearing on whether or not this property should be sold was legally excusable. I, or my spouse, currently reside in this property and I wish a further hearing so that I may assert my exemption rights under Code of Civil Procedure Section 690.31 and contest the sale of my home. I understand that the clerk of the court will notify me of the date and place for this hearing if I return this form immediately and that I must attend this hearing.

I declare under penalty of perjury that the foregoing is true and correct.
Executed on __________________ at ______________, California.

____
Signature of Debtor or Debtor's Spouse

* * * * *

REQUIRED NOTICE IF DEBTOR ABSENT FROM HEARING - CCP § 690.31f

CAPTION) No. ________________
) CLAIM OF EXEMPTION
________________________)

I, ____________________, declare:

I am the defendant in the above-entitled cause.

On ________________, 19____, the sheriff of the County of ______________, pursuant to a writ of execution, levied on the following-described property belonging to me: (set forth description).

The property is exempt from execution by virtue of the provisions of C.C.P. §_______.

The reason why the property is exempt is as follows: (Reasons must be specifically stated).

My address within this State for the purpose of permitting service by mail is (set forth address).

WHEREFORE, it is claimed that the property is exempt, be ordered exempt, and that the property be released pursuant to C.C.P. §690.50.

I declare under penalty of perjury that the foregoing is true and correct.

EXECUTED at ______________, California, on ____________, 19_____.

____
Declarant

****

The claim of exemption must be delivered to the levying officer within 10 days in the case of personal property and within 20 days in the case of real property, except in the cases of dwelling houses.

If property levied upon consists of earnings of the judgment debtor, each date that earnings are withheld from the judgment debtor shall be deemed to be the date such earnings were levied upon for the purpose of notice.

If plaintiff desires to serve a counter declaration, it must be served within 10 days in the case of real property or 5 days in the case of personal property from the time the affidavit of exemption is received from the levying officer. C.C.P. § 690.50(b).

CAPTION	No. ______________
	NOTICE OF MOTION FOR DETERMINATION OF CLAIM OF EXEMPTION
	Date: ______________
	Time: ______________
	Dept: ______________

TO THE DEFENDANT ________________ AND TO HIS ATTORNEY:

YOU AND EACH OF YOU WILL PLEASE TAKE NOTICE that on ________________, 19____, at the hour of ____________, or as soon thereafter as the matter may be heard, in Department ____ of the above-entitled court, plaintiff will move the court for an order determining that defendant's claim of exemption to ________________ property should not be sustained.

The motion will be made on the ground that defendant has heretofore filed his declaration of claim of exemption and plaintiff has filed a counter declaration contesting the claim of exemption, and that the property is not exempt. The motion will be based upon the provisions of C.C.P. §690.50(e), this notice of motion, the declarations of the respective parties, memorandum of points and authorities served and filed herewith, on all papers and records on file herein, and on such evidence oral and documentary as may be presented at the hearing on the motion.

DATED: ______________________

____
Attorney for Plaintiff

****

This motion may be instituted by either plaintiff or defendant. The motion must be made within 5 days after the counter declaration is filed. The hearing must be had within 15 days from the date of making the motion. The party making the motion shall give not less than 5 days' notice of the hearing to the levying officer and to the other party. C.C.P. §690.50(e).

Prior to the hearing either party may move the court for the sale of perishable property. C.C.P. §690.50(g).

	)	No. ____________
CAPTION	)	ORDER DETERMINING PROPERTY AS EXEMPT
____________________	)	

The motion of plaintiff came on regularly for hearing by the court before the undersigned on ___________, 19____. Plaintiff appeared by his attorney____________, and defendant appeared by his attorney_____________.

The court sitting without a jury having heard the evidence and receiving exhibits and considering the declarations and other papers on file herein and having the matter submitted, makes the following determination:

IT IS HEREBY ADJUDGED that the property is exempt from execution and that the sheriff of the County of ___________ is hereby ordered to release the property to the defendant forthwith.

DATED: ____________________________.

____
Judge

CAPTION) No. ________________

REQUEST FOR NOTICE OF SALE
[C.C.P. § 692(a)]

TO THE CLERK OF THE SUPERIOR COURT OF LOS ANGELES COUNTY:

PLEASE TAKEN NOTICE that the undersigned hereby requests that he be given notice by mail of any sale under execution issued on the judgment rendered in the ____________ Court of ____________________ County, California, in the following-entitled case: (Set forth name of case and case number).

The judgment was entered in Judgment Book ______ at page_______ on___________________, 19___.

It is further requested that on any writ of execution issued to you, you note thereon the fact that notice by mail has been requested by the undersigned.

The address to which notice of sale should be mailed is (set forth address).

DATED: ____________________________.

____
[Person requesting notice]

****

C.C.P. §692(a) provides that any person may file a written request for notice.

CAPTION) No. ______________

NOTICE OF SALE

NOTICE IS HEREBY GIVEN that the undersigned will sell on ________________, 19______, at _____A.M., on the Courthouse steps at the County Courthouse, ______________________Street, City of ______________, California, to the highest bidder, for cash, the following-described property: (Set forth description).

The sale is pursuant to a writ of execution issued out of the above-entitled court in the above-entitled action between plaintiff and defendant. The sale will be held at public auction.

DATED: __________________________.

____
Sheriff

	)	No. ____________
	)	
	)	NOTICE OF MOTION TO VACATE
	)	EXECUTION SALE
	)	Date:__________________
CAPTION	)	Time:__________________
	)	Dept:__________________
	)	
________________________	)	

TO____________________, JUDGMENT CREDITOR, AND TO HIS ATTORNEY, AND TO________________PURCHASER, AND HIS ATTORNEY:

YOU AND EACH OF YOU WILL HEREBY TAKE NOTICE that on _________________, 19______, at the hour of ______A.M., or as soon thereafter as the matter may be heard, in Department _______ of the above-entitled court, _________________ will move the court for an order vacating and setting aside the sale of the following-described property (describe property), which property was sold to______________________________, on __________________, 19____, made by the sheriff of__________ ______________County under a writ of execution issued on ___________________, 19___.

The motion will be based on the following grounds: (Set forth grounds).

The motion will be based on this notice of motion, the declaration of ____________________ attached hereto, and on the memorandum of points and authorities served and filed herewith and all other records and papers on file herein and such other evidence oral and documentary as may be presented at the hearing on the motion.

DATED: ___________________________.

____
Attorney for Defendant

****

Inadequacy of price alone will not authorize vacating a sale unless the price is so gross as to indicate fraud or misconduct. Baar v. Smith, 97 C.A. 398; Darden v. Reese, 88 C.A.2d 904.

The motion must be accompanied by a declaration setting forth the reasons for seeking an order to vacate the sale, such as inadequacy of the price or unfairness in the proceedings.

CAPTION

No. ________________

PETITION TO DETERMINE AMOUNT TO REDEEM

The petition of ______________, defendant, respectfully shows:

1. That upon an execution sale had in the above-entitled proceedings on______________, 19____, in the City of ______________, California, the real property of defendant was purchased. The description of the real property is: (Set forth description).

2. Your petitioner, as judgment debtor, desires to exercise his right to redeem as provided by §702 of the Code of Civil Procedure.

3. Your petitioner has tendered to said purchaser the total amount paid to said purchaser for the property plus interest, taxes, and fire insurance premiums as required by law, but said purchaser refuses to accept the redemption price.

4. That said purchaser demands of petitioner as part of the price of redemption the following amounts: (Set forth amounts).

5. Your petitioner alleges that the amount demanded by ______________________is in dispute for the following reasons (set forth reasons), and further contends that the amount tendered is the correct amount.

6. The petitioner has deposited with the Clerk of the Court the sum of $___________, which the petitioner contends is the correct amount less the amount in dispute.

WHEREFORE, your petitioner prays that this court determine this dispute existing between______________________and your petitioner and determine the amount required for redemption.

DATED: ______________________.

____
Attorney for Judgment Debtor

CAPTION

ORDER DETERMINING REDEMPTION PRICE

The petition of ______________________having come on for hearing on ______________, 19____, before the undersigned, upon notice duly given and by ______________________, purchaser, appearing by his counsel, and by______________________, judgment debtor appearing by his counsel, and the matter having been argued and evidence submitted, and good cause appearing therefor,

IT IS ORDERED that the sum of $___________ is determined to be the correct redemption price and that the amounts paid by ______________________to the Clerk of the Court is the amount necessary to redeem the property.

DATED: ______________________.

____
Judge of the Superior Court

CAPTION

No. ________________

NOTICE OF MOTION TO REVIVE JUDGMENT
[C.C.P. §708]

TO__________________________, DEFENDANT, AND TO _______________, HIS ATTORNEY:

YOU AND EACH OF YOU SHALL PLEASE TAKE NOTICE that on _______________, 19_____, at the hour of ________A.M., or as soon thereafter as the matter may be heard, in Department ____ of the above-entitled court, ____________________, the purchaser of the hereinbelow-described property, will move the court for an order reviving the original judgment heretofore entered in favor of__________________, plaintiff, in Civil Action No._______, recorded in Judgment Book _________, at page ________, on _________________, 19____, in________________County, California.

The original judgment is to be revived in the name of ___________________, the purchaser of the hereinbelow-described property in the sum of $_____________ with interest from_________ 19_____.

The description of the property is as follows: (Set forth description).

The motion will be based upon the provisions of C.C.P. §708 and on the ground that the purchaser at the sale failed to recover possession of the property because of irregularity in the proceedings concerning the execution sale at which the purchaser attempted to acquire the property.

The following facts constitute the irregularity of the sale: (Set forth reasons).

The motion will further be based on this notice of motion, the declaration of________________, on the memorandum of points and authorities served and filed herewith, and on other records and papers on file herein, and such oral and documentary evidence as may be presented at the hearing on the motion.

DATED: __________________________.

____
Attorney for Purchaser

****

A motion to revive a judgment is void unless made on notice to the defendant. Thompson vs. Cook, 20 C.A.2d 564.

The sale where property has already been homesteaded is not subject to execution within the meaning of C.C.P. §708. Heine v. Bloomer, 183 C. 398.

CAPTION) Case No.______________
)
) PETITION FOR WRIT OF PROHIBITION
)
__________________)

TO THE HONORABLE PRESIDING JUSTICE AND ASSOCIATE JUSTICES OF THE COURT OF APPEAL OF THE ____________ APPELLATE DIVISION OF THE STATE OF CALIFORNIA:

Your petitioner, by this petition for writ of prohibition respectfully alleges:

1. Petitioner is a defendant in that certain action entitled ___________vs. ____________________ now pending before respondent ________________court, case bears Superior Court No.______________.

2. Respondent is the Superior Court of __________ County, California and respondent __________is the judge thereof.

3. The real party in interest is the plaintiff in the action, ______________vs. ______________referred to above.

4. On____________, 19____, the above-entitled action was commenced by the filing of a summons and complaint and on_____________, 19____, your petitioner was served with a copy of the summons and complaint on__________, 19___, filed a demurrer thereto. A copy of the complaint and demurrer are attached hereto, marked Exhibits "A" and "B" respectively and made a part hereof.

5. The complaint seeks to recover damages for personal injury for a collision which occurred on__________, 19____. The action was commenced on__________, 19____, more than a year following the happening of alleged collision which it is claimed caused the injuries.

6. On___________, 19____, on hearing of the demurrer, respondent court overruled the demurrer on the ground that it had jurisdiction to proceed to try the case and over objection of the petitioner, threatens, and unless restrained by this Honorable Court, will proceed with the trial thereof. A copy of the order overruling the demurrer is attached hereto, marked Exhibit "C" and made a part hereof.

7. Respondent has no jurisdiction to proceed with the trial of said action, for the reason that the applicable statute of limitations provided by §________of the Code of Civil Procedure requires that the action be filed within a year from the date of the injury.

8. Your petitioner is a party beneficially interested in the proceeding, and the petitioner, respondent and real party in interest, are the parties who are affected by this petition.

9. Petitioner has no plain, speedy or adequate remedy in the ordinary course of law in that his only alternative, if this writ is not granted, is to proceed with a costly and time-consumming trial.

WHEREFORE petitioner prays:

1. That this court issue a writ of prohibition restraining respondent from proceeding with the trial and to show cause before this court, at a time and place to be designated by this court, why it should not be permanently enjoined from so doing.

2. For such other and further relief as this court deems just.

(If a peremptory writ is sought)

WHEREFORE petitioner prays:

1. That a date for hearing for this petition be set and on such hearing, a peremptory writ of prohibition be issued, permanently restraining respondent from proceeding with the trial in the above-entitled action and for such other and further relief as the court deems just.

Dated:_________________, 19____

____
Attorney for Petitioner

****

This petition must be verified.

A peremptory writ may be issued without an alternative writ if at least ten days notice is given, C.C.P. §1088 and 1105.

CAPTION) Case No.________________
)
) PEREMPTORY WRIT OF PROHIBITION
)
____________________)

THE PEOPLE OF THE STATE OF CALIFORNIA to ____________________ COURT:

WHEREAS a verified petition of___________was filed on____________, 19____, in the above-entitled court for a writ of prohibition absolutely restraining you from proceeding with the trial in the case entitled ___________ vs. ___________, number_________________and,

WHEREAS notice has been given and a hearing on the matter shown by said petition, having been held on________, 19____, and proof having been made to the satisfaction of this court that petitioner has no plain, speedy or adequate remedy at law and that this writ should issue, and good cause appearing therefor,

WE COMMAND YOU that you absolutely and permanently refrain from proceeding with the trial in this matter or from taking any other proceeding except to dismiss the case of _______________vs._______________.

Dated:________________, 19____.

____
Justice of the Court of Appeal

COURT OF APPEAL

OF THE STATE OF CALIFORNIA

_________ APPELLATE DISTRICT

DIVISION 1

JOHN JONES, Petitioner, vs. THE SUPERIOR COURT OF LOS ANGELES COUNTY, Respondent, RAY SMITH, Real Party in Interest.	)	Case No. ___________ PETITION FOR WRIT OF MANDATE

TO THE HONORABLE COURT OF APPEAL OF THE STATE OF CALIFORNIA, _____________ APPELLATE DISTRICT:

Petitioner respectfully petitions the above-entitled court for a writ of mandate to compel respondent court to enter its order striking the answer and entering judgment for plaintiff in the action referred to herein, and in this connection respectfully alleges as follows:

1. On _______________, 19___, petitioner filed an action in respondent court entitled ___________________ vs. ____________________, bearing Case No. _________. A copy of the summons and complaint are attached hereto as Exhibit "A" and made a part hereof.

2. The real party in interest filed an answer to the complaint on _____________, 19____, generally and specifically denying the allegations of the complaint. A copy of the answer is attached hereto as Exhibit "B" and made a part hereof.

3. Petitioner on _____________, 19____, filed a motion for summary judgment on the ground that the answer presented no triable issue of fact. Petitioner included in his motion a declaration in which it was alleged that the note was executed and that the balance thereon remains unpaid. A copy of the motion for summary judgment, together with supporting documents, is attached hereto as Exhibit "C" and made a part hereof.

4. On a hearing of the motion and after consideration of the declarations and counter declarations, the respondent court denied the motion.

5. Respondent court has acted in excess of its jurisdiction in refusing to grant the motion for summary judgment in that it was not established by the counter declaration that there is a triable issue of fact.

6. The action of respondent court results in the requirement that plaintiff will be compelled to go to trial. The trial will require several days and will place an unfair burden on plaintiff as well as on witnesses and jurors.

7. There is no appeal from the order herein complained of, and petitioner has no other adequate or speedy remedy at law.

WHEREFORE, petitioner prays that a writ of mandate be granted requiring respondent court to grant a motion for summary judgment and enter judgment for plaintiff.

DATED: ________________________, 19___.

____
Attorney for Petitioner

****

A writ of mandate is a proper remedy to compel the trial court to grant a motion for summary judgment. Declarations are sufficient to sustain a judgment in his favor. Iverson vs. Superior Court, 57 C.A.3d 168.

Petition for writ of mandate must be verified.

CAPTION) Case No.____________________
)
) ALTERNATIVE WRIT OF PROHIBITION
)
____________________)

THE PEOPLE OF THE STATE OF CALIFORNIA TO THE ____________________ COURT, GREETINGS:

The petition for a writ of prohibition on file herein, having been considered and good cause appearing therefor, for the issuance of the writ of prohibition,

WE DO COMMAND YOU, that pending further order of this Court, you desist and refrain from taking further action or proceedings, including__________________in the case of____________ vs.______________, case number______________and that you show cause before department___of this court, why you should not be permanently restrained from doing so.

The written return, if any, to this alternative writ is to be served and filed on or before __________, 19____.

Witness the Honorable ________________Judge (or Justice) of the _____________Court.

Attest my hand and the seal of this Court this_________ day of_____________, 19____.

____
CLERK

CAPTION) Case No.____________________
)
) ALTERNATIVE WRIT OF MANDATE
)
____________________)

THE PEOPLE OF THE STATE OF CALIFORNIA TO _______________, RESPONDENT:

The verified petition of _______________, the petitioner for an alternative writ of mandate commanding you to do the following (describe) having been presented to this court, and it appearing that said petitioner has no plain, speedy, or adequate remedy at law, and that an alternative writ of mandate should issue,

THEREFORE, WE COMMAND YOU, upon receipt of this writ that you ___________________or that you show cause before this court in department__________there of on____________, 19____ at the hour of ___________A.M. in the courthouse at______________ City of _______________, California, why you have not done so.

Witness the Honorable _____________Judge of the _____________________Court.

Attest my hand and seal of this court on_____________, 19____.

____
CLERK

CAPTION)   Case No.__________
)
) PETITION FOR WRIT OF ADMINISTRATIVE
) MANDAMUS
__________________)

Petitioner,___________by this verified petition, petitions this Court for a writ of mandamus under Code of Civil Procedure, §1094.5, directed to respondent, Registrar of Contractors, Department of Consumer Affairs, Contractors State License Board, and represents that:

1. Petitioner, at all times mentioned in this petition has been and, until action by the respondent, was licensed as a Class B Contractor under a license issued by the respondent and has engaged in the business of contracting in the City of Los Angeles, County of Los Angeles.

2. At all times mentioned in this petition, respondent has been and now is the agency charged with administering the provisions of §§ 7107, 7113, 7115, (Title 16, California Administrative Code, §76c), 7119, 7159 of the Business and Professions Code.

3. On or about______, 19____, under Government Code §§11503, 11504 and 11507 an accusation was filed with respondent alleging that petitioner had violated §7119 of the Business and Professions Code and alleging the existence of cause for disciplinary action against petitioner under §11503 of the Government Code. On or about July 13, 1973 a first supplemental accusation was filed against the petitioner alleging violations of the same sections. These notices were served on petitioner and within 15 days petitioner filed a notice of defense with respondent. On or about_______, 19____, a hearing was held in __________County before a hearing officer, who then rendered his proposed decision. On _______, 19____, respondent adopted that decision as its own, making the decision effective on______, 19____. A true copy of that decision is attached and labeled Exhibit "A".

4. As a condition precedent to the filing of this writ, petitioner has exhausted all administrative remedies available to him.

5. Petitioner has no adequate or speedy remedy at law and unless the relief sought herein is granted, petitioner will suffer irreparable damage.

6. Contemporaneously with the filing of this petition, your petitioner is requesting that the respondent prepare, at petitioner's expense, a full and complete record of the proceedings held before the hearing agency, including but not limited to the reporter's transcript of said proceedings. Petitioner is ready, willing and able to pay the costs of said record immediately when said costs have been ascertained.

7. Prior to the institution of the disciplinary proceedings herein petitioner had commenced construction activities on the following projects (describe):

At the time of the decision of the respondent these projects had not been completed. Your petitioner is willing, ready and able to complete said projects, but is unable to do so by virtue of the decision of the respondent. Not only will irreparable damage befall the petitioner if a temporary stay is not granted, but irreparable damage will also befall the contractees who still hold an expectation, and who have paid in part for that expectation, that your petitioner will complete the construction projects.

8. Petitioner seeks this writ on the basis that the findings are not supported by the evidence and on the further basis that the respondent abused its discretion in arriving at the findings which were not supported by the weight of the evidence.

It is further urged that the punishment meted out by the respondent is disproportionate to the alleged violations, assuming they are well founded. In order to adequately present to the Court petitioner's contentions to the effect that the tribunal abused its discretion, it will be necessary for the petitioner to present to this Honorable Court the transcript of the proceedings that took place on_______, 19____.

WHEREFORE, petitioner prays that:

1. An alternative writ of mandamus be issued ex parte.

2. An ex parte order be issued staying respondent's decision and ordering respondent to show cause why an order should not be granted further staying that decision.

3. A peremptory writ of mandamus be issued ordering respondent to set aside its decision.

4. Petitioner be afforded a full hearing as soon as the transcript becomes available.

5. Petitioner recover his costs in this action; and

6. Other relief that the Court deems proper.

____
Attorney for Petitioner

****

A temporary stay may be granted. C.C.P. §1094.5(f).

Deepwell v. Palm Springs, 239, C.A. 2d 63.

____________________,	Case No. __________
Petitioner,	PETITION FOR WRIT OF CERTIORARI, REQUEST FOR TEMPORARY STAY
vs.	
SUPERIOR COURT OF THE STATE OF CALIFORNIA FOR THE COUNTY OF LOS ANGELES,	
Respondent,	
_______________________,	
Real Party in Interest.	

The petitioner ___________ hereby petitions this court for a writ of certiorari directed to the respondent Superior Court in the State of California for the County of _____________, and by this verified petition alleges:

1. Petitioner is the attorney for____________, a witness in an action instituted in respondent Court entitled _________________vs._____________, bearing Case No. _______. The _____________in said action is named herein as the real party in interest.

2. Respondent Court is a Superior Court of the County of____________in the State of California, and at all times herein mentioned has exercised its judicial function in connection with the cause of action heretofore described.

3. ___________is a Commissioner of the Superior Court who, by virtue of the Constitution of the State of California, and by virtue of an order executed by ___________, the presiding Judge of respondent Court was presiding over the trial of the above-entitled matter as a judge pro tem. A stipulation enabling_____________to preside over the matter as Judge Pro Tem was executed by _______________and____________________, the plaintiff and defendant in that action, but was never executed by your petitioner.

4. Your petitioner was appearing as the attorney for____________, who was subpoenaed by the real party in interest to testify on his behalf. Your petitioner was representing the witness______________ for the reason that the testimony which the real party in interest was attempting to elicit was testimony that would tend to incriminate the witness_________________.

5. That your petitioner appeared before said court and objected to the questions being proferred to witness ___________and instructed said witness not to answer the questions. The court instructed and admonished petitioner not to interfere in the proceedings, and petitioner's continued efforts to advise his client resulted in the court holding petitioner in contempt and sentencing him to 5 days in jail and the imposition of a fine of $500.00. A copy of said order is attached hereto, marked Exhibit "A" and incorporated by reference.

6. That such action is beyond the jurisdiction of respondent Court because at no time had your petitioner stipulated that the Honorable____________could hear the matter as Judge Pro Tem.

7. That your petitioner has no plain, speedy or adequate remedy other than by this proceeding by a writ of certiorari.

8. That unless such order of respondent Court is stayed, petitioner will be compelled to be incarcerated in jail and to pay a fine to his injury and detriment.

WHEREFORE, petitioner prays:

1. That a writ of review issue out of this Court to the respondent Superior Court of the State of California for the County of__________ commanding it to certify fully to this court at a specified time and place the records and proceedings of the above-mentioned action so that it may be inquired into and determined by this court;

2. That the said action be fully heard and considered by this court, and that the order finding petitioner in contempt be found to be in excess of the respondent Court's jurisdiction and further that it be annulled and set aside;

3. That execution of the order of the Superior Court be stayed pending decision of this court;

4. For costs of this proceeding and for such other and further relief as this court deems just.

DATED: ______________________, 19____.

____
Attorney for Petitioner

CAPTION) Case No. ____________________

) RETURN ON WRIT OF REVIEW

________________________________)

The respondent named in the writ of review issued out of the above-entitled court on______________, 19____, in compliance with said writ, hereby makes its return transmitting herewith a certified copy of the entire proceedings held on ______________, 19____, whereby petitioner was held in contempt of court by the Honorable______________, Judge Pro Tem or the respondent Court. The respondent further states that the action was within the jurisdiction of respondent in all respects for the following reasons: (Set forth reasons).

DATED: ________________________.

____
Attorney for Respondent

****

The copies of the proceedings should be certified. Rule 56c.

	)	Case No. ______________
	)	
	)	WRIT OF CERTIORARI
CAPTION	)	
	)	
	)	
___________________________	)	

THE PEOPLE OF THE STATE OF CALIFORNIA TO THE PRESIDING JUDGE OF THE _____________ COUNTY SUPERIOR COURT, STATE OF CALIFORNIA, RESPONDENT:

The verified petition of _____________, petitioner, having been presented to this court, and representations having been made that said respondent court has held the petitioner in contempt of court, and that said action has exceeded your jurisdiction in the matter and that there is no appeal, nor any plain, speedy, or adequate remedy at law,

WE THEREFORE COMMAND YOU that you certify and return to this Court in Department _____ thereof, at _________________ Street, ________________, California, on the ____ day of _________________, 19____, at the hour of ___________, A.M., the entire, full and complete transcript and record of any proceeding relating to a holding of petitioner in contempt of court so that said proceedings may be reviewed by this court.

Pending said return and review, YOU ARE HEREBY COMMANDED TO RESTRAIN, AND ARE HEREBY RESTRAINED from taking any further actions or proceedings in this matter, including the imposition of a fine and execution of the jail sentence, pending determination of this court.

WITNESS the Honorable _______________, presiding Judge of the ________________ Court.

ATTESTED by my hand and seal of this Court, this _____ day of ______________, 19____.

____
Clerk

CAPTION)   Case No.____________
)
) COMPLAINT FOR FALSE IMPRISONMENT
)
___________________)

1. At all times herein mentioned, defendant was and now is, engaged in the operation of a department store in the City of________, County of_______, State of California.

2. At all times herein mentioned, defendant___________ was and now is a security guard employed by defendant company. At all times herein mentioned, each of the defendants was the agent and employee of the remaining defendants and were, at all times herein mentioned, acting within the scope and course of their authority.

3. On or about______, 19____, at the hour of________ a.m., plaintiff entered the department store of defendant with the intention of shopping for several items. While looking at an article of clothing offered for sale by defendant, defendant _____________approached plaintiff and asked plaintiff to step inside the security office. Plaintiff was told by defendant ______________that if she did not accompany defendant________ into the security office that she, plaintiff, would be handcuffed in the presence of the other customers.

4. Out of fear and possible increased embarrassment, plaintiff accompanied defendant___________into the security office and was then charged with the theft of an article of clothing. Plaintiff was shown an article of clothing and also handed what appeared to be a written statement containing a confession of theft and told that if she, plaintiff, did not sign the statement, she would be detained until she did so.

5. Plaintiff refused to sign the statement because she, in fact, was innocent and demanded that she be allowed to leave. At this point a handcuff was placed on one arm and the other portion of the handcuff was attached to a leg of the table thereby preventing plaintiff from leaving. One hour and 30 minutes thereafter, a member of the_______city police department arrived and after a discussion between defendant____________ and plaintiff, the police officer instructed defendant__________ to release plaintiff. Plaintiff was thereupon released and returned home.

6. Plaintiff was maliciously, unlawfully and wantonly deprived of her liberty for a period of two hours, was accused of having commited the crime of larceny and threatened with the disgrace of arrest. Defendant, the accuser, knew that plaintiff had committed no crime whatever and the acts of defendants herein were malicious and without due regard to plaintiff's liberty.

7. By reason of the foregoing, plaintiff was made nervous, sick and ill and suffered extreme emotional distress and has further suffered considerable embarrassment in her community, all to her damage in the sum of $_______.

8. As a further direct and proximate cause of said imprisonment, plaintiff suffered the following physical disorders, (describe) and was obliged to expend $________for medical treatment. Plaintiff is informed and believes and upon such information and belief alleges that further medical treatment will be required in an amount presently unknown. Plaintiff will amend the complaint when the true sums are ascertained.

WHEREFORE, plaintiff prays for judgment as follows:

1. For general damages in the sum of $__________.

2. Special damages in the sum of $_________.

3. Punitive damages in the sum of $_________.

4. For costs of suit and such other relief as the court deems just.

____
Attorney for Plaintiff

****

Penal Code §236.

Collyer vs. Kress, 5 Cal. 2d 175.

Parrott vs. Bank of America, 97 C. A. 2d, 14.

CAPTION) Case No.__________
)
) REQUEST FOR FINDINGS OF FACT AND
____________________) CONCLUSIONS OF LAW

COMES NOW ____________________and requests that findings of fact and conclusions of law prepared by ____________________required in Rule 232, Rules of Court and C.C.P. §632.

DATED: __________________, 19____.

____
Attorney for

CAPTION) Case No.__________
)
) OBJECTION TO FINDINGS OF FACT AND
) CONCLUSIONS OF LAW, AND SUBMISSION OF
____________________ COUNTER FINDINGS AND REQUEST FOR SPECIAL FINDINGS

__________________, defendant herein, hereby objects to the proposed findings numbers ____, ____, and ____, and the proposed conclusions numbers ____. ____, and ____ for the following reasons: (Set forth reasons.)

In place and instead of the proposed findings________ and____________, defendant proposes the following. (Hereby indicate proposed counter findings).

In place of the conclusions of law _______and_________ defendant hereby submits the following proposed conclusions of law. (Set forth proposed conclusions).

Request is hereby made for special findings on the following issues. (Here state the special findings on the desired).

DATED:__________________, 19_____.

____
Attorney for Defendant

****

CAPTION) Case No.________
)
) COMPLAINT FOR NEGLIGENT
) MISREPRESENTATION
________________________)

Plaintiff complains:

1. On or about ______, 19___, in the City of________, California, defendant falsely and fraudulently made the following representations to plaintiff: (Describe representations.)

2. The representations so made by defendant were in fact false for the following reasons: (Describe reasons, including true facts.)

3. At the time defendant made said representations, he had no sufficient or reasonable ground for believing said representations to be true in that he, the defendant, did not have information and data sufficient to enable him to make the determination whether the representations were true. At the time of making the representations, defendant concealed from plaintiff his lack of information and data that prevented him from making a true evaluation of the facts.

4. Plaintiff at the time the representations were made had no knowledge of their falsity, but in fact, believed them to be true. Plaintiff relied upon the representations of defendant and was not in the position to make an independent investigation for the following reasons: (Describe)

5. Had plaintiff known the true facts, he would not have taken the following action which he was induced to take: (Describe)

6. By reasons of the facts alleged, plaintiff has been damaged in the sum of $___________.

WHEREFORE plaintiff prays:

1. For judgment in the sum of $___________.

2. For costs of suit and such other relief as the court deems just.

____
Attorney for Plaintiff

****

See Civil Code §1710(2). See also Horrell vs. Santa Fe, 117 C.A. 2d 114.

CAPTION)
)
_____________)

COMPLAINT TO SET ASIDE FRAUDULENT CONVEYANCE

Plaintiff complains and for cause of action alleges:

I

At all times herein mentioned, defendant was and now is a resident of the County of Los Angeles, State of California.

II

On or about ___________ 19__, plaintiff secured a judgment against the defendant in the sum of ____________________ dollars, a copy of the judgment is attached hereto marked Exhibit "A" and incorporated herein as though set out in full.

III

On or about ___________________ 19___, defendant was the owner of that certain motor vehicle described as a 1976 Pontiac sedan bearing California license number ABC 123. Defendant at the time had no other property other than a small amount of cash not exceeding the sum of $________________.

IV

On __________________, 19__, defendant conveyed said property to defendant _________________________. Said conveyance was made without any consideration passing between the two parties and said conveyance rendered defendant insolvent.

WHEREFORE, plaintiff prays for judgment against the defendants as follows:

1. That said conveyance between the parties be set aside.

2. That plaintiff recover the sum of ___________________ plus interest therein at the rate of ___________ percent per annum from _____________ 19__ until paid.

3. That plaintiff recover costs and such other and further relief as the court deems just and proper.

Dated:__________

____
Attorney for Plaintiff

****

Where a fraudulent conveyance is made, the creditor with the matured claim may either have the conveyance set aside or disregard the conveyance and attach or levy execution. If the latter remedy is pursued, plaintiff may be faced with a third party proceeding with the conveyee.

CAPTION

Case No. ________________

COMPLAINT FOR WRONGFUL WITHHOLDING OF PROPERTY

Plaintiff complains and for cause of action alleges:

1. That on ___________________, 19____, a judgment was rendered in favor of plaintiff in an action in the above-entitled court. The name of that action was _________________ vs.__________________and numbered __________.

2. On ________________, 19___, a writ of execution was levied by the Marshal of ______________County upon said defendant, and said execution was returned unsatisfied.

3. Plaintiff is informed and believes and therefore alleges that in fact defendant has the following-described property which belongs to the judgment debtor: (Describe property).

4. Although plaintiff has demanded said property of defendant, defendant refuses to turn said property over to plaintiff, which refusal is wrongful, as defendant is without the right to said property.

5. Unless an order restraining further transfer of the property is made, plaintiff is informed and believes and therefore alleges that the defendant will wrongfully transfer the property to render it unavailable for execution.

6. On ________________, 19____, defendant and the judgment debtor were examined in supplemental proceedings, and in said proceedings each denied that the property was the property of said judgment debtor.

WHEREFORE, plaintiff prays:

1. That a judgment be had declaring the above-described property be turned over by defendant to the sheriff;

2. That the court restrain the further transfer of said property until ownership of the property can be determined;

3. For costs of this suit and for such other relief as the court deems just.

DATED: ______________________.

____
Attorney for Plaintiff

****

This procedure is authorized by C.C.P. §720.

CAPTION)
)
) COMPLAINT FOR INJUNCTION TO
) RESTRAIN CONSTRUCTION OF FENCE
________________________)

Case No.______________

1. At all times herein mentioned, the plaintiff was and now is the owner of and in possession of that certain parcel of real property in the County of__________, State of California, the legal description of which is. (describe)

2. At all times herein mentioned, defendant was and now is the owner of and in possession of that certain parcel of real property in the County of________, State of California, the legal description of which is (describe). Defendant's property is adjacent to plaintiff's property.

3. Between ______, 19___, and_______, 19____, a period when plaintiff was absent from his property, out of the country, defendant commenced the construction of a fence on plaintiff's property, 6 feet south of the north boundary line between the property of plaintiff and defendant. When plaintiff returned to the property, he observed the construction and was told by defendant, that he, defendant, had constructed the portion already existing. Said fence was constructed without the permission or consent of the plaintiff and is unlawfully maintained on plaintiff's land.

4. On or about_______, 19____, plaintiff notified defendant in writing that the fence was on his land and demanded in writing that the fence be removed, but defendant has failed and refused and still fails and refuses to remove the fence.

5. Defendant is continuing to construct the fence and unless enjoined by this court will build the fence in its entirety to the extent that plaintiff will be deprived of the use and benefit of a portion of his land.

6. Plaintiff has no adequate or speedy remedy at law and will suffer irreparable injury if defendant is not enjoined from continued construction and if defendant is not required to remove that portion of the fence which has already been constructed.

7. The injury complained of is continuous and unless it is enjoined, plaintiff will suffer irreparable injury and will be involved in continuing litigation with defendant and will suffer additional loss of use of said premises, all to his damage in the sum of $_____________.

WHEREFORE, plaintiff prays judgment as follows:

1. For an order enjoining defendant from continuing construction of the fence.

2. For an order compelling defendant to remove the fence.

3. For damages in the sum of $__________.

4. For costs of suit and such other relief as the court deems just.

____
Attorney for Plaintiff

****

An order requiring defendant to remove a fence is a mandatory injunction and it is likely that the plaintiff will be required to remove the fence himself and recover damages. Kettenhofen vs. Superior Court, 55 Cal 2d, 189.

CAPTION	)	Case No.____________
	)	
	)	DECLARATION IN SUPPORT OF REQUEST FOR PRELIMINARY INJUNCTION AND TEMPORARY RESTRAINING ORDER
	)	
	)	
____________________	)	

I, ______________ DECLARE:

I am the plaintiff in the within action. That on _________, 19____, at ____________, California, the defendant committed the following-described acts: (Set forth acts.)

The defendant was requested to cease and desist from the commission of such acts but he refused to do so, and continues to refuse to do so.

That as a result of said acts, as aforesaid mentioned, the plaintiff is, and will be irreparable damaged in the following way: (Describe.)

WHEREFORE, it is requested that a temporary restraining order and preliminary injunction be issued.

DATED: ________________, 19____.

____
Plaintiff

****

If the verified complaint for injunction adequately sets forth the above allegations, the affidavit is not necessary.

See local court rules on further requirements. For example, Los Angeles County requires at least 24 hours notification to defendant, where a temporary restraining order is sought.

CAPTION) Case No.__________
)
) TEMPORARY RESTRAINING ORDER AND ORDER
) TO SHOW CAUSE
______________________)

IT APPEARING TO THE SATISFACTION OF THE COURT upon the reading of the verified complaint of the plaintiff and the supporting affidavit and points and authorities that the case presented therein is a proper case for a temporary restraining order and that a temporary restraining order is necessary to prevent irreparable injury before the matter can be heard on notice;

THEREFORE IT IS ORDERED that defendant____________appear before this court in Department_____thereof on____, 19____, at the hour of____a.m., there and then to show cause, if any he may have, why a temporary injunction should not be ordered restraining and enjoining said defendant, and all persons acting on his behalf, from doing directly or indirectly the following described acts: (Describe.)

IT IS FURTHER ORDERED that defendant________be restrained pending the hearing on this order to show cause from doing any of the following described acts: (Set forth description of acts in detail.)

IT IS FURTHER ORDERED that a copy of the complaint herein and the affidavit and points and authorities and this order be served on defendant within____days prior to the hearing.

This order shall become effective upon the plaintiff filing a bond in the sum of $__________.

DATED:________________, 19_____.

____
Judge of the Superior Court

CAPTION) Case No.______________
)
) NOTICE OF MOTION FOR PRELIMINARY INJUNCTION
)
__________________)

Date:___________________
Time:___________________
Department:_____________

TO ______________DEFENDANT AND HIS ATTORNEY:

YOU, AND EACH OF YOU, SHALL PLEASE TAKE NOTICE, that on ________________, 19____, at the hour of____a.m. in Department __________of the above entitled court, plaintiff will move the court for a preliminary injunction enjoining defendant, directly or indirectly, from committing the following acts: (Describe acts in detail.)

Said motion will be made on the ground that an injunction is required to prevent irreparable injury to the plaintiff. The motion will be based on C.C.P., § 527, the declaration and points and authorities attached hereto, the papers and records on file herein, and such other evidence, oral and documentary, as may be presented at the hearing on this motion.

DATED:______________________, 19_____.

____
Attorney for Plaintiff

CAPTION)
)
) COMPLAINT TO SET ASIDE RELEASE
)
________________)

Case No.__________

Plaintiff complains:

1. At all times mentioned herein, plaintiff and defendant were, and are residents of the County of__________, California.

2. At all times mentioned herein, defendant insurance company was authorized and empowered by defendant driver to act, and did act, as the agent of defendant driver, and each and all things herein alleged to have been done by him, were done in the capacity of and as said agent, who at all times was acting within the scope of his authority.

3. On or about______, 19___, plaintiff was driving the following-described motor vehicle (describe), in the City of__________, California, in a northerly direction on ______________street, at the intersection of__________street. At that time and at that place, defendant driver was driving his motor vehicle, the description of which is (describe) in a _____________direction on_____________street. The defendant so carelessly and negligently operated his motor vehicle that it collided with the motor vehicle of plaintiff, causing plaintiff serious physical injuries.

4. As a proximate result of said impact, plaintiff was injured in his health, strength and activity, sustained injury to his body, which injury caused and continues to cause plaintiff great mental, physical and nervous pain and suffering. Plaintiff is informed and believes and thereon alleges that said injuries will result in some permanent disability to the plaintiff, all to his general damage.

5. As a further proximate result of said negligence, on the part of defendant driver, the plaintiff was required to, and did employ physicians and surgeons to examine and treat him and incurred medical and incidental expenses in the amount of $_____________and will incur additional expenses in the future in an amount presently unknown.

6. On or about________, 19____, defendant adjuster was acting as agent for defendant insurance company. At all times herein mentioned, defendant adjuster was authorized and empowered by defendant insurance company, who in turn, was authorized and empowered by defendant driver, and all of the things done by defendant adjuster were done in his capacity as an agent, within the scope of his authority.

7. On or about_______, 19____, defendant adjuster called on plaintiff at his home to settle and pay the personal injury claim. The adjuster told plaintiff that if plaintiff would sign certain papers, defendant adjuster would take care of everything and pay plaintiff's medical bills.

8. Relying upon the representation of defendant adjuster, plaintiff signed certain papers, which he later learned to be a general release.

9. Defendant adjuster knew that the forms were a general release and falsely represented to plaintiff that he and the remaining defendants would "take care of everything," while in fact obtaining from plaintiff a release in the sum of $________. Had plaintiff known the true effect of the release, he would not have signed it.

10. After plaintiff signed the papers, defendant adjuster left, took the papers with him and left no copies with the plaintiff, but left only a check in the amount of $___________.

11. Thereafter, plaintiff discovered the serious nature of his injuries and the effect of what he had signed. Plaintiff has been informed and believes, and thereon alleges that defendants contend that the papers he signed, constitute a release of all claims, known and unknown and that said document was so drawn for the purpose of defeating any rights plaintiff might have had, arising out of said accident. An actual controversy exists between the parties as to the effect of the aforesaid papers signed by plaintiff as a part of any right of action he may have to recover for his personal injuries.

WHEREFORE, plaintiff prays:

1. For a judgment declaring the release void.

2. For a judgment declaring the rights of the respective parties under the release.

3. For costs of suit and such other relief as the court deems just.

____
Attorney for Plaintiff

****

Cause of action for personal injuries against defendant driver may be joined as a separate cause of action.

CAPTION)
)
)
)
)
______________________)

Case No.______________

COMPLAINT AGAINST INSURANCE COMPANY
FOR REFUSING TO SETTLE CASE
WITHIN POLICY LIMITS

Plaintiff complains:

1. At all times herein mentioned, defendant insurance company was and now is, a corporation duly organized and existing under the laws of California and authorized to do business as an insurer by the insurance commissioner of said state.

2. At all times herein mentioned, plaintiff was the owner of the following described automobile, (describe).

3. On or about______, 19____, defendant insurance company executed and delivered to plaintiff a policy of insurance which covered, among other things, liability for bodily injury and property damage, incurred in connection with the operation of the above-described automobile. A copy of the policy is attached hereto, marked Exhibit "A" and made a part hereof.

4. By the terms of the policy, defendant agreed to the extent of $__________for each person and $__________for each accident,to pay on behalf of plaintiff which plaintiff may be obligated to pay by reasonable liability imposed by law as a result of bodily injury sustained by any person or persons, caused by the accident and arising out of the ownership, maintenance and use of the above-described automobile.

5. Defendant, in addition, agreed to defendant plaintiff in any suit against plaintiff seeking damages for bodily injury and/or property damage. Defendant reserved the right to make investigation, negotiation and settlement of any claim of suit against plaintiff.

6. On or about_______, 19____, while the above-mentioned policy was in full force and effect, plaintiff was driving said insured automobile on_________Street in the City of___________, California and was involved in a collision withan automobile owned and driven by___________________.

7. As a result of the collision, _____________ sustained personal injuries and property damage and thereafter filed an action in the Superior Court of___________County, State of California against plaintiff. A copy of the complaint in that action is attached hereto, marked Exhibit "B" and incorporated herein.

8. Immediately after the collision, plaintiff notified the defendant and defendant accepted the duty to, and did investigate and attempt to negotiate a settlement. Upon service of the summons and complaint upon plaintiff, plaintiff immediately forwarded same to defendant and defendant thereafter took exclusive charge of and prepared the defense of said action.

9. At all times herein mentioned, defendant assumed complete and exclusive control of said investigation, negotiations and defense.

10. Prior to the trial on the matter, the injured party in said action, offered both orally and in writing to settle the case for policy limits of $______________. Plaintiff herein urged defendant in writing to accept the offer of said settlement proposal and plaintiff advised defendant that if he failed to do so, plaintiff would hold defendant responsible for the entire amount of any judgment rendered against plaintiff, however much it might exceed policy limits.

11. Defendant refused to accept or discuss settlement or negotiate any compromise and defendant did not at any time, make any offer of settlement to the injured party in the abovementioned. suit.

12. The personal injury action was tried and resulted in a judgment against plaintiff in the sum of $_______________.

13. In addition, defendants knew or should have known that because of the nature of the personal injury action judgment in an amount in excess of policy limits was forseeable.

WHEREFORE, plaintiff prays:

1. For judgment in the amount of $________plus interest thereon from__________, 19____.

2. For costs of suit and such other relief as the court deems just.

____
Attorney for Plaintiff

****

A wrongful refusal of an insured to settle within policy limits gives rise to compensation for pecuniary loss and damages for mental distress. Purcell vs. Colonial Insurance, 20 C.A. 3d, 807. Crisci vs. Security Insurance, 66 Cal. 2d, 425.

CAPTION) Case No.___________
)
) COMPLAINT FOR DECLARATORY RELIEF
) AND INFLICTION OF MENTAL DISTRESS
_________________________) FOR FAILURE TO PAY PROCEEDS OF INSURANCE

Plaintiff alleges:

FIRST CAUSE OF ACTION

1. At all times herein mentioned, defendant insurer was and now is, a corporation organized to do business in the state of California as an insurer.

2. On or about_______, 19____, plaintiff purchased from defendant insurer, a policy of health and accident disability insurance. Under the terms of the policy, defendant agreed to pay a monthly indemnity of $_____________ should the plaintiff become disabled as a result of an injury.

3. At all times mentioned herein, plaintiff paid premiums on said policy and at the time of the injury sued on herein, said policy was in full force and effect.

4. On or about_________, 19____, the plaintiff suffered the following injuries, (describe). From and after said date, the plaintiff is now disabled.

5. On _________, 19____, plaintiff informed defendant insurer of the disability and demanded that the monthly payments commence forthwith. On_________, 19____, defendant advised the plaintiff it would make no payments to the plaintiff under the provisions of the policy on the ground that plaintiff's condition was a sickness and not an injury.

6. A controversy has risen between the parties as to whether plaintiff's condition constitutes an injury within the meaning of the policy.

SECOND CAUSE OF ACTION

7. Plaintiff refers to paragraphs________through _____________of his first cause of action and incorporates them herein as though set out in full.

8. Prior to the issuance of the policy and more particularly, on________, 19____, plaintiff was approached by _______________, an agent for defendant insurer. ___________ at that time solicited plaintiff to take out the insurance which is the subject of this action. During the course of said solicitation, the agent falsely and fraudulently represented to plaintiff that if the plaintiff were injured and thereafter disabled, the plaintiff would be entitled to the monthly indemnity of$______________.

9. The representations so made by the defendant company through its agent, were in fact false and fraudulent. The true facts were that the defendant company did not intend to cover all disability and further, that the defendant company intended to deal with the plaintiff in bad faith and with the intention of using any methods to avoid legitimate payments under the policy.

10. When the defendant company, through its agents, made such representations, it knew them to be false. Such statements were made with the intent to fraud and deceive plaintiff and to induce him to purchase the policy.

11. Plaintiff at the time said representations were made was ignorant of the falsity and believed them to be true. In reliance thereon, plaintiff was induced to, and did enter into the policy of accident and health insurance as hereinabove alleged. Had plaintiff known the true facts, he would not have purchased the policy.

12. As a direct and proximate result of the alleged false representations and the subsequent failure of defendant company to pay under the policy, the plaintiff was forced to employ the services of an attorney to prosecute the within action. The reasonable value of said attorney's services are__________.

13. At all times herein mentioned, the defendant insurance company knew that the benefits were essential to plaintiff's ability to sustain himself during his disability and the company knew that he qualified under the policy for the payments of the monthly installments. The conduct of the defendant as herein alleged, has been malicious and oppressive. As a result of said conduct, the plaintiff has suffered great mental anguish, mortification, humiliation and shame and has become sick and ill, all to his damage in the sum of $________.

14. The conduct of the defendant insurance company has been intentionally and wrongfully performed and has been malicious and oppressive, and thus plaintiff should be awarded punitive damages in the sum of $____________.

THIRD CAUSE OF ACTION

15. (Incorporation of previous paragraphs)

16. Plaintiff is informed and believes and thereon alleges that sometime prior to________, 19____, and continuing up to the present, defendants _________and__________conspired to defraud the plaintiff. Pursuant to the conspiracy, defendants, and each of them, did on__________, 19____, write a letter to plaintiff accusing him of misrepresentation with implied threats of criminal prosecution and civil litigation, at a time when each of the parties knew the statements contained therein were false. The letter was mailed to plaintiff for the sole purpose of frightening him into releasing the defendant company from any further obligation under the policy. A copy of the letter is attached hereto and made a part hereof by reference.

17. At the time the letter was mailed, the defendants, and each of them, were aware the plaintiff was totally disabled and that plaintiff was a man of limited education.

18. Plaintiff is informed and believes and thereon alleges that with all the knowledge as hereinabove alleged, defendants, and each of them, conspired to place fear and terror in the mind of plaintiff. As a proximate result of the acts performed by defendants, and each of them, in furtherance of the conspiracy, plaint-iff suffered extreme mental and nervous strain, all to his damage in the sum of $______________.

19. Plaintiff is informed and believes and thereon alleges that the defendants, and each of them, acted willfully, maliciously and without any right and authority in carrying out the hereinabove alleged conspiracy and plaintiff is, therefore, entitled to punitive damages in the sum of $________________.

WHEREFORE, plaintiff prays:

1. For a declaration of plaintiff's rights under the policy.

2. For general damages in the sum of $_________.

3. For punitive damages in the sum of $________.

4. For costs of suit and such other relief as the court deems just.

____
Attorney for Plaintiff

****

Fletcher vs. Western National Life, 10 C.A. 3d, 376.

CAPTION) Case No.______________
)
) COMPLAINT TO RECOVER PROCEEDS OF
) LIFE INSURANCE
________________________)

Plaintiff complains:

1. At all times herein mentioned, defendant ____________________ was and now is, an insurance corporation, duly organized and existing under the laws of the State of California.

2. On or about ____________, 19____, in consideration of the payment of an annual premium of __________ made by ____________________, defendant insurance company, by its duly authorized agents, executed and delivered to ____________________ the insured, in the City of __________________, County of ____________, California, a policy of life insurance bearing number _____________ wherein and whereby defendant insurance company insured the life of __________________, the deceased. The insurance became effective at ______________ o'clock on __________, 19____, and was a policy with a specific term expiring on ___________, 19____.

3. Said insurance policy named plaintiff beneficiary of said policy with the knowledge and consent of defendant.

4. Plaintiff was, at the time of said execution and delivery of the policy, the employer of ________________, the insured, and as such, had an insurable interest in the life of ______________________, the insured. (An insurable interest must be alleged if the beneficiary purchased the policy. An insurable interest can be held by a debtor, dependent, employer or assignee.)

5. On or about _________, 19____, prior to the expiration of the term of the policy, the insured died in the City of _________, County of ________, State of California.

6. Plaintiff and said insured performed each and every act required by them to be performed in accordance with the terms and conditions of said policy, including, but not limited to, the payment of premiums.

7. Said sum of $___________ due under the policy has not been paid, nor has defendant paid any part thereof and the sum of $_____________ is now due, owing and unpaid from defendant to plaintiff, with interest thereon at the rate of _______% per annum from _________, 19____.

WHEREFORE, plaintiff prays:

1. For judgment in the amount of $____________, plus interest at the rate of ____% per annum from __________, 19____.

2. For costs of suit and such other relief as the court deems just.

____
Attorney for Plaintiff

CAPTION) Case No.______________
)
) COMPLAINT AGAINST INSURANCE AGENT
) FOR FAILURE TO PROCURE INSURANCE
___________________)

Plaintiff complains:

1. At all times herein mentioned, plaintiff was the owner of the following-described motor vehicle, (describe).

2. At all times herein mentioned, defendant was, and now is, an individual licensed as an insurance broker with the insurance commissioner of the State of California and conducts his business in the City of_________, State of California.

3. On or about________, 19____, in the above-mentioned city, plaintiff and defendant entered into an oral contract wherein defendant agreed to place a policy of insurance on the above-described automobile covering the following perils, (describe).

4. On or about __________, 19____, defendant informed plaintiff that plaintiff was "covered" and that he, defendant, secured a "binder" on the policy.

5. Defendant, however, had failed and neglected to place such insurance.

6. On ________, 19___, said automobile was completely destroyed by fire, one of the perils against which the insurance policy allegedly covered.

7. As a proximate result of the negligent omissions and breach of the agreement to cover said automobile, plaintiff was damaged in the sum of $_______________.

WHEREFORE, plaintiff prays:

1. For judgment in the amount of $__________with interest thereon from__________, 19____.

2. For costs of suit herein and such other relief as the court deems just.

____
Attorney for Plaintiff

CAPTION) Case No.____________
)
) COMPLAINT BY INJURED PARTY AGAINST
) INSURANCE COMPANY TO COMPEL PAYMENT
____________________) OF JUDGMENT ENTERED AGAINST INSURED

Plaintiff complains:

1. At all times herein mentioned, defendant insurance company is and was a corporation organized under the laws of California and licensed as an insurance company by virtue of said laws.

2. On or about_________, 19___, and at all times herein mentioned,________________was the name insured in and under a policy of public liability and property damage insurance issued by defendant. A copy of that policy is attached hereto, marked Exhibit "A" and incorporated herein. The policy, among other things, provided that defendant would pay on behalf of the insured, all sums which the insured should become legally obligated to pay as damages because of bodily injury caused by accident, arising out of the ownership, maintenance or use of the automobile insured thereunder.

3. On or about_______, 19____, at the intersection of_________and____________streets, in the city of___________, California,_________________, the insured, while negligently operating the insured automobile, collided with the automobile of plaintiff and inflicted upon plaintiff severe personal injuries.

4. On or about_________, 19____, plaintiff commenced an action against____________insured in the_________court of_________________county, a copy of the summons and complaint in that action is attached hereto, marked Exhibit "B" and incorporated herein.

5. Trial was had on the above-entitled matter and a judgment was entered against _______________insured in the sum of $________________. A copy of that judgment is attached hereto, marked Exhibit "C" and incorporated herein.

6. By virtue of the terms and provisions of the insurance policy, hereinabove described, plaintiff was and is a third party beneficiary thereunder.

7. Although demand has been made against defendant, no part of the judgment hereinabove rendered, has been paid by defendant or any other person and there remains due, owing and unpaid, the sum of $___________.

WHEREFORE, plaintiff prays:

1. For the sum of $_____________, together with interest thereon at the rate of _______% per annum from________, 19____.

2. For costs of suit and such other relief as the court deems just.

____
Attorney for Plaintiff

****

See Barrera vs. State Farm, 71 Cal. 2d 659.

__________________)
) No.
) (Caption)
) COMPLAINT FOR DAMAGES AGAINST TITLE INSURANCE COMPANY
__________________)

Plaintiff alleges:

I

(Allegations of fictitious entities, capacity of parties, unknown parties, agency, residence, venue and jurisdiction must be set forth in separate paragraphs if appropriate.)

II

At all times herein mentioned defendant was and now is a corporation duly organized and existing under and by virtue of the laws of the State of California, having its principal place of business in ____________ County, California, and authorized by the Commissioner of Insurance to engage in the business of a title insurer in this state.

III

On ____________, 19__, at _______________, California, defendant for a valuable consideration issued to plaintiff its written policy of insurance No. ___________, a copy of which is attached hereto, marked Exhibit "A" and made a part hereof.

IV

By the express terms of said policy of title insurance defendant insured plaintiff against any loss or damage sustained by him not exceeding $______________ by reason of any defect in or lien or encumbrance on the title therein specified, to be vested at the date of said policy in plaintiff to a fee estate or interest in the real property. The real property in ___________ County, California, is described as follows:

V

On the date of issuance of said title insurance policy there was of record in the office of the County Recorder of ___________ County, California, a deed recorded in Book ___ at Page ____ of the Official Records of said county conveying to _______________ an easement for the right of way for the erection of an electric power line across said real property.

VI

Plaintiff discovered the existence of said easement on or about ____________, 19__.

VII

On ______________, 19__, immediately upon discovering said easement, plaintiff notified defendant in writing of said defect in title and has performed all other duties requisite to be performed by him under the terms and conditions of said policy.

VIII

The reasonable market value of title to said real property as described in said title insurance policy if not encumbered by said easement is $_____________.

IX

The reasonable market value of title to said real property as it actually exists encumbered by said easement is $____________.

X

By reason of the existence of said easement, as an encumbered property plaintiff has sustained damages in the sum of $__________.

WHEREFORE, plaintiff prays:

1. For damages in the sum of $____________; and

2. For costs of suit and such other and further relief as the court deems just.

____

Attorney for Petitioner

CAPTION)
)
______________)

COMPLAINT IN INTERPLEADER

Plaintiff complains of defendants and for cause of action alleges:

I

59

At all times herein mentioned, plaintiff was and now is an attorney at law and duly licensed to practice as such in the state of California.

II

On or about ________________19__, John Jones, a client of plaintiff, entered into a contract with Ray Smith and Ted Brown wherein it was agreed that Jones would sell to Smith and Brown the following described property: (set forth description) for the sum of $50,000. The sum of $50,000 was handed to plaintiff which plaintiff deposited in his client's trust account. Said amount still remains in the trust account.

III

By mutual agreement between the buyers and sellers, the sale was cancelled.

IV

Defendant Smith contends that the entire $50,000 belongs to him and defendant Ted Brown contends that half of the fund belongs to him.

V

Defendant Smith has demanded the payment by plaintiff of the $50,000. Defendant Brown has demanded of plaintiff the payment of $25,000.

VI

Plaintiff admits that neither he nor his client Jones have any right, title or interest in the $50,000. Plaintiff is ready, willing and able to pay the sum to the person legally entitled thereto but is unwilling and unable to determine which claimant is rightfully and lawfully entitled to the sum and therefore brings this action without collusion of either party to have the matter legally determined.

VII

Plaintiff has deposited the sum of $50,000 with the clerk of this court.

WHEREFORE, plaintiff prays:

1. That defendants be required to interplead their claims in said matter.

2. That plaintiff be discharged from all liability to defendants or either of them.

3. That plaintiff be awarded his costs and reasonable attorneys fees out of the funds.

____
Attorney for Plaintiff

****

CCP §386.

Either of the parties alleging an interest in the fund may answer. The answer is in the nature of a cross-complaint. Knapp vs. Nicoll, 112 C.A. 187. However, the document should be entitled an answer.

After a complaint or cross-complaint in interpleader has been filed, the court may restrain all parties from instituting further proceedings with respect to the fund. CCP §386(f).

CAPTION)
)
_______________)

DECLARATION OF STAKEHOLDER

I ______________________ declare:

That I am the defendant in the above entitled action. That the only relief sought against your declarant by the pleadings herein is for the payment of the sum of ___________ in that it is alleged that said sum is wrongfully withheld by your declarant.

Your declarant is a mere stakeholder of such monies and has no interest in them or any part thereof. Your declarant is willing to deposit said funds in the court or make any other disposition ordered by the court.

____
Stakeholder

****

Where the only relief sought against one of the defendants is the payment of a stated amount of money, the defendant may upon affidavit that he is a mere stakeholder apply to the court for an order discharging him from liability. CCP §386.5.

CAPTION)
)
_________)

NOTICE OF MOTION FOR LEAVE TO INTERVENE

TO THE FOLLOWING PARTIES AND THEIR ATTORNEYS:

YOU AND EACH OF YOU WILL PLEASE TAKE NOTICE that on ___________, 19___ at the hour of _________ a.m. in Department _____ of the above entitled court, ___________________________ will move this court for an order permitting him to intervene in the above entitled action.

Said motion will be made upon the grounds that _______________ has an interest in the matter in litigation. The motion will further be based upon the declaration and affidavit attached hereto, the provisions of CCP §387 and upon all papers and records on file herein and such other evidence, oral and documentary, as may be presented at the hearing on this motion.

Dated:________________ ______________________________
Attorney for

****

A motion to intervene may be made at any time before trial. CCP §387.

If the motion is granted and the intervening party files a complaint, a party served with the complaint must within 30 days after service answer or otherwise plead. CCP §387.

A trial court has discretion to deny intervention even where a direct interest is shown. People vs. Superior Court, 131 Cal. Rptr. 800.

The interest which entitles a party to intervene must be direct and of an immediate character. Socialist Workers vs. Brown, 53 C.3d 879.

Intervention may be denied if the reasons are outweighed by the rights of the original parties. Firemen's Fund vs. Gerlach, 56 C.A. 3d 299.

CAPTION) Case No.__________
)
) DISQUALIFICATION OF JUDGE FOR
) CAUSE
______________________)

I, ________________declare:

I am the plaintiff in the above-entitled matter.

That the Honorable__________, the judge before whom this matter is pending, is disqualified from hearing the case for the reason that he is an owner of a bond issued by ____________________, the defendant, a corporation in this matter.

Executed at_________________Californiaon _____________, 19____.

I declare under penalty of perjury that the foregoing is true and correct.

____

****

A judge may be disqualified for the following reasons:

1. If he has an interest in the action;

2. If he is a party to the action;

3. If he is related to a certain degree to parties or attorneys in the action;

4. If he has previously been involved in an action involving the same issues as an attorney;

5. Where he is prejudiced;

6. Where he has a physical or mental impairment.

The court may, however, still hear certain default matters, make certain orders in eminant domain proceedings. C.C.P. §170(a).

Once a declaration regarding disqualification has been filed, the judge must transfer the case or another judge must be appointed to hear the issue of disqualification.

CAPTION) Case No.____________
)
) DECLARATION OF PREJUDICE AGAINST
) JUDGE (C.C.P. §170.6)
________________________)

I,__________________, declare:

I am a party (or an attorney for a party) to the within action. That_____________, the judge, court commissioner or referee before the trial or the hearing for said action is pending, or to whom it is assigned is prejudice against the party or his attorney, or the interest of the party, or his attorney, so that declarant cannot, or believes that he cannot have a fair and impartial trial or hearing before such judge, court, commissioner or referee.

Executed at_________________California on___________, 19____.

I declare under penalty of perjury that the foregoing is true and correct.

____

****

Any party or attorney may establish prejudice by an oral or written motion without notice, supported by a declaration. C.C.P. §170.6. When the judge to whom the matter is assigned is known at least 10 days before the date set for trial, the motion shall be made at least 5 days before that date. If directed to the trial of a cause where there is a master calendar, the motion shall be made to the judge supervising the master calendar before the case is sent out. In no event shall a motion be entertained after the drawing of the name of the first juror or the making of an opening statement or after the swearing of the first witness. C.C.P. §170.6.

A judge may also be disqualified for actual bias under C.C.P. §170(5). In that event, the procedure of C.C.P. §170 must be followed.

CAPTION)
)
____________)

NOTICE OF MOTION FOR AN ORDER REQUIRING THE ENTRY OF SATISFACTION OF JUDGMENT

TO THE PLAINTIFF AND HIS ATTORNEY:

YOU AND EACH OF YOU SHALL PLEASE TAKE NOTICE that on _______________, 19___ at the hour of ____________a.m. in Department ________ of the above entitled court, defendant will move the court for an order compeling plaintiff to execute and acknowledge a satisfaction of judgment or in the alternative for an order that the court enter satisfaction of judgment without execution by plaintiff. Defendant will also move for the sum of $100.00 to be paid by plaintiff as forfeiture.

Said motion will be made upon the ground that the judgment heretofore rendered has been fully and completely satisfied by payment (or that payment has been tendered and refused). Said motion will be based upon this notice, the affidavit, points and authorities attached hereto and all other papers and records on file herein and upon such other evidence, oral and documentary, to be presented at the hearing on the motion.

Dated:____________________

____
Attorney for Defendant

****

This motion should be accompanied by points and authorities and an affidavit setting forth that the amount of the judgment has been paid in full or that the amount has been tendered and refused or conditionally accepted. CCP §675.

ORDER FOR ENTRY OF JUDGMENT

CAPTION)
)
____________)

The motion of defendant for an order requiring plaintiff to execute and acknowledge a satisfaction of judgment or in the alternative for an order of the court to enter satisfaction of judgment came on regularly for hearing before the undersigned on ____________ 19___, upon notice duly given.

____________________appeared as counsel for defendant and ____________________ appeared as counsel for plaintiff. Evidence, oral and documentary, was presented and received. The matter was argued and submitted to the court.

It is therefore ordered that the motion of defendant be granted. The clerk is ordered to enter satisfaction of judgment upon the records of this court. It is further ordered that plaintiff shall pay forthwith to defendant the sum of $100.00.

Dated:________________ __________________________
Judge

****

CAPTION)
)
)
____

DEMAND FOR SATISFACTION OF JUDGMENT

TO ________________________Plaintiff and to his attorney:

PLEASE TAKE NOTICE that by reason of the payment in full of your judgment against defendant entered on _____________, 19___ in judgment book ________ at page _________, a satisfaction thereof should be executed and recorded.

Therefore, demand is hereby made upon you pursuant to the provisions of CCP §675 for a satisfaction of said judgment. Failure to furnish the satisfaction of judgment within 15 days from this notice will subject you to all damages plus the forfeiture of the sum of One Hundred Dollars.

Dated:______________

____
Attorney for Defedant

****

CAPTION) Case No.__________
)
) JUDGMENT AFTER COURT TRIAL
)
______________________)

THE CAUSE CAME ON REGULARLY FOR TRIAL on ______________________,19_____, in Department________of the above-entitled court, the Honorable_____________Judge, presiding, sitting without a jury, a jury having been waived.

Plaintiff appeared by attorney__________________and defendant appeared by attorney______________. Evidence, oral and documentary was presented by both parties and the cause was argued and submitted for decision.

Findings of fact and conclusions of law have been waived in open court by both parties.

IT IS ORDERED, ADJUDGED, AND DECREED that plaintiff shall have judgment against defendant in the sum of $__________, together with interest thereon at the rate of________% from ______________, 19____, with costs in the sum of $__________.

DATED:_______________, 19____

____
Judge

CAPTION) Case No._____________
)
) MOTION FOR JUDGMENT NOTWITHSTANDING
) VERDICT
____________________)

TO THE HONORABLE________________, JUDGE OF THE ABOVE-ENTITLED COURT:

_________________, the party against whom the verdict in the above-entitled action was rendered, hereby moves the court, for judgment notwithstanding the verdict, of the jury herein.

The motion is made on the following grounds:

(1) There is no evidence of sufficient substantiability to support a verdict in the____________favor and a directed verdict for_______________, the moving party should have been granted.

The motion is also made on the grounds upon which the directed verdict, heretofore made was supportive and on the additional ground that there was not sufficient evidence to support the following finding, (describe).

The motion shall be based on the entire evidence presented at the trial and on the pleadings, records and files herein and the memorandum of points and authorities served herewith.

The motion will be heard at the same time and place as_____________'s motion for a new trial, notice of which is served and filed concurrently herewith, which will be set by the court pursuant to Code of Civil Procedure, §661.

Dated:_____________, 19____

____
Attorney for

****

Motion for judgment notwithstanding the verdict must be made within the period specified by C.C.P. §659, the section dealing with motion for new trial.

Motions for judgment notwithstanding the verdict are covered in C.C.P. §629.

<u>Estate of Arnold</u>, 16 Cal. 2d, 573, <u>Estate of Franco</u>, 50 C.A. 3d, 374.

CAPTION	)	Case No.______________
	)	
	)	JUDGMENT NOTWITHSTANDING VERDICT
	)	
____________________	)	

The above-entitled cause came on regularly for trial on________, 19____, in Department _____of the above-entitled court, the Honorable _______________Judge presiding. Plaintiff appeared by his attorney_______________and defendant by his attorney_______________.

A jury of_________persons was regularly impaneled and sworn to try the action. Witnesses on the part of each party were sworn and examined. After hearing the evidence, the arguments of counsel and instructions of the court, the jury retired to consider their verdict and thereafter returned a verdict as follows, (describe verdict).

Thereafter ___________________duly moved the court for judgment in his favor notwithstanding the verdict and said motion came on regularly to be heard before this court on ____________, 19____, the above attorneys appearing for their respective parties.

The motion was argued and submitted and the court being fully advised, and good cause appearing therefor:

IT IS HEREBY ORDERED AND ADJUDGED:

That the motion for judgment in favor of __________________notwithstanding the verdict is hereby granted.

That judgment entered herein on said verdict on ______________, 19____, is hereby vacated and set aside.

That_______________, the moving party, have judgment in his favor on the following terms, (describe).

That_______________, the moving party shall recover from______________, costs in the sum of $______________.

Dated: _______________, 19____.

____
Judge

CAPTION)
)
)
)
________________________)

Case No.________________

NOTICE OF MOTION FOR JUDGMENT ON THE PLEADINGS

Date:____________________
Time:____________________
Department:______________

NOTICE IS HEREBY GIVEN that on________, 19____, at the hour of_______a.m., in Department ______of the above entitled court,_________________will move the court for an order for a judgment on the pleadings in favor of________________ against ________________________.

The motion will be made on the grounds that the answer (or complaint) on file herein is defective for the following reasons: (Set forth reasons.)

The motion will be made on the basis of the notice of motion, the declaration and points and authorities attached hereto, the papers and records on file herein and such other evidence, oral and documentary as may be adduced at the hearing on the motion.

DATED:_________________, 19_____.

____
Attorney for

****

The motion for judgment on the pleadings is used to perform the function of a general demurrer and, like a demurrer, is confined to the four corners of the pleading. Colberg vs. California, 67 Cal 2d, 408. Hospital Council vs. Superior Court, 30 C. A. 3d, 331.

The motion may be made by either party, either prior to, or at the trial.

Generally the grounds available for a general demurrer are the same grounds available in a motion for judgment on the pleadings.

There is no statutory authority for a motion for judgment on the pleadings. The law is derived from the cases. If the motion is made on the day of trial, it may be made orally without notice. Macbeth vs. West Coast, 83 C.A. 2d, 96.

CAPTION)   Case No.____________
)
)   DEMAND FOR JURY TRIAL
)
____________________________)

COMES NOW the plaintiff and demands trial by jury herein.

____
Attorney for

****

Trial by jury may be waived:

1. By failing to appear at trial;

2. By filing a written consent;

3. By oral consent in open court;

4. By failing to announce that a jury is required;

5. By failing to deposit with the clerk the required jury fees.

C.C.P. §631.

CAPTION)
)
)
)
______________________)

Case No.__________

NOTICE OF MOTION TO SET ASIDE JURY WAIVER

Date:___________
Time:___________
Department:_____

TO_________________AND TO HIS ATTORNEY:

PLEASE TAKE NOTICE that on__________, 19___, in Department_______of the above-entitled court, at the hour of_______a.m., ___________will move the court for an order setting aside the jury waiver.

The motion will be made on the ground that this is an action for_____________and is a proper case for trial by jury. That the waiver was due to the moving party's mistake, inadvertence, surprise or excusable neglect and that the interests of justice will be served by a jury trial.

The motion will be based on the provisions of C.C.P. §631, this notice of motion, the declaration and points and authorities attached hereto, the records and papers on file herein and such other evidence as may be presented at the hearing.

DATED:_________________, 19____.

____
Attorney for

****

The court has discretion to set aside a jury waiver. Davis vs. Conant, 10 C. A. 2d, 73.

CAPTION	)	Case No.____________
	)	
	)	COMPLAINT FOR REFUND OF SECURITY DEPOSIT
	)	
__________________________	)	

Plaintiff complains:

1. On or about______, 19____, defendant leased to plaintiff the following described premises, (describe). A copy of the lease is attached hereto, marked Exhibit "A", and made a part hereof.

2. The lease provided, among other things, that plaintiff deposit with defendant the sum of $_________as security for plaintiff's performance of all the conditions of the lease. Said security deposit was to be returned to plaintiff on expiration of the lease if all conditions therein were performed.

3. On or about______, 19___, plaintiff deposited with defendant the sum of $____________ as a security deposit.

4. The lease expired on__________, 19___, at which time plaintiff vacated the premises. Plaintiff has performed all the conditions of the lease and is entitled to the return of the security deposit.

5. Defendant has failed and refused and continues to fail and refuse to return to plaintiff the security deposit to plaintiff's damage in the sum of $__________________. Defendant's retention of plaintiff's security deposit is in bad faith and without justification and plaintiff is thereby entitled to exemplary damages in the amount of $200.00.

WHEREFORE, plaintiff prays:

1. For damages in the amount of the deposit of $______________.

2. For interest at the rate of______% per annum from__________, 19____.

3. For exemplary damages in the sum of $200.00.

4. For costs of suit and such other relief as the court deems just.

____
Attorney for Plaintiff

****

Civil Code §1950.5 provides that if security deposit was made on or after January 1, 1971, exemplary damages, not to exceed $200.00 may be recovered.

Bauman vs. Islay, 30 C.A. 3d, 752.

CAPTION) Case No.______________
)
) COMPLAINT FOR DAMAGES FOR
) TERMINATING UTILITY SERVICE
________________________)

Plaintiff complains:

1. At all times herein mentioned, defendant was and now is, the owner of that certain apartment building described as follows, (describe).

2. At all times herein mentioned, plaintiff resided in apartment___________in the above-described property under a month to month tenancy.

3. On or about________, 19____, defendant, with the intent to terminate plaintiff's tenancy of the premises did willfully and maliciously turn off the water service to plaintiff's apartment. Plaintiff was without these services for a period of 7 days.

4. As a direct and proximate cause of defendant's action, plaintiff has suffered and is suffering general damages in the amount of $______________.

5. Plaintiff is entitled to punitive damages under Civil Code §789.3 in the amount of $100.00 per day during the period he has been deprived of the utility service for the reason that at the time defendant terminated the service, he knew he was committing a prohibitive act that would subject him to civil penalties.

WHEREFORE, plaintiff prays:

1. For general damages in the amount of $__________.

2. For punitive damages in the amount of $_________.

3. For attorney's fees as provided in Civil Code §789.3.

4. For costs of suit and such other relief as the court deems just.

____
Attorney for Plaintiff

****

Civil Code §789.3.

Plaintiff must prove that landlord knew he was committing a prohibitive act that could subject him to a civil penalty. Hale vs. Morgan, 68 C.A. 3d, 291.

CAPTION) Case No.__________
)
) COMPLAINT FOR DAMAGES FOR WRONGFUL
) EVICTION
______________________)

Plaintiff complains:

1. At all times herein mentioned, defendant was and now is the owner of that certain improved real property described as follows, (set forth description.)

2. On or about________, 19___, plaintiff and defendant entered into an agreement wherein defendant would lease to plaintiff a portion of the above-described property, described as follows (set forth the portion, such as a store, or an apartment). The term of the lease was for a period of one year, commencing on ______________, 19___, and ending________, 19____.

3. On or about________, 19____, during the term of the lease, defendant wrongfully evicted plaintiff from the premises by breaking into the premises, removing the plaintiff's personal property, changing the lock and refusing to allow the tenant back on the premises.

4. (Allege the following if a constructive eviction.) On or about_________, 19___, defendant constructively evicted plaintiff by interfering with plaintiff's right to quiet enjoyment by the following acts, to wit: by allowing the premises to become inhabitable and infested with vermin and rodents. As a result thereof, plaintiff vacated the premises on _________, 19____.

5. As a proximate result of defendant's eviction of plaintiff from the premises, plaintiff has suffered general damages in the sum of $_________________.

6. As a further result of defendant's eviction, plaintiff has incurred the following special damages, including moving expenses, loss of good will and the sum of $_____________ advanced for future rent:

7. The acts of defendant were willful, wanton, malicious and justified the awarding of punitive damages in the amount of $_____________.

WHEREFORE, plaintiff prays:

1. For general damages in the sum of $________.

2. For special damages in the sum of $________.

3. For punitive damages in the sum of $_______.

4. For costs of suit and such other relief as the court deems just.

____
Attorney for Plaintiff

****

A tenant wrongfully evicted may recover damages. The eviction may be either actual or constructive. Buckner vs. Azulai, 251 C.A. 2d, Supp. 1013. Groh vs. Kover, 221 C.A. 2d, 611.

Special damage cases: Beckett vs. City of Paris, 14 Cal 2d, 633, Sierad vs. Lilly, 204 C.A. 2d, 770, Asell vs. Rodrigues, 32 C.A. 3d, 817.

Punitive damages are also recoverable, Tooke vs. Allen, 85 C.A. 2d, 230.

CAPTION)
)
) COMPLAINT FOR REMOVAL OF FIXTURES
) INSTALLED IN GOOD FAITH
______________________)

Case No.____________

Plaintiff complains:

1. At all times herein mentioned, defendant was and now is the owner of the following described real property, (describe).

2. On or about________, 19____, defendant leased to plaintiff the above-mentioned property for use as a laundromat under a lease for a period of one year. A copy of the lease is attached hereto, marked Exhibit "A" and made a part hereof.

3. During the period of plaintiff's tenancy, plaintiff attached certain improvements to the leased premises, thinking in good faith and under the erroneous belief that he had a right to do so. The improvements consisted of the following, (describe).

4. Plaintiff's tenancy of the leased premises will expire on_______, 19____.

5. Defendant refuses to allow plaintiff to remove the improvements although plaintiff has offered, and still offers to pay defendant, the total estimated damages proximately resulting from the affixing and removal of the improvements.

6. Removal of the improvements can be accomplished within a period of_______days at an estimated total cost of $______________to compensate for the damages proximately resulting from such removal.

7. Plaintiff elects to exercise his rights to remove the improvements pursuant to the provisions of Civil Code §101.35 and offers to pay into court the sum of $_________, the estimated damages or other sum as found by the court as a condition to the entry of an interlocutory judgment authorizing the removal of the improvements.

WHEREFORE, plaintiff prays:

1. For judgment declaring plaintiff's right to remove the improvements and compelling defendant to permit removal.

2. For judgment determining and ordering plaintiff to pay defendant the amount of damages proximately resulting from the affixing and removal of the improvements.

3. For costs of suit and such other relief as the court deems just.

____
Attorney for Plaintiff

****

This action is authorized by Civil Code §101.35

CAPTION) Case No.__________
)
) COMPLAINT - UNLAWFUL DETAINER
)
__________________)

Plaintiff complains:

1. At all times herein mentioned, defendant was and now is a resident of the__________County, State of California.

2. The property sought to be recovered is located at__________street, ___________California, in the County of ____________________and in the___________judicial district.

3. On or about________, 19____, plaintiff leased to defendant the above-described premises under an oral (or written) lease for a month to month tenancy, for a monthly rental of $_____________, payable on the______day of each and every month commencing __________, 19____.

4. Pursuant to said lease, (or tenancy), defendant went into possession of said premises on or about________, 19____ and continues in possession.

5. Defendant has not paid the following rental installments required by the terms of said tenancy, to wit; April 1st to April 30th - $100.00, May 1st to May 31st - $100.00, or a total sum of $200.00.

6. On________, 19___, plaintiff served on defendant a written notice stating that the amount of rent due to be paid in full or that defendant shall deliver possession of the premises within 3 days after service of the notice. (And stating plaintiff's election to declare a forfeiture of the lease.) A copy of the notice is attached hereto, marked Exhibit _____and made a part hereof.

7. More than 3 days have elapsed since the service of said notice, but no part of said rent has been paid. Plaintiff is entitled to the immediate possession of said premises.

8. Defendant continues in possession of said premises without the permission of plaintiff and such continuance is willful, intentional and deliberate and entitles plaintiff to treble damages.

9. The reasonable rental of the premises is the sum of $________per day and damages to plaintiff caused by defendant's unlawful detention have accrued at said rate since ___________, 19___, the end of the 3 day period and will continue to accrue at said rate so long as defendant remains in possession.

WHEREFORE, plaintiff prays:

1. For possession of the premises.

2. For damages at the rate of $__________per day from _________, 19____, for each day defendant continues in possession of said premises and that said amount be trebled.

3. For rent of said premises, now due and unpaid in the sum of $____________.

4. For interest on said rent, at the legal rate from the date each installment became due.

5. For costs of suit and such other relief as the court deems just.

____
Attorney for Plaintiff

****

C.C.P. §1174.

CAPTION) Case No.______________
)
) COMPLAINT FOR UNLAWFUL DETAINER
)
__________________)

Plaintiff complains:

1. At all times herein mentioned, defendant was and now is, a resident of the County of_______________.

2. The real property, possession of which is sought in this action, is situated in___________County, California, (or in ______________judicial district).

3. On or about________, 19___, plaintiff leased to defendant, certain premises, commonly known as (describe) under a written lease, (or a month to month tenancy) for a monthly rental of $___________, (or for a period of one year for a total yearly rental of $________) payable on the_______day of each month commencing on _____________, 19___. A copy of said lease is attached hereto, marked Exhibit "A" and made a part hereof.

4. Pursuant to the provisions of the lease, defendant took possession of the property, on or about _______________, 19___, and continues to occupy said property.

5. On___________, 19____, subsequent to the termination of the term of the lease, plaintiff caused to be served on defendant, a written notice declaring said tenancy to be terminated, at the expiration of 30 days after service of the notice on defendant and requiring defendant to deliver possession of the premises to plaintiff, on or before expiration of said 30 day period. A copy of said notice is attached hereto, marked Exhibit "B" and made a part hereof.

6. The 30 day period has expired and plaintiff is entitled to the immediate possession of said premises.

7. Defendant continues in possession of said premises without plaintiff's permission or consent. Said continuance by defendant is willful, intentional and deliberate and entitles plaintiff to treble damages.

8. The reasonable rental of the premises is the sum of $_______per day and damages to plaintiff caused by defendant's unlawful detention have accrued at that rate since __________, 19____ and will continue to accrue at that rate so long as defendant remains in possession of the premises. By the terms of the lease, it is provided that if an action is instituted, for the possession of said property, plaintiff shall be entitled to attorney's fees, a reasonable amount of attorney's fees is $______________.

(If appropriate add paragraph.....the amount of $____________remains as unpaid rent for the period of ________, 19____, to____________, 19____.)

WHEREFORE, plaintiff prays:

1. For possession of the property .

2. For judgment for unpaid rent in the amount of $________________.

3. For damages in the amount of $___________ (treble damages).

4. For attorney's fees in the amount of $_________________.

5. For costs of suit and such other relief as the court deems just.

____
Attorney for Plaintiff

****

Civil Code §1946, Civil Code §789.

Buck vs. Morrossis, 114 C.A. 2d, 461.

CAPTION)
)
)
)
________________)

Case No.__________

COMPLAINT FOR INTENTIONAL INFLICTION OF EMOTIONAL DISTRESS

Plaintiff complains:

1. At all times herein mentioned, defendant was and now is a resident of________County, California.

2. At all times herein mentioned, defendants ____________and______________were the agents and employees of co-defendant_____________and with respect to the events sued on herein, were acting within the course and scope of such agency and employment.

3. On or about_______, 19___, prior to the commencement of this action, plaintiff leased from defendant that certain dwelling in the City of______, California, known as apartment ____________, __________street,__________California.

4. On or about_____, 19___, defendant presented himself at the apartment of plaintiff and entered the apartment without notice by letting himself in with a passkey. At that time, present with plaintiff were the following people: (describe such as relatives, employers, others where outrageous conduct would cause embarrassment).

5. Although plaintiff's rent was not yet due, defendant told the plaintiff in the presence of the above-mentioned individuals that he, plaintiff, was behind in the rent and that if the rent was not paid forthwith, defendant would call the police. Defendant shouted at plaintiff in a rude, violent and outrageous manner.

6. Defendant's action was intended to cause plaintiff emotional distress and to suffer humiliation, mental anguish and physical discomfort. Defendant's conduct was willful and malicious and therefore entitles plaintiff to punitive damage.

7. As a proximate cause of the above-mentioned conduct of defendant, plaintiff suffered humiliation, mental anguish, emotional and physical distress and has been injured in mind and body as follows, (describe).

8. As a proximate cause of the above-mentioned conduct, plaintiff was required to, and did employ physicians and surgeons to treat and care fo him in connection with the injuries suffered. The exact nature and extent of the expenses is not yet ascertained and plaintiff will seek leave to amend the complaint when the amounts are determined.

WHEREFORE, plaintiff prays:

1. For general damages.

2. For medical expenses according to proof.

3. For punitive damages.

4. For costs of suit herein and such other relief as the court deems just.

____
Attorney for Plaintiff

****

A plaintiff must plead and prove outrageous conduct by the defendant, the defendant's intention to cause emotional distress, the plaintiff's suffering and actual and proximate causation. Fletcher vs. Western National, 10 C.A. 3d, 376.

Threatening one with a crime for civil liability has been considered emotional distress.

Defendant's conduct must be outrageous and must go beyond the reasonable bounds of decency. Cornblith vs. First Maintenance Supply, 268 C.A. 2d, 564. For a case on privilege see, Kachig vs. Booth, 22 C.A. 3d, 626.

CAPTION ______________________	Case No. ______________ COMPLAINT FOR TRESPASS

Plaintiff complain and for cause of action alleges:

1. (Allegations as to capacity, residence, and agency of parties).

2. (Allegations of fictitious defendants.)

3. At all times mentioned herein plaintiffs were and now are the owners and in possession of that certain real property located in Los Angeles County, the legal description of which is: (Set forth description), and which is commonly known as ____________________Street, ___________________, California.

4. On or about _____________, 19____, defendants, and each of them, wrongfully entered on said property without plaintiff's consent and against his will, and committed the following acts of damage: (Set forth acts).

5. As a proximate cause of the trespass of defendants, plaintiff sustained damages to the land in the following manner: (Set forth damage), all to plaintiff's damage in the sum of $_______________.

6. In committing the trespass, defendants, and each of them, were guilty of malice in that they deliberately and willfully committed the act of trespass for the purpose of injuring plaintiff and his land, and by reason thereof plaintiff is entitled to punitive damages in the additional sum of $_______________.

WHEREFORE, plaintiff prays:

1. For judgment in the amount of $________________ general damages;

2. For judgment in the amount of $________________ punitive damages;

3. For costs of suit herein; and

4. For such other relief as the court deems just.

DATED: ___________________, 19____.

____
Attorney for Plaintiff

CAPTION)
)
)
)
________________)

Case No.____________

COMPLAINT FOR DAMAGES AGAINST LANDOWNER

Plaintiff complains:

1. At all times herein mentioned, defendant was and now is, a resident of________County, California, and further was and now is, the owner of that certain described real property commonly known as ______________, the legal description of which is__________________________________.

2. On or about _____, 19___, plaintiff was on said premises as a business visitor for the mutual benefit of himself and defendant for the following purpose, (describe business purpose).

3. (Alternate Allegation) On or about__________, 19___, plaintiff was on the premises of defendant with the knowledge, permission and consent of defendant and was a guest at plaintiff's hotel which was situated on defendant's premises.

4. (Another Alternate Paragraph) On or about __________, 19___, plaintiff was a pedestrian walking on public sidewalk adjacent to defendant's premises where the following dangerous activity was taking place, (describe).

5. At said time and place, defendant so negligently owned, maintained and controlled his premises and the fixtures and improvements thereon, that a railing attached to a stairway providing entry to said building, collapsed,causing plaintiff to fall to the ground and to suffer the injuries and damages hereinbelow complained of.

6. (Alternate Allegation) At said time and place, defendant so negligently owned, maintained and operated his premises that while in the process of removing a tree, defendant negligently caused the branch to fall from the tree,which branch struck plaintiff as plaintiff was walking along the sidewalk as hereinabove described.

7. (Alternate Allegation) At various times, prior to__________, 19___, numerous persons were on defendants' premises and became engaged in fights and other dangerous activity and defendants knew of such conduct and that such conduct was likely to occur in the future and to constitute an unreasonable risk of harm to persons lawfully on defendants' premises who were not participants in such activities. On__________, 19___, defendant negligently and carelessly failed to take precautions to prevent such activities and on said date, fight ensued between two patrons of defendants and one patron threw a bottle which struck plaintiff in the head.

8. (Alternate Allegation) On or about __________, 19____, and prior thereto, there existed on defendant's premises an abandoned well, the opening of which was covered by a thin piece of plywood. Said plywood was covered with dirt and grass so as to render the opening of the well unknown by persons passing across the premises. Said condition was known to, or in the exercise of reasonable care should have been known to defendant. Defendant knew, or should have known that plaintiff and others might walk across the opening without knowledge of the opening and would not, in the exercise of reasonable care, obtain knowledge of the opening. Notwithstanding these facts, defendant failed to warn the plaintiff, or others, of the danger either personally or by other means.

9. As a proximate result of said negligence, plaintiff was injured in his health, strength and activity and sustained physical injuries to his body and shock to his nervous system, all of which have caused him, and will cause him great mental and physical pain and suffering, all to his general damage in the sum of $__________________.

10. (Alleged Special Damages, such as medical expenses and loss of earnings).

WHEREFORE, plaintiff prays:

1. For general damages.

2. For medical and hospital expenses according to proof.

3. For loss of earnings according to proof.

4. For costs of suit and such other relief as the court deems just.

____
Attorney for Plaintiff

****

General damages shall not be specified in a dollar amount. C.C.P. §425.10.

See the case of Rowland vs. Christian, 69 Cal. 2d, 108.

Taylor vs. Centenniel Bowl 65 Cal. 2d, 114.

Louie vs. Hagstrom, 81 C.A. 2d, 601.

Violation of statute may constitute negligence per se. Nunnelley vs. Edgar, 36 Cal. 2d, 493.

Duty to persons outside premises: Coole vs. Haskins, 57 C.A. 2d, 737.

CAPTION) Case No.________
)
) COMPLAINT FOR DAMAGE TO PROPERTY
) ON PLAINTIFF'S LAND
____________________)

1. At all times herein mentioned, plaintiff was and now is the owner of, and in possession of that certain parcel of real property in the County of________, the legal description of which is. (Give legal description)

2. At all times herein mentioned, defendant was and now is the owner of and in possession of certain real property in the County of_________, State of California, the legal description of which is (Set forth legal description). Defendant's property is adjoining plaintiff's property.

3. On ______, 19____, and at all times prior thereto, plaintiff erected and maintained a fence on the north boundary of said property. Said fence separated plaintiff's property from that of defendant.

4. On ______, 19____, defendant willfully and maliciously and with the intent to injure plaintiff and his property destroyed and removed said fence of plaintiff.

5. As a direct and proximate cause of said destruction by defendant, plaintiff was forced to construct a new fence between his property and that of the defendant, at a cost of $_________________.

6. Said acts of defendant and the destruction and removal of the fence were willful and malicious and plaintiff is therefore entitled to punitive damages in the sum of $_________.

WHEREFORE, plaintiff prays for judgment as follows:

1. For damages in the sum of $_________.

2. For punitive damages in the sum of $_______.

3. For costs of suit and such other relief as the court may deem just.

____
Attorney for Plaintiff

CAPTION) Case No.____________
)
) COMPLAINT TO ESTABLISH BOUNDARY LINE
) AND QUIET TITLE
_____________________)

Plaintiff alleges:

1. At all times herein mentioned, plaintiff was and now is the owner in fee simple, and in possession of that certain real property in___________County, commonly known as _______________, the legal description of which is as follows: (Set forth legal description.)

2. At all times herein mentioned, defendant______________ was and now is the owner in fee simple, and in possession of that certain real property contiguous to plaintiff's property in _________________County, commonly known as _______________, the legal description of which is: (Set forth legal description.)

3. The above-described properties of plaintiff and defendant adjoin each other in the following manner. (Set forth boundary lines.) A copy of map identifying the properties and setting forth the boundaries is attached hereto, marked Exhibit "A" and incorporated herein.

4. The defendants sued herein as "all other persons unknown claiming any right, title, estate , lien or interest in the real property described in the complaint, adverse to plaintiff's ownership, or any cloud upon plaintiff's title thereto" are unknown to plaintiff. Those defendants, and each of them, claim some right, title, estate , lien or interest in the real property adverse to plaintiff's ownership and this claim, or these claims constitute a cloud upon plaintiff's title.

5. Defendants, and each of them claim some right, title, estate, lien or interest in and to the land of plaintiff hereinabove described and dispute and deny that the true correct boundary line between their respective properties is as follows, (Set forth plaintiff's contended boundary line.) but contend instead that the true and correct boundary line, runs as follows: (Set forth defendants' claim.) Defendants' claim is without any right whatsoever and defendants are without any right, title, estate, lien or interest whatsoever in the aforementioned real property or any part thereof.

WHEREFORE, plaintiff prays judgment against defendants, and each of them as follows:

1. That they be required to set forth each and every claim they may assert in and to plaintiff's land and to the location of the boundary line set out above.

2. That the court establish the true and correct location of the boundary line.

3. That plaintiff's title in and to his land above-mentioned be quieted and that it be adjudged that the plaintiff is the owner in fee and entitled to the possession of the land and that the true, correct location of the boundary line between plaintiff's land and defendants' land is as described in this complaint and that none of the defendants has any right, title, estate, lien or interest in and to the land of plaintiff.

4. That defendants, and each of them, be forever enjoined and restrained from claiming or serving any claim, or interest, in and to the plaintiff's land, or any portion thereof or from interfering with the boundary line established by this court, or attempting to do so.

5. For costs of suit incurred herein and for such other relief as the court deems just.

DATED: _____________, 19____.

____
Attorney for Plaintiff

****

Quiet title actions are controlled by C.C.P., §738.

The caption must name as defendants "all other persons unknown, claiming any right, title, estate, lien or interest in the real property described in the complaint adverse to the plaintiff's ownership or any cloud upon plaintiff's title thereto."

When boundaries have been disturbed by an earthquake, an action may be brought under the Cullen Earthquake Act. C.C.P., §751.50 through 751.65.

____________________)
)　　　　　　　　No.
)　(Caption)
)　　　　　　COMPLAINT FOR DAMAGES FOR
____________________)　　　　REMOVAL OF SUBJACENT SUPPORT

Plaintiff (or petitioner) alleges:

I

(Allegations of fictitious entities, capacity of parties, unknown parties, agency, residence, venue and jurisdiction must be set forth in separate paragraphs if appropriate.)

II

Plaintiff is and at all times mentioned herein was the owner of and in possession and control of that certain real property in Los Angeles County, California described as follows:

III

Defendant is and at all times herein mentioned was the owner of a certain sub-surface interest in said land, which is described as follows:

IV

On or about ___________, 19__ and until ____________, 19__ defendant caused certain excavations to be made on his property in an area subjacent to the aforementioned property owned by plaintiff, which excavations are described as follows:

V

At all times prior to ____________, 19__,when such excavations were made, plaintiff's land in its natural state was receiving subjacent support from the land excavated on by defendant.

VI

On or about ______________, 19__, as a proximate cause of such excavations plaintiff's land was deprived of its subjacent support and the earth and soil thereon settled and subsided into defendant's excavation, all to plaintiff's damage in the sum of $__________.

WHEREFORE, plaintiff prays:

1. For damages in the sum of $___________; and

2. For costs of suit herein incurred and for such other relief and the court deems just.

____
Attorney for Plaintiff

CAPTION)
)
_____________)

NOTICE OF LIS PENDENS

Notice is hereby given that in the above entitled action plaintiff has instituted an action to quiet title to the real property, the legal description of which is:

(Set forth legal description)

The purpose of the action is to quiet title to the above described property in the name of the plaintiff.

The parties to the action are:

(Set forth the names of the parties to the action)

Dated:____________________

____
Attorney for Plaintiff

****

CCP §409

CAPTION)
)
________)

NOTICE OF MOTION TO
EXPUNGE LIS PENDENS

TO ____________________ Plaintiff and to ____________________, his attorney:

YOU AND EACH OF YOU WILL PLEASE TAKE NOTICE that on ______________, 19___, at the hour of ______________ a.m., in Department ________ of the above entitled court, defendant will move the court for an order expunging the notice of lis pendens heretofore recorded in the office of the County Recorder of ______________ County, California in Volume ________, page ________ of the Official Records of said County Recorder, and for an order awarding attorneys fees and costs.

Said motion will be based upon the grounds that (set forth the grounds).

The motion will also be made upon this notice, the declaration of ________________, all papers, records and documents on file herein and upon such other evidence, oral and documentary, as may be adduced at the hearing on this motion.

Dated: ______________

____
Attorney for Defendant

****

This notice must be served not less than 20 days prior to the hearing.

CAPTION)
)
)
____

DECLARATION IN SUPPORT OF MOTION TO EXPUNGE LIS PENDENS

I, __________________________declare:

That I am the owner of the real property described in the notice of lis pendens, a copy of which notice is filed as set forth in the notice of motion.

That plaintiff has filed the above action seeking an order quieting title in his name.

The action is not undertaken in good faith for the following reasons: (Set forth reasons).

The notice of is pendens constitutes a cloud upon declarant's title to the real property and is preventing him from consummating a sale thereof. The declarant is willing and able to provide an undertaking to indemnify plaintiff for all damages which he may incur if the notice is expunged. If the notice is not expunged, defendant will suffer the loss in profits and be subject to further liability if the pending sale is not concluded.

WHEREFORE, declarant prays that the court may make an order expunging the notice of lis pendens or in the alternative, that the court require your declarant to provide an undertaking in a sum sufficient to indemnify the plaintiff for all damages which he might incur as a condition to making such an order.

Executed at _________________, California on __________________, 19___.

I declare under penalty of perjury that the foregoing is true and correct.

____
Defendant

****

CAPTION) Case No.____________
)
) COMPLAINT FOR MALICIOUS PROSECUTION
) OF CIVIL ACTION
____________________)

Plaintiff complains:

1. At all times herein mentioned, defendant was and now is a resident of the County of_________, State of California.

2. On or about_________, 19___, the defendant commenced a civil action against plaintiff by filing a summons and complaint in the Superior Court of___________County, containing the following alleged cause of action, (describe). The action was numbered______and was entitled ______________vs. __________________and claimed damages in the sum of $___________.

3. On or about_________, 19____, plaintiff was served with a copy of the summons and complaint.

4. On or about___________, 19____, defendant voluntarily dismissed said action against plaintiff.

5. Defendant acted without probable cause in instituting the above-mentioned action against plaintiff for the following reasons, (describe) and further, he did not honestly and reasonably believe that there were grounds for said action for the following additional reasons, (describe).

6. As a proximate cause of defendant's commencing the above-mentioned action, plaintiff has been damaged in the sum of $__________________.

7. Defendant's conduct in bringing the above-mentioned action against plaintiff was malicious and willful and done with an improper motive or purpose and with the intent to injure plaintiff, (specify specific facts justifying this allegation).

8. As a further proximate result, plaintiff incurred costs in the sum of $__________for attorney's fees.

9. Defendant's conduct was willful and malicious to the extent that plaintiff is entitled to punitive damages in the sum of $______________.

WHEREFORE, plaintiff prays:

1. For compensatory damages in the sum of $__________.

2. For punitive damages in the sum of $___________.

3. For costs of suit and such other relief as the court deems just.

____
Attorney for Plaintiff

****

Davis vs. Local Union Number 11, 16 C.A. 3d, 686. Rich vs. Siegel 7 C.A. 3d, 465. Kassen vs. Bledsoe, 252 C.A. 2d, 810.

Attorney's honest belief in claim may be a defense. Tool Research vs. Heningson, 46 C.A. 3d, 675.

CAPTION) Case No.______________
)
) COMPLAINT FOR MALICIOUS
) PROSECUTION OF CRIMINAL ACTION
)
__________________)

Plaintiff complains:

1. At all times mentioned herein, defendant was and now is, a resident of the City of_______, County of________, State of California.

3. On or about_______, 19____, defendant initiated a criminal proceeding against plaintiff by causing to be filed with the District Attorney of__________County, a felony complaint, charging plaintiff with violation of the crime of_____________, Penal Code §_________. A warrant was issued for the arrest of plaintiff and the warrant was executed and plaintiff was arrested on_________, 19____ and was retained in custody for_________hours until bail was posted and thereafter charged by said complaint at an arraignment on_______, 19____ and held for preliminary hearing.

4. Preliminary hearing was held on______, 19___ in Division_______of the Municipal Court, __________Judicial District,_______County, California in a proceeding titled People of the State of California vs.______________________, Case No._________. At the end of that proceeding, the matter was dismissed by the court for lack of evidence. The court also found that there was no probable cause for the issuance of the warrant or the arrest of the plaintiff.

5. Defendant acted without probable cause in the initiating the prosecution of plaintiff and in presenting the facts to the District Attorney for the issuance of the complaint for the following reasons, (describe). Defendant did not honestly, reasonably and in good faith believe plaintiff to be guilty of the crime charged, and in fact knew plaintiff was not guilty for the following reasons, (describe.)

6. Defendant's conduct in initiating the proceedings was malicious and done with the intent to annoy, harrass and injure plaintiff.

7. As a proximate result of the criminal prosecution, initiated by defendant, plaintiff has been damaged in the sum of $____________.

8. As a further proximate result of the criminal prosecution, plaintiff has incurred the following expenses, (describe such as bail, attorney's fees, investigation fees, etc.).

9. Defendant's malicious acts, as described above, justify the awarding of punitive damages in the sum of $________.

WHEREFORE, plaintiff prays:

1. For damages in the sum of $__________.

2. For punitive damages in the sum of $________.

3. For costs of suit and such other relief as the court deems just.

____
Attorney for Plaintiff

****

Centers vs. Dollar Market, 99 C.A. 2d, 534. Bertero vs. National General, 13, Cal. 3d, 43.

Bulkey vs. Klein, 206 C.A. 2d, 742. (The Bulkey case contains an allegation for false imprisonment.)

Hardy vs. Vial, 48 Cal. 2d, 577.

If favorable termination is not alleged, it may be attacked by demurrer or affirmative defense.

CAPTION) Case No.____________________
)
) COMPLAINT-MEDICAL MALPRACTICE
____________________)

Plaintiff complains:

1. Defendant at all times herein mentioned was, and now is a resident of County of____________, State of California and further, at all times herein mentioned was and now is a physician and surgeon duly licensed to practice medicine in the State of California.

2. Plaintiff has and now does hold himself out to possess that degree of skill, ability and learning common to medical practitioners in the community of_____________, California.

3. Defendant ______________hospital is a corporation organized and existing under the laws of the State of California with its principal place of business in _____________County, California and now is, and at all times herein mentioned was, operating a general hospital.

4. (Set forth fictitious defendant allegation)

5. (Set forth agency allegation)

6. On or about _______, 19___, plaintiff was experiencing the following symptoms, (describe) and on_________, 19____, consulted defendant physician for the purpose of obtaining diagnosis and treatment of said symptoms and to do all things necessary to care, cure and treat said symptoms and whatever illness might be causing said symptoms. Defendant physician agreed to diagnosis plaintiff's illness and disorder and to care and treat for said disorder and to do all things necessary and proper in connection with said treatment and diagnosis.

7. On or about_______, 19____, defendant physician admitted plaintiff as a patient to_____________hospital. Said defendant hospital agreed and undertook to care and treat plaintiff and to assist defendant physician in carrying out the treatment and to do all things necessary and proper in connection thereto. Plaintiff paid said hospital in consideration of said services the sum of $_____________. Defendant so negligently examined plaintiff and diagnosied his condition and so negligently treated and cared for plaintiff's disorder, plaintiff was caused to, and did suffer the injuries and damages hereinafter set forth.

8. Defendant hospital so negligently and carelessly cared for plaintiff and assisted defendant physician in that defendant hospital administered the drug____________instead of the drug________________so that plaintiff was caused to, and did suffer injuries and damages hereinafter set forth.

9. As a proximate result of the negligence of each of the defendants, plaintiff suffered injuries, both physical and mental in the following respects, (describe). In addition, the disorder for which he was originally hospitalized and for which he originally consulted the physician was aggrevated and plaintiff suffered great physical and mental pain and suffering and permanent disability, all to his general damage.

10. As a further proximate result of the negligence of defendants, and each of them, plaintiff has incurred and will continue to incur medical, hospital and related expenses and the amount of such expenses is presently unknown to plaintiff and plaintiff will amend this complaint to set forth the exact amounts when they become ascertained.

11. At the time of said injuries, and prior thereto, plaintiff was employed as a____________and as a further proximate result of the negligence of the defendants, and each of them, plaintiff was prevented from attending to his occupation from __________, 19____, through____________, 19____, and lost earnings for said period. Plaintiff is informed and believes and on such information and belief alleges that he will continue to be prevented from attending to his occupation for a period in the future and will thereby lose further earnings. The full amount of such loss of earnings is presently unknown to plaintiff, and plaintiff will seek leave to amend this complaint when the true amount has been ascertained.

WHEREFORE, plaintiff prays:

1. For general damages.

2. For medical and related expenses according to proof.

3. For loss of earnings.

4. For costs of suit and such other relief as the court deems just.

____
Attorney for Plaintiff

****

Prior to filing an action against a health care provider, a plaintiff must give each defendant at least ninety (90) days notice of his intention to commence the action. C.C.P. §364. If the notice is served within ninety (90) days prior to the expiration of the statute of limitations, the statute of limitations is extended for an additional ninety (90) days. Health care providers are described in C.C.P. §364.

See Civil Code §333.2(a) for recoverable damages. See also C.C.P. §667.

See also Business and Professions Code §6146(a) on attorney's fees.

See C.C.P. §425.10 on allegation of general damages.

CAPTION	)	Case No.__________________
	)	
	)	COMPLAINT FOR MALPRACTICE AGAINST
	)	ATTORNEY
______________________	)	

Plaintiff complains:

1. At all times herein mentioned, defendant was an attorney at law, duly licensed as such, in the State of California and engaged in said practice in the County of____________, California. The events sued on herein occurred in the County of __________________, California.

2. On or about___________, 19___, at _______________, California, defendant attorney's office, plaintiff retained defendant attorney to represent plaintiff in connection with injuries sustained by plaintiff as the result of an automobile collision which occurred on _________, 19____. At such time and place, defendant accepted such employment and agreed to perform such services for plaintiff. A written retainer agreement was executed, a copy of which is attached hereto, marked Exhibit "A" and incorporated herein.

3. At all times herein mentioned, defendant failed to exercise reasonable care and skill in the performance of said legal services in that defendant carelessly and negligently failed to file a summons and complaint on or before __________, 19____, the anniversary date of the statue of limitations.

4. As a proximate result of defendant's negligence, plaintiff was foreclosed from recovering any amount as a result of the collision hereinabove referred to. Plaintiff is informed and believes, and upon such information and belief alleges, that such claim was at all times mentioned, meritorious and plaintiff would have recovered judgment on such claim in the sum of $________. At all times herein mentioned, the party against whom the claim existed was insured by_______________insurance company for public liability in the sum of $________________.

5. As a proximate result of the negligence hereinabove stated, plaintiff's cause of action against __________________ for personal injuries has been rendered worthless, all to plaintiff's damage in the sum of $________________.

WHEREFORE, plaintiff prays:

1. For judgment in the amount of $__________.

2. For costs of suit and such other relief as the court deems just.

____
Attorney for Plaintiff

****

Hege vs. Worthington, 209 C.A. 2d, 670.

CAPTION) Case No.__________
)
) COMPLAINT FOR BREACH OF CONTRACT AND
) TO FORECLOSE MECHANIC'S LIEN
____________________)

Plaintiff alleges:

FIRST CAUSE OF ACTION

1. At all times mentioned herein, plaintiff was and now is, a corporation organized and existing under the laws of California, and is a general building contractor, duly licensed as such under the laws of the State of California.

2. At all times herein mentioned, defendant was and now is, the owner of that certain real property in__________ County, California, the legal description of which is, (set forth legal description).

3. On or about________, 19______, in__________, California, plaintiff and defendant entered into a written contract wherein and whereby it was agreed that plaintiff would construct on the above-mentioned property of defendant, the following described improvement, (describe). It was agreed that plaintiff would furnish all necessary labor, services and equipment to be used in the construction and defendant agreed to pay, upon the completion of said construction, the sum of $__________. A copy of the contract is attached hereto, marked Exhibit "A" and made a part hereof.

4. Between the date of_______, 19___, and ____________, 19____, plaintiff performed the work and labor and furnished all necessary services, materials and equipment necessary for the completion of the construction of the work of improvement and performed all other conditions, covenants, and promises under the contract.

5. Plaintiff has paid the claims of all claimants, subcontractors, and materialmen who have funished labor, services, equipment and materials as required under the master contract.

6. The whole of the real property mentioned above on which the work of improvement is situated, is required for the convenient use and occupation of the work of improvement.

7. Although demand has been made therefor, no part of the contract price, except the sum of $__________ has been paid, and the sum of $__________remains due, owing and unpaid.

SECOND CAUSE OF ACTION

8. Plaintiff incorporates each and every allegation of paragraphs _______through_______ inclusive of the first cause of action as thought set out in full.

9. After plaintiff completed the contract on or about_________, 19____, plaintiff duly filed and recorded his claim of lien, duly verified by the oath of____________. Said claim of lien was filed in book_____, page___ of the official records of___________County. A copy of said claim of lien is attached hereto, marked Exhibit "B" and made a part hereof. The claim of lien was recorded within ________days of________, 19_____, the date being the date of the recording of a notice of completion by defendant, (or the completion of the work if no notice of completion was filed).

10. In this claim of lien, plaintiff claimed a mechanic's lien on the work of improvement and real property for the amount of the unpaid contract price alleged. Said price is the reasonable value of all labor, materials, services and equipment plaintiff has furnished. Plaintiff has further incurred indebtedness in the sum of $_________, the necessary costs of recording and verifying the claim of lien.

11. Defendants _______and________ claim to have some right, title or interest in the above-described real property, the exact nature of which claims is presently unknown to plaintiff, but which claims plaintiff alleges are subordinate to the claim of lien of plaintiff.

WHEREFORE, plaintiff prays:

1. For the sum of $___________on the first cause of action, with interest at the rate of_____% per annum from ___________, 19____.

2. A decree declaring that the rights, claims, ownership, liens, titles and demands of defendants are subsequent to and subject to the lien of plaintiff.

3. A decree declaring that the mechanic's lien claim be foreclosed and that the usual judgment be made for the sale of the property according to law, and that the proceeds be applied in payment of the amounts, including interest at the rate of_____% per annum from______, 19____.

4. Judgment for any deficiency should the proceeds from the sale be less than the amount of plaintiff's claim.

5. Judgment allowing plaintiff to become a purchaser at the foreclosure sale.

6. For costs of suit and such other relief as the court deems just.

____
Attorney for Plaintiff

CAPTION) Case No.__________

) NOTICE OF INTENTION TO MOVE FOR A NEW TRIAL

____________________________)

Date:_______________
Time:_______________
Department:_________

TO______________________AND TO HIS ATTORNEY______________:

PLEASE TAKE NOTICE that the above named plaintiff intends to, and will move the court, for a new trial. Motion will be made at a time set by the court. The motion will be made upon the following grounds: (Set forth only appropriate grounds.)

1. Irregularity in the proceedings of the court or jury.

2. Misconduct of the jury.

3. Accident or surprise which ordinary prudence could not have guarded against.

4. Newly discovered evidence material to the moving party, which could not with reasonable diligence have been discovered and introduced at the trial.

5. Excessive or inadequate damages.

6. Insufficiency of the evidence to justify the verdict or the verdict or decision is against the law.

7. Errors in law occurring at the trial and excepted to by the moving party.

The motion will be based upon the declarations and points and authorities submitted herewith and upon the evidence, oral and documentary to be presented at the hearing on the matter.

DATED:___________________, 19______

____

****

The date of hearing is not set forth in the motion for new trial. Time is set by the judge or clerk and five days notice must be given by the clerk. C.C.P. §661. The court must pass on the motion within 60 days after the entry of judgment or 60 days after the notice of intention to move for new trial.

CAPTION) Case No.______________
)
) ORDER GRANTING NEW TRIAL
)
)
_______________________)

The motion of plaintiff for a new trial, having been heard and presented on__________, 19____, with _______________ appearing as attorney for plaintiff and___________appearing as attorney for defendant, and the matter having been submitted and argued, and good cause appearing therefor:

IT IS HEREBY ORDERED that a new trial be granted on the ground of________________and for the following reasons: (Describe reasons.)

The matter is set for trial on____________, 19_____.

DATED:___________________, 19_____.

____
Judge

****

The order passing on the determination of the motion must state the ground or grounds relied on by the court.

On appeal, from an order granting a new trial, the order shall not be affirmed on the ground of insufficiency of the evidence or upon the ground of excessive or inadequate damages unless the ground is stated in the order and the reasons are specified. C.C.P. §657.

The court must be specific and identify the deficiencies in terms of the evidence for granting the motion. Scala vs. Witt, 3 Cal. 3d, 359.

The requirement that the reasons be specified is mandatory. Krueger vs. Meyer, 48 C.A. 3d, 760.

The notice of intention to move for a new trial must be filed either before the entry of judgment or within 15 days of the mailing of the notice of entry of judgment or within 180 days after the entry of judgment, whichever is earliest. C.C.P. §659.

Where the application is made on the basis of grounds 1 through 4, it must be made upon affidavit. In all other cases, the application may be made upon the minutes of the court. The affidavits must be filed within 10 days of the notice of motion, and opposing parties shall have 10 days after the service of the moving parties' affidavits in which to file counter affidavits.

CAPTION	)	Case No.________________
	)	
	)	NOTICE TO PRODUCE
	)	
____________________	)	

TO______________PLAINTIFF, AND TO HIS ATTORNEY:

NOTICE IS HEREBY GIVEN that at the trial of this action, now set for_________, 19_____, at _________a.m., in Department________of the above-entitled court, the following documents now in your possession and control will be required and you are hereby requested to produce the original thereof, (describe documents).

YOU ARE FURTHER NOTIFIED that if you fail to produce the originals of said documents, secondary evidence of their contents will be introduced.

DATED:__________________

____
Attorney for Defendant

****

Evidence Code, §1503 permits the introduction of secondary evidence if a party, after a request, fails to produce the originals.

______________________)))) ______________________)	(Caption)	No. COMPLAINT TO ABATE A NUISANCE AND FOR A PERMANENT INJUNCTION

Plaintiffs (or petitioners) allege:

I

(Allegations of fictitious entities, capacity of parties, unknown parties, agency, residence, venue and jurisdiction must be set forth in separate paragraphs if appropriate.)

II

At all times mentioned herein plaintiffs were and now are the owners and in possession of that certain dwelling house in the County of Los Angeles, California described as follows:

III

At all times mentioned herein and since ______________, 19__, defendant has resided in a dwelling house which is contiguous to and directly north of the property of plaintiffs hereinabove described.

IV

Since ______________, 19__ and continuously thereafter defendant has maintained on his premises a number of domestic and wild animals which include 13 dogs, one weasel, one coyote and three lion cubs. The presence of said animals constitutes a private nuisance in that between the hours of 12 a.m. and 6 a.m. daily said animals incessantly bark, yowl, whine and make other noises. Said noises are unreasonable and not necessary and have disturbed the quiet enjoyment of plaintiffs and has injuriously affected plaintiffs' enjoyment of their property.

V

Prior to ______________, 19__ plaintiffs were not disturbed by any of the unnecessary and unreasonable noises, since prior to that time defendant did not keep and maintain said animals on the premises.

VI

On ________________, 19__ plaintiffs in writing notified defendant that the manner in which defendant has and does maintain his premises was and is a nuisance, and requested defendant to discontinue the manner in which and the times at which said animals are maintained and allowed to make excessive noises. Notwithstanding said notice by plaintiffs to cease and desist, defendant has refused and still refuses to cease and desist therefrom.

VII

By reason of said unnecessary and unreasonable noise the value and enjoyment of plaintiffs' premises have been and are greatly impaired and great nervous distress and suffering have been caused to plaintiffs, to their damage in the sum of $__________.

IX

Unless restrained by order of this court, defendant will continue said acts and will cause irreparable damages to plaintiffs. Plaintiffs have no plain, speedy or adequate remedy at law and injunctive relief is expressly authorized by Section 731 of the Code of Civil Law.

WHEREFORE, plaintiffs pray judgment against defendant as follows:

1. That this court order that defendant be permanently restrained and enjoined from maintaining said animals on the premises except in such a manner that animals will not emanate noise;

2. That defendant be permanently enjoined from maintaining an excess of two animals on said premises;

3. That plaintiffs recover from defendant the sum of $____________ as damages; and

4. For costs of suit herein and for such other and further relief as the court deems just.

____

Attorney for Plaintiffs

CAPTION)
)
) APPLICATION FOR ORDER SHORTENING
) TIME
________________)

Case No.____________

I________________declare:

I am the attorney for______________in the above-entitled matter. I make this application for order shortening time for service of the______________and in support of said application declare that it is necessary that the time for service be shortened to not later than_________ days before the time appointed for the hearing, by reason of the following facts, (describe).

Executed at Los Angeles, California, on________, 19________.

I declare under penalty of perjury that the foregoing is true and correct.

____
Attorney for

APPLICATION HAVING BEEN MADE AND GOOD CAUSE APPEARING THEREFOR,

IT IS ORDERED that the time for serving the notice of motion of______________be shortened so that the same may be served together with a copy of this order on ____________, the opposing party, not later than______days before the time of the hearing of the motion.

Dated:______________________

____
Judge

CAPTION)
)
)
____

NOTICE OF MOTION TO BRING IN NEW PARTY

TO ____________________ AND TO HIS ATTORNEY:

YOU AND EACH OF YOU are hereby notified that on ______________, 19___, at the hour of ______________ a.m., in Department _______ of the above entitled court, plaintiff will move the court for an order bringing in _______________ as party defendant.

The motion will be made upon the grounds that in the absence of _________________________, complete relief cannot be had among the present parties to the action. The motion will further be based upon the provisions of CCP §389a, upon the declaration and points and authorities filed herewith, the papers and records on file herein and upon such other evidence, oral and documentary, to be presented at the hearing on this motion.

Dated: _____________

____
Attorney for Plaintiff

****

A person who is subject to service of process and whose joinder will not deprive the court of jurisdiction over the subject matter of the action shall be joined if in his absence complete relief cannot be accorded among the existing parties or if he claims an interest relating to the subject of the action and is so situated that the disposition of the action in his absence may impair his ability to protect that interest or leaves other persons already parties subject to a risk of incurring double obligations. CCP §389.

If the person described above cannot be joined, the court may either continue the action without him or dismiss the action without prejudice. CCP §389b.

Sanders v. Fuller, 45 C.A. 3d 994.

CAPTION)
)
________________)

NOTICE OF MOTION TO SUBSTITUTE PARTY

TO THE FOLLOWING PARTIES AND THEIR ATTORNEYS:

YOU AND EACH OF YOU are hereby notified that on ______________, 19__ at the hour of ___________ a.m. in Department _____ of the above entitled court, the moving party herein will move the court for an order substituting _______________ as plaintiff in this action.

The motion is made on the ground that subsequent to the commencement of the action, plaintiff _______________ assigned and transferred all of his right, title and interest in this action to the above named _____________________.

The motion will be based upon the provisions of CCP §385, this notice of motion, the declaration and points and authorities attached hereto, the papers and records on file herein and such other evidence, oral and documentary, to be aduced at the hearing on the motion.

Dated:_________________

____
Attorney for

****

The authority for this procedure is found in CCP §385. In the case of a transfer of interest, the action may be continued in the name of the original party or the court may allow the person to whom the transfer is made to be substituted in the action.

The motion may also be used to substitute a personal representative in place of a party who has died after the commencement of the action.

CAPTION)
)
_______________)

NOTICE OF MOTION TO CONTINUE ACTION AFTER DEATH OF PARTY

TO THE ___________________ and his attorney and to _________________ attorney for defendant:

YOU AND EACH OF YOU will please take notice that on _________________, 19___ at the hour of _________________ a.m. in Department ______________ of the above entitled court, plaintiff will move the court for leave to continue the above-entitled action against _______________________________________, the personal representative of the defendant, now deceased.

Said motion will be made upon the grounds that the defendant has died after the commencement of the action and the action herein does not abate upon the death of the defendant and will be based upon CCP §385. The motion will further be based upon the declaration and affidavit attached hereto, the records, papers on file herein and such other evidence, oral and documentary, as to be presented at the hearing on the motion.

Dated: ___________________

____
Attorney for Plaintiff

****

CCP §385 permits an action to continue, if it is the type of action that does not abate. A copy of the complaint must be served on the insurer.

The court may order the appointment of a personal representative and his substitute as a defendant. P.C. §630 and §707.

This procedure is essential or a judgment rendered if the defendant is dead, will be void. Bliss vs. Speier, 193 C.A. 2d 125.

CAPTION) Case No.____________
)
) COMPLAINT FOR PARTITION OF REAL PROPERTY
)
________________)

Plaintiff complains:

1. The real property which is the subject of this partition action, is commonly known as ____________ street, ________________, California, and has the following legal description, (describe).

2. The interests in the property, both those of record, and those otherwise known to plaintiff, or reasonably apparent from an inspection of the property, owned or claimed by all persons, are as follows:

a. Plaintiff has a present interest in fee in an un-divided one-half of the property as a tenant in common.

b. _______________ has an un-divided one-half interest in fee as a tenant in common.

(Set forth other interests, such as remainders or unknown interests.

(If there is a future interest, set forth the names of those who will take the remainer.)

3. The liens and encumbrances on the property appearing of record or otherwise known to plaintiff, or apparent from an inspection of the property are as follows, (describe).

4. _________________ is the wife of ____________ and may claim a community property interest in the property. However, it is alleged that she has no interest and is joined as a defendant for a judicial determination of that fact.

5. Partition is sought of the fee estate between ________________ and _______________, tenants in common. Sale of the property and a division of the proceeds would, under the circumstances, be more equitable than division of the entire property for the following reasons, (reasons must be stated in ordinary and concise language).

6. Prior to the commencement of this action, plaintiff procurred a title report concerning said property at an expense of $_______________ and that sum is reasonable and plaintiff is entitled to reimbursement thereof. The title report will be kept available for inspectión and use by the parties at _________________, _____________ California.

WHEREFORE, plaintiff prays:

1. For a partition of the present and future interests of the property.

2. For an order that the property be sold and the proceeds be distributed as follows, (describe).

3. For costs of suit and such other relief as the court deems just.

____
Attorney for Plaintiff

****

The new partition law is found in C.C.P. §§ 872.010 through 874.240. Both real and personal property may be partitioned pursuant to these sections, with some exceptions.

The plaintiff must join as defendants all persons having, or claiming interest of record or actually known to the plaintiff or reasonably apparent from an inspection of the property. These persons should be named in the caption. C.C.P. § 872.510.

If a person to be named is dead, the plaintiff must join the personal representative or file a declaration indicating that the person is dead, in which the case the testate and intestate successors shall be joined. C.C.P. §872.530.

CAPTION) Case No.__________
)
) ANSWER TO COMPLAINT FOR PARTITION
)
_______________)

COMES NOW the defendant, and answering for himself alone, admits, denies and alleges as follows:

1. This answering defendant admits that he is the record owner of an undivided one-half interest and a tenant in common with plaintiff in the property described in the complaint.

2. Defendant admits generally the allegations contained in paragraphs ____, ____, and ____ of plaintiff's complaint and denies generally and specifically each and every other allegation contained in said complaint.

FIRST AFFIRMATIVE DEFENSE

3. This answering defendant has the following claim for contribution by virtue of the following, (describe right to contribution and basis of the right).

WHEREFORE defendant prays:

1. That partition be granted and ordered as prayed for in the complaint.

2. That defendant be awarded the sum of $____________in addition to sums realized by the sale.

3. For costs of suit and such other relief as the court deems just.

____
Attorney for Defendant

****

The answer must contain any interest the defendant has, or claims in the property, any facts, tending to controvert the material allegations of the complaint or any facts justifying the sale of the property, if defendant initially seeks sale. C.C.P. §872.410.

CAPTION)   Case No.________________
)
)   ORDER APPOINTING REFEREE
)
__________________)

Pursuant to the consent of ______________and ____________, parties to this action, ________________is hereby appointed as referee to sell the property which is the subject of this action.

The referee is instructed to sell the property in the following manner, (describe order of sale, whether sale is to be public or private, the manner in which parcels are to be sold off, etc.,).

The referee shall file an interim report on or before ________, 19___and a final report on or before _______, 19____.

Compensation for the referee shall be fixed as follows, (describe) and his expenses shall be paid as follows, (describe).

Bond shall be fixed in the amount of $__________.

Dated: ______________, 19____.

____
JUDGE

****

The court may, with the consent of the parties, appoint 3 referees to divide or sell the property, or the court may appoint any referee otherwise unqualified, with the consent of the party. C.C.P. §§ 873.010 through 873.050.

__________________)
)
) (Caption)
)
__________________)

No.

INTERLOCUTORY JUDGMENT OF PARTITION

IT IS ORDERED, ADJUDGED AND DECREED:

1. Plaintiff and defendant are owners as tenants in common of of a fee simple interest in the following described real property in the County of Los Angeles, California:

2. There are no liens and encumbrances of record on said property and there are no other interests, estates of said property owned or possessed by any other person other than those herein set forth.

3. Said real property is situated such that partition cannot be made without great prejudice to the owners.

4. _______________ and _______________ are hereby appointed as referees with authority to sell said property at public auction to the highest bidder for cash on notice duly given in the manner required for the sale of real property on execution, or at a private sale in the event that referees shall determine that a private sale would be most beneficial to all parties having interest therein, in which event said private sale shall be conducted in the manner as required in private sales of real property of estates of deceased persons.

5. Said referees after making the sale of said real property are hereby directed to report to this court their proceedings thereon, and on confirmation of the sale of said real property by this court and the payment of the purchase price thereof, said referees are hereby authorized and directed to execute and deliver a deed of the real property sold to the purchaser thereof.

6. Unless modified by any order confirming sales hereafter entered, the proceeds from said sale shall be applied after the confirmation of said sale as follows:

a. To pay a just proportion of the general costs of this action;

b. To pay the costs of the referees, including fees and disbursements; and

c. To pay the residue in equal shares among plaintiff and defendant.

____
Judge of the Superior Court

CAPTION) Case No.________________
)
) COMPLAINT FOR DISSOLUTION OF
) PARTNERSHIP, ACCOUNTING AND APPOINTMENT
__________________) OF RECEIVER

Plaintiff complains:

1. At all times herein mentioned, defendant was and now is, a resident of _____________County, California.

2. On or about_________, 19____, plaintiff and defendant entered into a written partnership agreement at_________, California, for the purpose of conducting the business of ____________________, under the parnership name of_____________, with its principal place of business at ___________________. A copy of the partnership agreement is attached hereto, marked Exhibit "A" and made a part hereof.

3. Thereafter, the partnership commenced a business and ever since has been, and now is, operating the business at the above address and has acquired and owns assets exceeding the value of $______________________.

4. (Alternate Allegation) On or about_________, 19____, defendant sold partnership assets described as follows, (describe), which had the value of $___________. The loss of said assets has resulted in loss to the partnership of plaintiff in the sum of $_____________. The above-described asset was sold without the knowledge or consent of plaintiff and was not sold in the scope of the partnership business. Plaintiff is informed and believes and upon such information and belief, alleges that the sum of $_____________was received for said asset and that said sum has been retained and misappropriated by defendant.

5. (Alternate Allegation) Since__________, 19____, and on numerous occasions thereafter, defendant has from time to time, collected receipts and profits due the partnership and has converted them to his own use and has not deposited them in the partnership account. Defendant refused, and still refuses to account to plaintiff for said receipts although plaintiff has requested and demanded such an accounting.

6. (Alternate Allegation) On___________ and ______________and on numerous occasions thereafter, defendant has repeatedly withdrawn amounts from the partnership profits in excess of his agreed share, the total sum of said overdraw is $________________________.

7. (Alternate Allegation) On or about__________, 19____, defendant took exclusive possession of the premises of the partnership business, changed the locks on the door and has retained and still retains possession of the assets, books accounts, and records of said partnership and at all times since, has excluded, and still excludes plaintiff from participating in the management of the partnership premises and excludes plaintiff from entering the partnership property.

8. (Alternate Allegation) Differences have arisen between plaintiff and defendant as to the manner in which the partnership business should be conducted and the participation of each partner in the business, to such an extent, that it is in the best interests of all partners that the partnership be dissolved.

9. (Alternate Allegation) By the terms of the partnership agreement, plaintiff and defendant agreed to actively engage in the management and business of the work and do certain designated tasks during designated hours. Since__________, 19____, defendant has willfully and wrongfully neglected, failed, and refused to participate in the business of the partnership and, in fact, has been absent from the operation of the business since the above date.

10. (Alternate Allegation) Since ________, 19____, the partnership has been operating at a substantial loss and the loss is the result of________________. Plaintiff is informed and believes, and upon such information and belief, alleges that the business of partnership in the future can be carried on, only at a loss and further continuance will greatly diminish and probably destroy plaintiff's share of the partnership assets.

11. By reason of the acts and conduct above, defendant has breached the partnership agreement and has otherwise so conducted himself in matters relating to the partnership that it is not reasonably practicable for the partnership business to be carried on between the parties.

12. Unless a receiver is appointed to take possession of all the monies and accounts of the partnership and to receive accounts receivable, the affairs of the partnership will lead to waste, destruction and deterrioration. Plaintiff has no adequate remedy at law and unless a receiver is appointed, plaintiff will suffer great and irreparable loss and damage.

13. (Alternate Allegation) Plaintiff desires to continue the operation of the partnership business by himself during the term of the partnership agreement and desires to be placed in exclusive possession of the partnership business. Plaintiff is ready, willing and able to conduct the business and is further willing to pay defendant the value of his interest, if any, exclusive of the value of good will, less damages pursuant to Corporation Code, §15038.

14. Since the commencement of said business, the plaintiff has fully complied with all the terms and conditions of the partnership agreement and has fully performed all the obligations therefor. Plaintiff desires a dissolution and an accounting, but defendant has failed and refused and continues to fail and refuse to provide same.

WHEREFORE, plaintiff prays:

1. That the partnership be dissolved.

2. For an accounting of the affairs of the partnership from the date of its formation to the present and that plaintiff have judgment against defendant for such sums as may be found due and owing in such accounting.

3. That a receiver be appointed to take possession of the property and the assets of the partnership to wind-up the affairs of the partnership and to operate the business until its dissolution.

4. (Alternate Prayer) For an order allowing plaintiff to be permitted to continue the business of the partnership and to have and retain ownership and possession of the partnership assets on payment to the defendant of amount pursuant to Corporation Code §15038.

5. That the property of the partnership, both real and personal be sold, and the debts and accounts receivable owing to the partnership be collected, the partnership debts and liabilities be paid, and the surplus divided between plaintiff and defendant.

6. That defendant be enjoined, pending the outcome of this action, from in any way having to sell, assign,hypothecate or otherwise encumber the assets of the partnership or from diverting the business thereof to the personal advantage of defendant.

7. For costs of suit and such other relief as the court deems just.

____
Attorney for Plaintiff

****

See Corporation Code, §15032. Stowe vs. Matson, 94 C.A. 2d, 678.

The grounds for dissolution by court are found in Corporation Code §15032.

Galich vs. Brkich 103, C.A. 2d, 187. Fretz vs. Burke, 247 C.A. 2d, 749.

On accounting: All partners must be made parties to the action, Rudnick vs. Delfino, 140 C.A. 2d, 260.

Caption)
)
)
)
___________________)

COMPLAINT TO ESTABLISH
EXISTENCE OF FATHER/CHILD
RELATIONSHIP
Civil Code § 7004(a)(1)

Plaintiff alleges:

1. On __________,19____, ________________was duly appointed as guardian ad litem of ______________, the minor child who is the subject of this action.

2. ________________ is a minor child who is a resident of the County of Los Angeles. Said child was born on _____________,19____.

3. __________________is the natural mother of said minor child.

4. ____________________, a resident of Los Angeles County is presumed to be the father of ______________, the minor child by virtue of the fact that he and________________, the child's natural mother,were married to each other. The marriage was terminated by annulment on________________,19_____. The minor child was born______ days thereafter.

5. ____________________does not have funds or other property with which to support said minor child. Further, it is necessary for_______________to retain the services of an attorney to prosecute this action. _______________does not have funds to pay an attorney. ________________, the father of said minor child, does have sufficient funds to pay child support and attorney's fees. The sum of $____________is a reasonable amount for the monthly support of said minor child and the sum of $______is a reasonable amount for attorney's fees.

6. It is in the best interests of said minor child that custody be awarded to the mother with rights of reasonable visitation reserved to the father.

WHEREFORE, plaintiff prays:

1. For a judgment declaring that there exists a relationship of father and child between defendant and _____________, the minor child;

2. For an order requiring defendant to pay directly to _____________the sum of $_______for the support of said minor child;

3. For an order requiring defendant to pay the sum of $________as attorney's fees;

4. For an order awarding custody of said minor child to _____________with visitation fixed as follows:

5. For actual costs incurred in this action;

6. For such other relief as the Court deems just and proper.

____
Attorney for Plaintiff

Caption)
)
)
)
______________________)

COMPLAINT TO ESTABLISH NONEXISTENCE OF FATHER/ CHILD RELATIONSHIP
CC § 7006(a)(2)

Plaintiff alleges:

1. Plaintiff is informed and believes and upon such information and belief, alleges that defendant________________is the natural mother of ________________, a minor child born on _________,19___. Said minor child is a resident of Los Angeles County, State of California.

2. On or about ______,19___, plaintiff discovered that defendant was claiming that plaintiff is the father of said minor child. Plaintiff is informed and believes and upon such information and belief, alleges that defendant bases said claim on the presumption contained in Civil Code §_________.

3. Plaintiff denies that he is the father of said minor child and further denies that he, or his conduct, falls within the presumption of Civil Code §______. Plaintiff further denies that any allegations made by defendant are true.

4. Plaintiff has never had sexual intercourse with defendant, nor has he ever been married to or attempted to marry the defendant. Plaintiff has never consented to being named as the father on the birth certificate of said minor child. Plaintiff, neither by court order or by a written promise is obliged to support the child. Plaintiff has never received the child into his home and has never openly held the child out to be his natural child. Plaintiff does not fall within the provisions of Evidence Code § 621. Plaintiff has never consented to the artificial insemination of the defendant.

WHEREFORE, plaintiff prays:

1. For a judgment declaring that there is no father and child relationship between plaintiff and said minor child_____________;

2. For costs of suit incurred and for such other relief as the court deems just and proper.

____
Attorney for Plaintiff

Caption	)))))	JUDGMENT DECLARING EXISTENCE OF FATHER/CHILD RELATIONSHIP

This action came on regularly for trial on ____________, 19_____, ________________ appeared as attorney for Plaintiff, ________________ appeared as attorney for Defendant.

Evidence, oral and documentary, was presented and received by the court. After hearing and submission of the matter, the court finds that the allegations in the complaint are true and that the plaintiff is entitled to the relief prayed for.

THEREFORE, IT IS ORDERED, ADJUDGED AND DECREED as follows:

1. That ________________ is the father of ______________, the minor child;
2. That ________________ is ordered to pay directly to ____________ the sum of ________________ per month, payable ________________ for the support of said minor child;
3. That ________________ is ordered to pay to __________________, the sum of __________________ for attorney's fees.

Dated: ______________

____
Judge

CAPTION) Case No.______________
)
) REQUEST FOR STATEMENT OF DAMAGES
)
______________________)

TO THE PLAINTIFF______________AND TO HIS ATTORNEY:

THE DEFENDANT___________HEREIN, HEREBY REQUESTS that within 15 days from the service of this request, you serve a responsive statement setting forth the nature and amount of damages being sought by your complaint. This request is being submitted pursuant to the provisions of C.C.P. §425.11.

____
Attorney for Plaintiff

****

In personal injury or wrongful death actions, in the Superior Court, the amount of damages sought shall not be stated in the complaint or cross complaint. C.C.P. §425.10.

The procedure of C.C.P. §425.11 shall be followed.

The request may be served on the plaintiff at any time and the plaintiff shall serve a responsive statement as to the damages within 15 days thereafter.

If no request is made, a statement setting forth the nature and amount of damages must be given either before a default is taken or in the contested case at least 60 days prior to the date of trial.

If a request is made and a response is not given, defendant may petition the court to order the plaintiff to serve the responsive statement.

CAPTION)
)
) RESPONSIVE STATEMENT OF DAMAGES
)
________________________)

Case No.____________

COMES NOW the plaintiff and in response to defendant's request for statement of damages, submits the following:

SPECIAL DAMAGES

1. Dr.________ $__________
2. Hospital________ $__________
3. Medication________ $__________
4. Wage loss__________ $__________
5. Other specials______ $__________

GENERAL DAMAGES

$________________

Special damages not yet ascertained will be submitted at the time of pretrial.

____
Attorney for Plaintiff

CAPTION)
)
) NOTICE OF MOTION TO REQUIRE
) RESPONSIVE STATEMENT
______________________)

Case No.______________

Date:__________
Time:__________
Department_____

TO THE PLAINTIFF_________________AND TO HIS ATTORNEY:

YOU AND EACH OF YOU WILL PLEASE TAKE NOTICE that on________, 19____, at the hour of_______a.m. in Department____ of the above-entitled court, defendants will move the court for an order requiring plaintiff to furnish a responsive statement of the nature and extent of damages sought in the within case.

The motion will be made on the basis that since the filing of the summons and complaint and service thereof on defendant, defendant has served on plaintiff a request for a responsive statement pursuant to C.C.P. §425.11. More than 15 days have elapsed since the service of the request and plaintiff has not responded.

The motion will further be made on the contents of this notice of motion, the declaration and points and authorities attached hereto, the records and papers on file herein and such other evidence, oral and documentary to be presented at the hearing.

DATED:______________, 19___.

____
Attorney for Defendant

CAPTION) Case No.______________
)
) COMPLAINT FOR DAMAGES FROM DOG AND TO
) REMOVE DOG
________________________)

Plaintiff complains:

FIRST CAUSE OF ACTION:

1. At all times herein mentioned, defendant was and now is a resident of the County of_________, State of California.

2. At all times herein mentioned, and specifically on or about_______, 19___, defendant was the owner of that certain German Shepherd Dog which was kept on defendant's premises at______________ Street, ___________________California.

3. At all times herein mentioned, plaintiff was lawfully walking on____________Street, which is a public street in the City of___________, County of__________, State of California.

4. While plaintiff was lawfully walking on the abovementioned street, the aforementioned dog attacked and bit the plaintiff.

5. As a proximate result of the action of said dog, plaintiff sustained the following injuries, (describe) all to his damage in the amount of $______________.

6. As a further proximate result of the actions of defendant's dog, plaintiff was required to and did employ physicians and surgeons to examine, treat and care for him and incurred additional medical expenses for hospital bills in the approximate amount of $__________________ to date. Plaintiff is informed and believes, and on such information and belief alleges, that he will incur some additional medical expenses, the exact amount of which is unknown. Plaintiff will ask leave of the court to amend his complaint to insert the correct amount of such medical expenses when the same has been ascertained.

7. As a proximate result of the action of defendant's dog, plaintiff suffered a loss of income and earnings and his earning ability is, and will be impaired and diminished by reason of said injuries and he will continue to suffer a further loss of earnings and income for an indefinite period of time. Plaintiff prays leave to amend the complaint and insert the true amount when they have been ascertained.

8. As a proximate result of the action of defendant's dog, plaintiff suffered tears to his clothing in the following respects: (Describe.) The clothing was rendered totally unusuable and the reasonable value of the clothing is $_________________.

SECOND CAUSE OF ACTION:

9. Plaintiff incorporates and realleges each and every allegation of paragraphs 1 through 5 of the first cause of action as though set out in full.

10. Plaintiff is informed and believes and on such information and belief, alleges that the aforementioned dog has bitten the following human beings (Set forth names and addresses.) in the same city and county.

11. It is necessary to determine whether the present condition of the dog is such that it should be destroyed.

WHEREFORE, plaintiff prays:

1. For general damages in the sum of $____________.

2. For medical and incidental expenses according to proof.

3. For damages for loss of income and earnings and earning capacity.

4. For damages to personal property in the sum of $________.

5. For removal and destruction of the dog.

6. For costs of suit herein and such other relief as the court deems just.

DATED:_______________, 19____.

____
Attorney for Plaintiff

****

The owner of any dog is liable for damages suffered by any person who is bitten by the dog while in a public place or lawfully in a private place, including the property of the owner of the dog, regardless of the former viciousness of the dog, or the owner's knowledge of such viciousness. Civil Code § 3342.

Any person may bring an action in the Municipal Court against the owner of an animal to have the animal removed where the dog has bitten human beings at least on two separate occasions. Civil Code, § 3342.5.

CAPTION) Case No.____________________
)
) COMPLAINT FOR NEGLIGENCE
) (DANGEROUS CONDITION ON SIDEWALK)
____________________)

Plaintiff complains:

1. At all times herein mentioned, defendant City of____________, was a municipal corporation existing under and by virtue of the laws of the State of California.

2. At all times herein mentioned, defendants ____________and____________were the agents and employees of said defendant city, and in doing the things sued on herein, were acting in the scope of their authority as such agents and with the permission and consent of defendant city.

3. At all times herein mentioned, ________street was and is a public street and highway running in a general ________________direction within said city.

4. At all times herein mentioned, defendant city had control and the duty of constructing, maintaining and repairing said street and adjacent sidewalks and keeping them in a safe condition for public use within its corporate limits.

5. On or about________, 19____, defendant city, through its agents and employees, while carrying on its duties of maintaining and repairing said streets in a safe condition, did so negligently and carelessly carry out said duties, that the following condition existed on the sidewalk, (describe).

6. Said dangerous condition created an unreasonable risk of harm to pedestrians using said sidewalk in a lawful and careful manner and said dangerous condition on the sidewalk was not reasonably apparent and could not be anticipated by a person using the sidewalk with reasonable care.

7. At all times herein mentioned, defendants and each of them, had notice, or should have known of the dangerous condition of said sidewalks. Said condition had existed for a substantial period of time before ________, 19___. The exercise of due care should have imparted knowledge to defendants that the dangerous condition existed.

8. On or about________, 19____, as a proximate result of said dangerous condition, while plaintiff was walking on the sidewalk, he tripped over the defect described above, and fell to the ground and received serious injuries thereby.

9. (Allege general damage allegations).

10. (Allege special damages).

WHEREFORE, plaintiff prays:

1. For judgment in the sum of $_______general damages.

2. For judgment in the amount of $____________ for medical expenses.

3. For judgment in the amount of $____________ for loss of earnings.

4. For costs of suit and such other relief as the court deems just.

____
Attorney for Plaintiff

****

Peters vs. San Francisco, 41 Cal. 2d, 419. Gentekos vs. San Francisco, 163 C.A. 2d, 691.

CAPTION) Case No.________________
)
) COMPLAINT FOR NEGLIGENCE
) (DANGEROUS CONDITION OF HIGHWAY)
___________________)

Plaintiff complains:

1. At all times mentioned herein, defendant State of________________ is, and was, a state in the United States.

2. At all times herein mentioned, defendant ________________, was the Director of Public Works of said state and in failing to do the things hereinafter mentioned was acting within the course and scope of his employment.

3. At all times herein mentioned, highway_______ was a state public highway in the state of ________________ and was operated, managed and maintained by defendant.

4. On or about________, 19____ and prior thereto, defendants in carrying out their duties of repairing and maintaining said highway in a safe condition, negligently caused the following condition to exist, (describe). Said condition was at a point on the highway which was approximately ______feet west of a curve on the highway and due to said curve, said condition could not be observed by a motorist exercising reasonable care and traveling in a ________direction while approaching said curve.

5. Defendant failed to place a sign or other device designed to warn motorists of the unsafe condition and said dangerous condition was not apparent or would not have been anticipated by a person exercising due care in approaching the curve.

6. Defendants and each of them, had the authority and the funds and other means available to them to have posted signs or other marking devices which would have warned of the dangerous condition.

7. On or about_______, 19____, plaintiff was driving and operating the following-described motor vehicle, (describe) in a ____________direction on said highway at a point where defendant had failed to place and maintain proper safety signs, signals or other warning devices to inform motorists of the dangerous condition which existed beyond the curve. As a proximate result of said negligence of defendant, plaintiff's automobile (describe what happened, such as striking an abuttment) and thereafter turned over, causing plaintiff serious physical injuries.

8. As a proximate result of the negligence of defendants, plaintiff was injured in his health, strength and activity and sustained bodily injury and shock and injury to his nervous system. Said injuries have caused, and continue to cause plaintiff great physical and mental pain and suffering. Plaintiff is informed and believes and upon such information and belief alleges that said injuries will result in his permanent disability to his general damage.

9. (Allege special damages such as medical expenses, loss of earnings, etc.,).

10. On or about__________, 19____, plaintiff duly presented to defendant his claim for the damages sought herein. A copy of said claim is attached hereto, marked Exhibit "A" and made a part hereof. On________, 19____, defendant rejected said claim.

WHEREFORE, plaintiff prays:

1. For damages in the sum of $__________.

2. For special damages according to proof.

3. For costs of suit and such other relief as the court deems just.

____
Attorney for Plaintiff

****

See Government Code §840.2 and 815.2 . See also Government Code §835. See Government Code §945.4 and §915 and the presentation of claims as a prerequisite to filing the action.

Fackrell vs. San Diego, 26 Cal. 2d, 196. Gentekos vs. San Francisco, 163 C.A. 2d, 691. Doeg vs. Cook, 126 Cal. 213.

CAPTION) Case No.______________
)
) COMPLAINT FOR PERSONAL INJURY AND
) PROPERTY DAMAGE
__________________________)

Plaintiff alleges:

1. Defendant is and at all times herein mentioned was, a resident of ___________County, California.

2. Plaintiff is ignorant of the true names and capacities of each of the defendants sued herein as Does 1 through 10 inclusive and therefore, sues said defendants by such fictitious names. Defendant will seek leave to amend the complaint to allege their true names and capacities when the same has been ascertained.

3. Plaintiff is informed and believes and based upon such information and belief alleges that each of the defendants named herein as a Doeis negligently responsible in some manner for the occurrences herein alleged and plaintiff's injuries as herein alleged were proximately caused by defendants' negligence.

4. At all times herein mentioned, defendant_____________ was the owner of the following described automobile. (Set forth description.)

5. At all times herein mentioned, defendant_____________ was the agent and employee of defendant____________ and in committing the acts herein alleged, was acting within the scope and authority of his agency and employment.

6. At all times herein mentioned, defendant_____________ was driving and operating the above-described motor vehicle with the consent, permission and knowledge of____________defendant.

7. (Include if appropriate.) At the time defendants ________________________furnished and entrusted the above-described automobile to defendant________________, they knew or should have known that the defendant was unfit to drive the above-described motor vehicle and that his driving would create an unreasonable risk of harm and danger to persons and property.

8. (Allege if appropriate.) At all times herein mentioned, defendant___________knew, or should have known that the automobile above-described was in a dangerous and defective condition and unfit to be operated on the public highways.

9. (Allege if appropriate.) At all times herein mentioned, defendant_____________was a person under 18 years of age and the son of defendants____________. At the time____________defendant was driving the automobile with the knowledge, permission and consent of defendants____________________. At the time of the events sued on herein, defendant______________, the minor, was a licensee, using a California Driver's License, the application of which was signed and verified by his parents, defendants_________.

10. At all times herein mentioned, plaintiff was and now is the owner of the following described motor vehicle. (Set forth description.)

11. At all times herein mentioned, ____________and____________ streets are intersecting public highways in the City of__________, County of_____________, running in a north/south and east/west direction respectively.

12. On or about ________, 19____, at or about the hour of ______a.m., plaintiff was operating the above-described motor vehicle on___________street in a general________direction, at or near the intersection of_________and __________streets.

13. At the same time and place, defendants, and each of them, negligently, carelessly and recklessly entrusted, managed, maintained, drove or caused to be driven the above-described motor vehicle of defendant on____________street in a general ______________direction so as to proximately cause it to collide with plaintiff's automobile and to proximately cause the injuries and damages hereinbelow described.

14. As a proximate cause of the negligence of defendants, and each of them, and the resulting collision, plaintiff was injured in his health, strength and activity, sustaining injury to his body and shock and injury to his nervous system and person, all of which injuries have caused, and continue to cause plaintiff great physical, mental and nervous pain and suffering, all to plaintiff's general damage.

15. As a further proximate result of the negligence of defendants, and each of them, plaintiff was required to, and did employ physicians and surgeons for medical examination and treatment and incurred medical and hospital expenses in the following amounts. (Describe amounts.) Plaintiff will be obliged to incur further medical and hospital expenses in an amount presently unknown.

16. At the time of the collision hereinabove described, plaintiff was employed in the capacity of ___________ and was earning an average monthly income in the amount of $___________. As a further proximate result of the negligence of defendants, plaintiff was prevented from attending to his usual occupation and has been damaged in the sum of $______________.

17. By reason of the negligence of defendants, plaintiff will in the future be prevented from attending to his usual occupation for a period of time not yet ascertained.

18. Immediately prior to, and at the time of collision, plaintiff's above-described automobile was in good mechanical condition and as a further proximate result of defendant's negligence, the automobile was damaged and depreciated to the extent of _____________________.

19. As a further proximate cause of the negligence of defendants, plaintiff has lost the use of his motor vehicle for a period of __________ days and was damaged thereby in the sum of $_________________.

WHEREFORE, plaintiff prays judgment as follows:

1. For general damages.

2. For all present and future medical and incidental expenses according to proof.

3. For loss of earnings according to proof.

4. For repairs to plaintiff's automobile in the sum of $________________.

5. For loss of use of the automobile in the sum of $________________.

6. For costs of suit herein incurred and for such other relief as the court deems just.

DATED: ____________________, 19____.

____
Attorney for Plaintiff

****

C.C.P. §425.10 provides that the complaint for personal injuries shall not state the amount of damages demanded.

For statutes on vicarious liability, see Vehicle Code §'s 17150 through 17159

CAPTION) Case No.______________
)
) COMPLAINT FOR DAMAGES, NEGLIGENCE
)
_______________________)

Plaintiff alleges:

1. At all times mentioned herein, defendant was and now is, the owner of that certain real property described as follows, (describe). The improvement on said property consists of a single family dwelling.

2. At all times herein mentioned, plaintiff was and now is, a tenant and the sole occupant of said dwelling house. Plaintiff occupies said dwelling house on a month to month oral tenancy.

3. On or about _______, 19____, defendant hired _________________, an independent contractor to install a water heater in said premises. _______________so carelessly and negligently installed the water heater that a connecting pipe ruptured and sprayed hot water on plaintiff, causing him severe injuries thereby.

4. As a proximate result of said negligence, plaintiff was damaged and injured in his health, strength and activity and sustained injuries to his body and nervous system, all of which has caused him great mental, physical and nervous pain and suffering.

5. As a further proximate result of said negligence, plaintiff was required to and did employ physicians and surgeons to treat and care for him and incurred medical expenses in the sum of $________________.

WHEREFORE, plaintiff prays:

1. For general damages in the sum of $___________.

2. For medical expenses according to proof.

3. For costs of suit and such other relief as the court deems just.

____
Attorney for Plaintiff

****

A landlord is strictly liable if an independent contractor defectively installs a water heater on the leased premises, Golden vs. Conway, 55 C.A. 3d, 948.

Other case on landlord's liability: Rowland, vs. Christian, 69 C.A. 2d, 108, Brennan vs. Cockrell, 35 C.A. 3d, 796; Green vs, Superior Court, 10 Cal. 3d 616; Fakhoury vs. Magner, 25 C.A. 3d, 58.

CAPTION)   Case No.
)
)   ANSWER TO COMPLAINT FOR NEGLIGENCE
)
____________________)

(Alleges Denials)

FIRST AFFIRMATIVE DEFENSE

1. At the time and place of the collision, sued on herein, plaintiff did not exercise ordinary care, caution or prudence to avoid the accident and the resulting damages, if any sustained by plaintiff, were proximately caused and contributed to by the negligence of plaintiff in the following manner, (describe) and plaintiff's damages, if any, are thus reduced by his negligence.

SECOND AFFIRMATIVE DEFENSE

2. At all times relevant, at the time of the accident and before plaintiff was aware of the hazards involved in his activities and had full knowledge of the conditions and risks existing. He voluntarily assumed said risks and his assumption of said risks was the sole proximate cause of his injuries, if any.

WHEREFORE, defendant prays:

1. That plaintiff take nothing by his complaint.

2. That defendant be awarded costs of suit and such other relief as the court deems just.

____
Attorney for Defendant

****

Although contributory negligence and last clear chance have been abolished, his negligence must be specifically pleaded to avail defendant of the defense of comparative negligence. Lei vs. Yellow Cab, 13 Cal. 3d, 804.

Lei vs. Yellow Cab, is also an excellent case on the topic of assumption of risk.

CAPTION)   Case No.__________
)
) COMPLAINT FOR DAMAGES BY A THIRD PERSON
) DUE TO ACCIDENT CAUSED BY NEGLIGENT
____________________) REPAIR OF BRAKES

Plaintiff complains:

1. At all times herein mentioned, defendant garage was engaged in the business of repairing automobiles and specifically brakes.

2. At all times herein mentioned, defendant driver was the owner and operator of that certain motor vehicle described as follows: (Set forth description.)

3. At all times herein mentioned defendant's workers were the agents, servants and employees of defendant garage and did the acts hereinafter complained of, in the course and scope of said agency and employment.

4. Defendant garage in the repair and maintenance of brake systems of automobiles knew that the automobiles upon which he made repairs and adjustments were to be used on the public highways and further knew that should brakes be defectively repaired, the automobiles repaired by defendant garage would present an unreasonable risk of harm to third persons. Defendant garage owed a duty to persons who presented their vehicles for repairs of brake systems as well as to those who were present on the public highways to use reasonable care in the repair of brake systems.

5. On or about______, 19_____, defendant driver took his automobile to defendants for the repair and adjusting of his brakes.

6. On__________, 19____, defendant driver was told by defendant garage that the brakes were fully repaired and in excellent working condition.

7. On or about _______, 19____, plaintiff was driving the automobile in__________California, and attempted to brake and stop the automobile. Due to the negligence and carelessness of the defendants, and each of them, in connection with the repair and adjustment of said brakes, the brakes failed to stop the automobile and the automobile collided with plaintiff, causing him severe injuries thereby.

(Allege items of damage, special and general. See other personal injury complaints.)

WHEREFORE, plaintiff prays:

1. For general damages in the sum of $__________.

2. For special damages in the sum of $_________.

3. For damages for property destroyed in the sum of $__________.

4. For costs of suit and such other relief as the court deems just.

____
Attorney for Plaintiff

CAPTION) Case No.____________
)
) COMPLAINT FOR NEGLIGENT REPAIRS OF
) AUTOMOBILE
________________________)

Plaintiff complains:

1. Defendant at all times herein mentioned, was and now is, the owner and operator of an automobile repair facility located at:_______________.

2. At all times herein mentioned, defendants __________ and_____________were the agents, servants and employees of defendant________________garage company and committed the acts hereinafter described in the course and scope of said employment and agency.

3. At all times herein mentioned, plaintiff was, and now is the owner of the following described motor vehicle. (Set forth description.)

4. On ________, 19___, plaintiff presented the automobile to the defendant garage for the purpose of having defendant make certain repairs to said automobile. Defendant stated to plaintiff that he would make such repairs for a certain consideration, which consideration plaintiff agreed to pay.

5. Defendant garage at all times herein mentioned held itself out as a facility which repaired motor vehicles in a workmanlike and safe manner and plaintiff, being induced by such implied representations, selected defendant garage to repair his motor vehicle.

6. Defendants so negligently and carelessly repaired the automobile that within two hours of delivery to plaintiff after the repairs were made, the following occurred: (Describe)

7. As a direct and proximate result of said negligence plaintiff incurred expenses in the sum of $______________, for the additional repairs of said damage and was further deprived of the use of the automobile for a period of_____________.

WHEREFORE, plaintiff prays for judgment:

1. For damages for further repairs in the sum of $__________________.

2. For damages for loss of the use of the vehicle in the sum of $____________.

3. For costs of suit herein and such other relief as the court deems just.

____
Attorney for Plaintiff

CAPTION) Case No.____________
)
) COMPLAINT-INJURIES DUE TO FOOD
) POISONING
____________________)

Plaintiff complains:

1. On or about ______, 19___, defendant owned and operated a certain restaurant located at _________. Defendant operated and still operates said restaurant and in connection with said operation solicits the patronage of members of the public as customers and offers to furnish to said customers foods for consumption on the premises.

2. At all times herein mentioned defendant, through advertising and otherwise, attempted to create for himself a general reputation in the locality for serving excellent food. Defendant did in fact enjoy a general reputation for serving excellent and wholesome food. Defendant expressly and impliedly warranted to the public and to plaintiff, a member of the public, that the various foods offered to the public and to plaintiff for consumption, were clean, wholesome and free from harmful and injurious foreign substances. A copy of his menu is attached hereto, marked Exhibit "A" and incorporated herein as though set out in full.

3. On or about ______, 19_____, in reliance upon the above-mentioned warranties and reliance upon the reputation of the defendant for skill, experience and judgment in the preparation and service of food, plaintiff entered said restaurant and ordered for plaintiff's consumption a quiche and paid the price for said food.

4. Plaintiff ate the food and at the time of eating it could not by taste, or from a reasonable inspection, determine that the food was not reasonably fit for human consumption. The food, in fact, was not fit for human consumption and contained injurious and foreign substances and poisons.

5. As a direct and proximate result of plaintiff eating the above-mentioned quiche, plaintiff became violently ill within an hour thereafter and required immediate hospitalization.

6. After the discovery by plaintiff of said breach of warranty of defendant and within a reasonable time thereafter, plaintiff, in writing, advised the defendant of its breach of warranty.

7. As a proximate result of the breach of warranty by defendant, plaintiff suffered the following injuries: (describe) Plaintiff was hospitalized and was obliged to obtain medical services and has incurred expenses from the hospital, physician, laboratory and pharmacy. The extent and nature of the expenses is presently unknown and plaintiff will ask leave to amend the complaint when the true value has been ascertained.

(Set forth allegations for loss of earnings, if appropriate.)

8. As a proximate cause of said breach of warranty, plaintiff has been generally damaged in the sum of $__________.

SECOND CAUSE OF ACTION

9. Plaintiff refers to each paragraph of the first cause of action and realleges them as though set out in full.

10. Defendant, engaging in the business of preparing, distributing and selling food to the general public, owed a duty to the general public and to plaintiff in particular, to use reasonable care to see that the food sold was fit for human consumption and free from poisonous substances.

11. Defendant failed and neglected to use reasonable care in the preparation and selling of the quiche and by reason of this negligence, plaintiff was caused to be served an unwholesome quiche which plaintiff purchased and ate.

WHEREFORE, plaintiff prays:

1. For judgment in the sum of $_______general damages.

2. For judgment in the sum of $_______special damages.

3. For costs of suit herein and such other relief as the court deems just.

____
Attorney for Plaintiff

****

If filed in Superior Court, general damages shall not be alleged, C.C.P. §425.10.

For a case on food poisoning consult Mix vs. Ingersoll, 6 Cal. 2d, 674.

CAPTION)   Case No.________________
)
)   COMPLAINT FOR DAMAGES
)   (SLIP AND FALL)
________________)

Plaintiff complains:

1. At all times herein mentioned, defendant was and now is, a resident of the County of_________, State of California and operated a sole-proprietorship under the fictitious firm name of_____________________, in the City of_________, California.

2. At all times herein mentioned, defendant was in possession of, and owned, operated and maintained and controlled that certain business establishment located at __________street, ____________California, and on___________, 19____, plaintiff was on said premises of defendant for the purpose of purchasing an item which was on display in defendant's store for sale to the general public.

3. At all times herein mentioned, defendant carelessly and negligently maintained, said premises in a defective, dangerous and unsafe condition, in that defendant allowed accumulations of foreign matter to remain on the floor, to the extent that the floor was rendered slippery and unsafe and dangerous to persons using it, including plaintiff. Defendant failed to warn plaintiff and others of said dangerous,defective and unsafe conditions, although defendant knew, or should have known, of the condition of the floor.

4. While walking on the floor, plaintiff slipped and fell and sustained serious injuries as hereinbelow described.

5. As a proximate cause of the negligence of defendant, plaintiff was injured in his health, strength and activity, and sustained injury to his body and to his nervous system, all of which injuries have caused, and continue to cause plaintiff great mental, physical and nervous pain and suffering. Said injuries will result in some permanent disability to plaintiff all to his general damage.

6. As a further proximate cause of said negligence, plaintiff was required to, and did incur expenses for physicians and surgeons, hospitals and drugs and other related expenses, all to his damage in an amount presently unknown. Plaintiff will seek leave to amend the complaint to assert the exact amounts when they have been ascertained.

(Set forth other special damages, such as loss of earnings, etc.)

WHEREFORE, plaintiff prays:

1. For general damages.

2. For special damages in the amount of $_________.

3. For costs of suit and such other relief as the court deems just.

____
Attorney for Plaintiff

****

<u>Goldsmith vs. Mills</u>, 130 C.A. 2d, 493. <u>Clayton vs. J. C. Penny</u>, 186 C.A. 2d, 1.

CAPTION)
)
) COMPLAINT FOR DAMAGES
) (PRODUCTS LIABILITY)
_______________)

Case No.____________

Planintiff complains:

1. Plaintiff is, and at all times herein mentioned was, a resident of __________County, State of California.

2. Defendant manufacturer is, and at all times herein mentioned was, a corporation organized and existing under the laws of the State of California, engaged in the manufacture of the following-described product, (describe). Said products were designed and manufactured for sale to be used by members of the general public. As part of its business, defendant designed, manufactured and assembled the specific______________hereinafter referred to.

3. Defendant supplier is, and at all times herein mentioned was, a corporation organized and existing under the laws of the State of California, with its principal place of business in______________California, and was engaged and is engaged in the business of designing and manufacturing certain component parts to wit; ________________and supplying them to defendant manufacturer. Plaintiff is informed and believes, and on such information and belief alleges, that as a part of its business, defendant supplier designed, manufactured and supplied to defendant, the following, (describe).

4. Defendant retailer is, and at all times herein mentioned was, an individual and a resident of______________of California, and at all times herein mentioned was engaged in the business of selling at retail to members of the general public, at its principal place of business in______________California, the hereinabove described products.

5. Plaintiff is informed and believes and on such information and belief alleges that defendant manufacturer intended the products manufactured be used for the following purpose, (describe).

6. Plaintiff is informed and believes and upon such information and belief alleges that defendant supplier manufactured and sold to defendant manufacturer, the above-described parts, intending them to be used in the following manner, (describe).

7. Plaintiff is informed and believes and on such information and belief alleges that defendant retailer sold said products with the knowledge that said products would be used in the following manner, (describe).

(If strict liability is sought such as in the case of automobiles, machinery, which is inherently dangerous, the above paragraphs are required.)

8. On or about________, 19____, plaintiff purchased from defendant retailer the following described item, (describe). Said item was manufactured, designed and assembled by defendant manufacturer and contained component parts (describe) manufactured by defendant supplier.

9. At the time of the purchase, the product was defective and unsafe for the intended purpose in that the component part consisted of a ______________which was made part of_________ metal, rather than ____________metal.

10. On or about_______, 19___, plaintiff was operating said machinery and in the course of the operation, the plywheel separated from the drive shaft and struck plaintiff in the head and eye, proximately causing him damages hereinbelow described. The separation of the flywheel was the proximate result of the defective ________________furnished by supplier to manufacturer.

(Set forth items of general and special damages.)

WHEREFORE plaintiff prays:

1. For judgment for general damages for $___________.

2. For judgment for special damages $__________and $____________.

3. For loss of earnings in the sum of $_________.

4. For costs of suit and such other relief as the court deems just.

____
Attorney for Plaintiff

****

Barth vs. Goodrich Tire, 265, C.A. 2d, 228. Read vs. Safeway, 264 C.A. 2d, 404.

CAPTION) Case No.__________

)
) COMPLAINT FOR BREACH OF WARRANTY-
) FOREIGN SUBSTANCE IN CONTAINER
) (WITH ALTERNATE ALLEGATIONS FOR
____________________) EXPLODING BOTTLES)

Plaintiff complains:

1. Defendant bottling company, at all times herein mentioned was and now is engaged in the general business of manufacturing, bottling and selling and distributing to the retail trade for resale to the general public, a beverage under the style and trade name of Tired Blood.

2. Defendant______________market is and at all times herein mentioned has been engaged in the general retail business and in connection therewith, sells and distributes to the general public certain beverages intended for human consumption, including Tired Blood.

3. On or about ________, 19___, plaintiff purchased from defendant market a bottle of Tired Blood. Plaintiff at the time believed the beverage to be pure, harmless and wholesome by virtue of the fact that prior to the purchase of said bottle, defendants and each of them, represented expressly and impliedly to the general public and to defendant that the bottle contained wholesome beverages free of impurities, poisons and free of defects in the bottle which could cause an unreasonable risk of harm to the public, including plaintiff.

4. At all times herein mentioned, each of the defendants knew, or should have known, that plaintiff, a member of the general public, could or would purchase the bottle of Tired Blood and would rely on the warranty and representation made by each of the defendants.

5. Relying on said warranty, on or about_______, 19___, plaintiff, after having purchased the bottle of Tired Blood, drank the contents therein and immediately became violently ill and required hospitalization. The contents of the bottle included portions of a dead, putrid and decomposed beaver and other waste and refuge material.

(Alternate paragraph if alleging exploding bottle)

6. Defendants, and each of them, expressly and impliedly represented and warranted to the public and to the plaintiff that the container was of merchantable quality and was safe and fit in every respect and was free from defect in material and that the glass had been properly tested before being offered for sale.

7. Defendants, and each of them, breached their warranties in that the glass was not safe and fit and was not free from defects in material and workmanship.

8. On or about _____, 19____, when plaintiff attempted to remove the metal cap of said glass container, the container exploded, burst, and fragments of the glass flew into various parts of plaintiff's body, including his face and eyes.

(The following paragraphs now refer to either cause of action)

9. As a direct and proximate result of said breach, plaintiff has incurred expenses for hospital care, doctors, nurses and other medical expenses, the exact amount of said expenses is not yet known to plaintiff, and plaintiff will seek leave to amend the complaint when the full nature and extent has been ascertained.

10. Within a reasonable time after discovery of said breach of warranty, plaintiff in writing notified defendants of said breach.

11. In addition to the above damages and as a proximate cause of defendants' breach of warranty, plaintiff suffered general damages in the sum of $__________.

SECOND CAUSE OF ACTION

12. Plaintiff incorporates each and every allegation of each paragraph contained in the first cause of action and makes them a part hereof by reference.

13. By reason of the business in which defendants were engaged in manufacturing, bottling and selling and distributing food to the general public, they owed a duty to the general public and more particularly to plaintiff, to use reasonable care to see that the product sold by them was fit for reasonable consumption and that the containers did not pose upon the public an unreasonable risk of harm.

14. Defendants failed and neglected to use reasonable care in the manufacturing, bottling, selling and distributing of said beverage and by reason of their negligence, plaintiff suffered special and general damages as hereinabove set forth.

WHEREFORE, plaintiff prays:

1. For judgment in the sum of $__________.

2. For judgment in the sum of $______for special damages.

3. For costs of suit herein and such other relief as the court deems just.

____
Attorney for Plaintiff

****

General damages are not alleged for personal injury matters filed in Superior Court. C.C.P. §425.10

For appropriate cases, see Vallis vs. Canada Dry, 190 C.A. 2d, 35.

CAPTION) Case No.____________
)
) COMPLAINT TO DETERMINE MARITAL RIGHTS
) AND TO IMPOSE CONSTRUCTIVE TRUST
____________________)

Plaintiff complains:

1. At all times herein mentioned, plaintiff and defendant were, and now are, residents of ____________County of California.

2. On or about_______, 19____, plaintiff and defendant entered into an oral agreement wherein and whereby it was agreed that the parties would live together, and hold themselves out to the general public as husband and wife. It was further agreed that plaintiff would render her services as a companion and homemaker to defendant and that plaintiff and defendant would combine their efforts and earnings and would share equally any and all property accumulated as a result of their efforts, whether individual or combined.

3. (Alternate allegation for implied contract)
On or about _________, 19____, plaintiff and defendant commenced living together and held themselves out to the general public as husband and wife. Prior to living together, plaintiff was employed in the following capacity, (describe) and was in the process of developing a career as (describe). At defendant's request upon living together, plaintiff ceased working and gave up the following career opportunities, (describe). Plaintiff at the time gave up her career with the belief that she would serve as a companion and homemaker for defendant and assist defendant in the development of his career and business activities and that the two of them would remain together and share the benefits of defendant's career. Defendant knew, or should have known that plaintiff harbored this belief and knew that plaintiff would not have given up her career, if she had known that defendant did not intend to share the benefits of their joint relationship regardless of the origin of said benefits.

4. On or about__________, 19___, plaintiff and defendant separated and plaintiff demanded of defendant an accounting of the accumulations during the period when plaintiff and defendant were living together and further demanded her proportion of the accumulations during that period. Defendant has refused to render an accounting and provide plaintiff with her proportion and still refuses to do so.

5. As a consequence of said breach, (of the express or implied contract), plaintiff has suffered damage in an amount presently unknown in the approximate amount of $_______.

WHEREFORE plaintiff prays:

1. For judgment requiring defendant to render an accounting setting forth the exact nature and extent of the accumulations of the parties during the period while they lived together.

2. Judgment in the amount of $________, an amount equal to one-half of said accumulations, less liabilities incurred.

3. For judgment in the amount of $__________the reasonable value for her services during the period while they were living together.

4. For the imposition of a constructive trust upon the accumulations that were acquired between __________and ________________.

5. For costs of suit and such other relief as the court deems just.

____
Attorney for Plaintiff

****

A plaintiff may sue to enforce an express contract and/or an implied contract. In the absence of an express contract, the court should inquire into the conduct of the parties to determine whether the conduct demonstrates an implied contract. Agreement of partnership or joint venture - the courts may also employ the doctrine of Quantum Meruit and equitable remedies such as a constructive or resulting trust. Marvin vs. Marvin, 18 Cal 3d, 660.

______________________)		No.
)		
)	(Caption)	COMPLAINT TO QUIET TITLE
)		TO REAL PROPERTY
______________________)		(Adverse Possession)

Plaintiff (or petitioner) alleges:

I

(Allegations of fictitious entities, capacity of parties, unknown parties, agency, residence, venue and jurisdiction must be set forth in separate paragraphs if appropriate.)

II

At all times herein mentioned plaintiff is and was the owner of that parcel of real property in Los Angeles County, California, described as follows:

III

Plaintiff, by himself, has been in the actual, open, notorious, exclusive, hostile and adverse possession of the aforementioned real property continuously for more than 20 years prior to the filing of the complaint herein, claiming to own this property in fee against the whole world, and by himself has paid all taxes of every kind levied or assessed against the property and which were payable during the period of more than five years continuously immediately preceding the filing of the complaint herein.

IV

Defendant ____________ claims some right, title, estate, lien in the aforementioned real property adverse to plaintiff's ownership and such claim constitutes a cloud on plaintiff's title. Such claim is without any right whatever and said defendant has no right to title, estate, lien or interest whatever in the aforementioned property, or in any part thereof.

V

The defendants herein named as "all persons unknown claiming any right, title, estate, lien or interest in the real property described in the complaint adverse to plaintiff's ownership, or any cloud on plaintiff's title thereto," are unknown to plaintiff. Such defendants and each of them claim some right, title, estate, lien or interest in the aforementioned real property adverse to plaintiff's ownership, and such claim or claims constitute a cloud on plaintiff's title. Such claim or claims are without any right whatever and these defendant's have no right, title, estate, lien or interest whatever in the aforementioned property or in any part thereof.

WHEREFORE, plaintiff prays:

1. That defendants and each of them be required to set forth the nature of their claims and that all adverse claims of these defendants and each of them be determined by decree of this court;

2. That this judgment declare and adjudge that plaintiff is the owner of the aforementioned real property and that defendants and each of them have no estate or interest whatever in and to said property; that defendants be forever enjoined from asserting any claim whatsoever in or to the aforementioned real property or any part thereof; and

3. For costs of suit herein incurred and for such relief as the court deems just and property.

____

Attorney for Plaintiff

(The summons and complaint must be captioned with language naming unknown defendants. In addition, the complaint must be verified and a notice of lis pendans must be filed.)

______________________)
)
) (Caption)   No.
)
______________________)   COMPLAINT FOR QUIET TITLE TO REAL PROPERTY

Plaintiff (or petitioner) alleges:

I

(Allegations of fictitious entities, capacity of parties, unknown parties, agency, residence, venue and jurisdiction must be set forth in separate paragraphs if approriate.)

II

At all times herein mentioned plaintiff was, and now is, the owner in fee of that certain real property in the County of Los Angeles, California, described as follows:

(Set forth description of property.)

III

The above-named defendants who are designated as "all other persons unknown claiming any right, title, estate, lien or interest in the real property described in the complaint adverse to plaintiff's ownership" are unknown to plaintiff. Said defendants and each of them claim some right, title, estate, lien or interest in said real property adverse to plaintiff's ownership, and said claim or claims constitute a cloud upon plaintiff's title.

IV

Defendant ______________ claims and asserts an interest in said real property adverse to plaintiff and the claim or claims of said defendant are without any right whatever. Said defendant has no right, title, estate, lien or interest whatever in said real property or in any party thereof.

WHEREFORE, plaintiff prays that defendants be required to set forth the nature of their claims and that all adverse claims of defendant ______________ be determined by a decree of this court and that said decree recite and adjudge that plaintiff is the owner of said real property and that defendants have no estate or interest whatever in said real property, and for such other and further relief as the court deems just and proper.

____

Attorney for Plaintiff

CAPTION)
)
)
)
______________)

Case No.____________

COMPLAINT TO COMPEL RECONVEYANCE AND QUIET TITLE FOR BREACH OF RESTRICTIVE COVENANT

Plaintiff complains:

1. At all times herein mentioned, plaintiff and defendant were and are, residents of the County of____________, California. The real property, which is the subject of this action, is located in ______________County, California.

2. Plaintiff herein is the grantee and successor in interest in and to all the right, title and interest of ______________, defendant's grantor of the following-described real property, (describe) and to all restrictions, reservations, conditions, covenants and reversionary interests thereto by virtue of a deed dated __________, 19____, which was duly filed in the office of the County Recorder of___________County, California on_____________, 19____ in book_____, page_______ of the records of said County Recorder. A copy of the deed is attached hereto, marked Exhibit "A" and made a part hereof.

3. Prior to________, 19___, defendant's grantor ______________was the owner in fee of that certain real parcel of property by way of the above-mentioned grant deed, the legal description of which is, (describe).

4. On or about__________, 19____, said grantor conveyed to plaintiff the above-described real property by a certain grant deed, executed and delivered by grantor to plaintiff herein. The deed was thereafter recorded on________, 19___in the office of the County Recorder of ______________County, California in book_____, page______of the official records of the recorder of said county.

5. Said deed contained the following conditions and restrictions, to wit; that the conveyance was made and accepted on the express condition that the grantee shall not erect or maintain at said property, any building or improvement which is operated as a business which conducts on-sale liquor activities, nor shall any such business be maintained on said premises.

6. The deed further provides that restrictions shall be binding upon all heirs, administrators, executors or assigns of said grantee and in the event of a breach of the grantee or anyone thereafter taking from the grantee, in that event and without previous notice or demand, the estate created in the grantee os his assigns, etc., will at once terminate and become void and the land and premises shall revert to grantor, his successors or assigns in fee simple absolute. A copy of said deed with said conditions is attached hereto, marked Exhibit "B" and incorporated herein.

7. Said deed, on the delivery thereof, accepted by defendant on said conditions.

8. On or about_______, 19____, defendant breached the condition by obtaining from the Alcholic Beverage Control Board, a license to operate a saloon and since __________, 19____, defendant has operated a saloon and has sold alcholic beverages on the premises.

9. Said acts constitute a breach of said conditions and the estate of defendant and said property has terminated and become void and the land has reverted to plaintiff in fee simple absolute without any claim, right, title or interest therein or thereto in favor of defendant.

10. After the breach of said condition, plaintiff exercised his right of re-entry, reversion and forfeiture. On or about_______, 19____, and prior to the commencement of this action, plaintiff demanded of defendant the possession of the premises, but defendant failed and refused and still fails and refuses to deliver the premises to plaintiff.

WHEREFORE, plaintiff prays:

1. That defendant be commanded to convey the real property to plaintiff and give plaintiff possession thereof.

2. That plaintiff be declared to be the owner in fee simply absolute of said real property without any right, title or interest therein remaining in defendant.

3. That the title of said property be quieted in plaintiff as against defendant, and all persons claiming to be under defendant and that defendant be perpetually enjoined from asserting any claim whatsoever against said property.

4. That plaintiff be adjudged in possession of the real property and that plaintiff be given possession of such property.

5. That the property be adjudged to have reverted to plaintiff.

6. For costs of suit and such other relief as the court deems just.

____
Attorney for Plaintiff

****

Defendant could set up as affirmative defenses, change in conditions or failure of grantor to enforce restrictions on similar lots. Wolff vs. Fallon, 44 Cal. 2d, 695.

Defendant could also cross-complain to cancel restrictions.

It is also possible that the restriction is not a covenant running with the land which may be enforced by subsequent grantee. Civil Code §1462. Young vs, Cramer, 38 C.A. 2d, 64. See Civil Code §§1434 through 1432 on conditions involving forfeitures .

For a good distinction between conditions and covenants, see Knight vs. Black, 19 C.A., 518.

See also Trahms vs. Starrett, 34 C.A. 3d, 766.

________________)
)
) (Caption)
)
________________)

No.

DECREE QUIETING TITLE

The above-entitled cause came on regularly for trial on ________________, 19__ in Department _____ of the above-entitled court, the Honorable ________________ Judge presiding. The matter was held as a court trial, ______________ appeared as attorney for the plaintiff and _________________ appeared as an attorney for the defendant.

Witnesses having been called and sworn and evidence both oral and documentary having been introduced in behalf of the parties and the court having heard and considered the same and argument of counsel and the cause having been submitted for decision and the court being fully advised in the premises and the court heretofore having made its written findings of fact and conclusions of law.

NOW, THEREFORE, IT IS HEREBY ORDERED, ADJUDGED AND DECREED:

1. That at the time of the commencement of this action title to the subject real property described as follows:

was and now is vested in ________________ as owner in fee simple absolute.

2. That _______________ has no estate, right, title, lien or interest whatever in or to said property or any part thereof.

3. Said title of said _______________ is hereby forever quieted against any and all claims of said _______________ and said ________________ is perpetually enjoined and restrained from setting up or making any claim to or upon the real property above described or any part thereof.

____

Judge of the Superior Court

CAPTION	No. ______________
	NOTICE OF MOTION FOR APPOINTMENT OF RECEIVER
	Date:______________
	Time:______________
	Dept:______________

TO__________________DEFENDANT AND TO HIS ATTORNEY:

YOU AND EACH OF YOU ARE HEREBY NOTIFIED that on __________ __________, 19____, at the hour of _____ A.M., in Department ____ of the above-entitled court, plaintiff will move the court for an order appointing a receiver.

The motion will be made on the grounds that the property which is the subject of the action is in danger of being lost or materially injured and will be based upon the provisions of C.C.P. §564, this notice of motion and the affidavit attached hereto, and all papers, records and documents on file herein, and evidence, oral and documentary to be adduced at the hearing on this motion.

DATED: __________________________.

____
Attorney for Plaintiff

****

An affidavit setting forth the basis of the contentions why the property is in danger should be attached, or the allegations may be included in a verified complaint.

CAPTION	No. ________________
	DECLARATION IN SUPPORT OF APPLICATION FOR RECEIVER

I, ___________________, declare:

I am the plaintiff in the above-entitled cause. I am the mortgagee of that certain real property described in the verified complaint on file herein.

The amount of the mortgaged debt owing by the defendant is the sum of $____________. The value of the property is $____________, and said sum is insufficient to discharge said mortgage.

On or about______________, 19____, defendant abandoned the property. There is presently no person caring for or occupying said property. Several acts of vandalism have already occurred and there is reason to believe that additional vandalism and other dangerous elements will seriously reduce the value of the property.

EXECUTED at Los Angeles, California, on________________, 19______.

I declare under penalty of perjury that the foregoing is true and correct.

____
Plaintiff

CAPTION

No. ______________

EX PARTE APPLICATION FOR APPOINTMENT OF RECEIVER

I, ________________, declare:

On______________, 19____, plaintiff filed the above-entitled action seeking the appointment of a receiver.

It is necessary that a receiver be appointed to preserve and maintain the property.

An emergency exists with respect to the property for the reason that it has been abandoned and has on two occasions been victimized by vandals to the extent that the property has been partially dismantled. Since the property is unattended, irreparable injury would result if the property remains unattended during the time it would take for a hearing for the appointment of a receiver.

The names, addresses and telephone numbers of the persons in actual possession of the property are (set forth names, addresses and telephone numbers).

The use being made of the property by the persons in possession is (set forth uses).

________________, of________________, California, is nominated as receiver, and such nominee is not an attorney of a party to the action, nor an interested party in the action, nor related to any judge of the court.

WHEREFORE, declarant prays that:

1. The court appoint ________________ ex parte, as receiver to take charge of the above-described property.

I declare under penalty of perjury that the foregoing is true and correct.

EXECUTED at Los Angeles, California, on______________, 19_____.

____
Plaintiff

****

Superior Court Rule 238 requires the above allegations for an ex parte appointment, and, in addition, if the party is part of a plant equipment or stock in trade of a business, facts must be alleged to show that the appointment of a receiver will not stop or seriously interfere with the operation of the business.

If any of the above matters are unknown to the applicant or cannot be ascertained by the exercise of due diligence, the applicant may be excused from setting them forth, in which case he shall fully state the matters unknown and the efforts made to acquire the information.

CAPTION	No. ____________________
	ORDER APPOINTING RECEIVER

The motion of the plaintiff for the appointment of a receiver came on regularly for hearing before the undersigned on __________, 19______. Notice was duly given, and the plaintiff and defendant each appeared by their respective attorneys, and good cause appearing therefor,

IT IS HEREBY ORDERED that upon the filing of a bond by the plaintiff in the sum of $__________ that __________________ be appointed receiver of the property described in the verified complaint on file herein with the power and duties to take charge of the property, to collect all income therefrom, and to maintain and conserve the property pending further order of this court.

IT IS FURTHER ORDERED that said ________________________ prior to his entry upon his duties take an oath to perform said duties faithfully and further that he execute an undertaking to the State of California for the faithful performance of said duties in the amount of $______________.

DATED: ______________________________.

____
Judge of the Superior Court

CAPTION	No. ______________
	ORDER TO SHOW CAUSE WHY EX PARTE APPOINTMENT SHOULD NOT BE CONFIRMED
	Date:_________________
	Time:_________________
	Dept:_________________

TO________________________DEFENDANT:

The court, having on the _____day of____________, 19_____, upon the ex parte application of the plaintiff, appointed ____________________ of__________________, California, a receiver for the following-described property (set forth description),

IT IS HEREBY ORDERED that defendant appear before this court on _________________, 19____, at the hour of____________ A.M., in Department ______, in the County Courthouse at ____________________Street, Los Angeles, California, then and there to show cause if any he may have why the appointment of the receiver should not be confirmed. A copy of the complaint and declaration of _______________________and points and authorities shall be served with this order.

DATED: ______________________.

____
Judge of the Superior Court

****

See Rules of Court 239 and 240.

____________________)
)   No.
) (Caption)
)   COMPLAINT FOR RESCISSION
____________________)

Plaintiff (or petitioner) alleges:

I

(Allegations of fictitious entities, capacity of parties, unknown parties, agency, residence, venue and jurisdiction must be set forth in separate paragraphs if appropriate.)

II

On or about ____________, 19__ defendant was the owner of that certain parcel of improved real property in Los Angeles County, California, described as follows:

On that date defendant by a grant deed conveyed said property to plaintiff and plaintiff paid to defendant the sum of $___________, which was the total cash price.

III

Prior to the date of the conveyance defendant had constructed the improvement on said property, which consists of an office building, with a total square footage of 1560 square feet.

IV

At the time of said construction and at the present time Los Angeles Building Code Ordinance No. _______ required that in the framing of a structure the supporting studs, beams and rafters must conform to the following specifications:

At all times defendant had knowledge of the above requirements of aforesaid ordinance.

V

On the date of the conveyance and on dates prior to the conveyance and for the purpose of inducing plaintiff to purchase said real property and with the intent to deceive and defraud plaintiff, defendant intentionally, willfully and fraudulently concealed from plaintiff that said supporting structures did not conform with the ordinance.

VI

Plaintiff at no time prior to or on the date of the conveyance knew or had cause to believe that the internal structures had been unlawfully constructed. A reasonable inspection of the property would not have revealed the unlawful construction, since the constructed components were completely enclosed by walls and siding.

VI

By reason of the unlawful construction, plaintiff has been notified by the Department of Building and Safety that it will be necessary to demolish the building.

VII

On _______________, __ plaintiff notified defendant in writing of his intent to rescind the sale of the real property and offered to return to defendant the property and everything of value which he had received under the sale, and demanded of the defendant the return to him of all money paid under said sale.

VIII

Defendant made said representations maliciously and with the intent to defraud plaintiff and plaintiff is thus entitled to punitive damages in the amount of $___________.

WHEREFORE, plaintiff prays:

1. That the court order that the sale of said real property be rescinded and that plaintiff be restored to all consideration paid by him;

2. For punitive and exemplary damages in the sum of $_______; and

3. For costs of suit herein and for such other relief as the court deems just.

____

Attorney for Plaintiff

CAPTION) Case No.__________
)
)
) COMPLAINT FOR REFORMATION
__________________)

Plaintiff complains:

1. At all times herein mentioned, plaintiff and defendant were and are, residents of the City of________, County of____________, State of California.

2. On or about_______, 19____, plaintiff and defendant entered into a written agreement, wherein and whereby it was agreed that plaintiff would manufacture and defendant would accept and pay for, the following described items, (describe). A copy of the agreement is attached hereto, marked Exhibit "A" and made a part hereof.

3. Due to a mistake on the part of plaintiff, said agreement did not represent the true intent of the parties in that the agreement calls for the manufacture of 2,500 items, when in truth and in fact, plaintiff was to manufacture 250 items.

4. Defendant knew or had reason to know of the mistake, in that the price for 250 items was so disproportionate to 2,500 items. Defendant had caused the above-mentioned items to be manufactured by plaintiff and other vendors on numerous previous occasions and knew approximately what the cost of each item should be.

5. Said written agreement should have read, that plaintiff had agreed to manufacture and deliver 250 items, which was the true intent of the parties, instead of 2,500 items.

6. Plaintiff discovered the error on or about _________, 19____, and thereafter notified defendant and asked for a revision of the written agreement to conform to the true intent of the parties. However, defendant refused and continues to refuse to do so.

WHEREFORE, plaintiff prays:

1. That the written agreement be reformed to show the real intent of the parties, to wit; that plaintiff agrees to manufacture 250 items.

2. For costs of suit and such other relief as the court deems just.

____
Attorney for Plaintiff

****

Reformation will be granted when, through fraud, mutual mistake or a mistake of one party, the agreement does not truly express the intention of the parties. Civil Code §3399.

The ultimate facts that form the basis of the right to reformation must be pleaded with particularity. Girard vs. Miller 214, C.A. 2d, 266.

Lemoge vs. County of San Mateo, 46 Cal. 2d, 659.

CAPTION)
) Case No.____________
)
) COMPLAINT TO REFORM DEED
)
____________________)

Plaintiff complains:

1. On or about_____, 19_____, plaintiff and defendant entered into a written agreement wherein and whereby defendant agreed to convey to plaintiff, that certain real property described as follows: (Set forth legal description.)

2. A copy of the contract, a copy of which is attached hereto, marked Exhibit "A" and made a part hereof, contained a map, the shaded area of which was the parcel agreed to be conveyed.

3. On or about ________, 19_____, pursuant to the written agreement, defendant conveyed to plaintiff, a grant deed, A copy of the grant deed is attached hereto, marked Exhibit "B" and made a part hereof. Due to a mistake on the part of the defendant, the deed failed to convey all the property agreed on. The correct legal description should be: (set forth correct legal description) whereas the legal description contained in the conveyed deed is as follows: (Set forth description.)

4. Plaintiff took possession of the property believing that the deed described all the property agreed to be conveyed by the underlying contract.

5. On or about________, 19_____, plaintiff discovered the mistake of the deed and requested the defendant to have the mistake corrected, but the defendant refused and continues to refuse to do so.

WHEREFORE plaintiff prays:

1. That the deed be reformed to express the true intended conveyance.

2. For costs of suit herein and for such other relief as the court deems just.

DATED:________________, 19_____.

____
Attorney for Plaintiff

****

Civil Code §3399 applies to reformation of deeds and contracts. Welsher vs. Glickman, 272 C.A., 2d 134.

CAPTION

Case No. ______________

NOTICE OF MOTION TO QUASH SERVICE OF SUMMONS
[C.C.P. §418.10]

Date: ______________
Time: ______________
Dept: ______________

TO ________________, PLAINTIFF, AND TO ________________, HIS ATTORNEY:

YOU AND EACH OF YOU WILL PLEASE TAKE NOTICE that on ______________, 19___, at the hour of __________, A.M., in Department ____ of the above-entitled court, defendant will, by special appearance only, move the court for an order quashing service of summons allegedly made upon him by virtue of the fact that the court does not have jurisdiction over the person of the defendant.

The motion will be made on the ground that the defendant is not a resident of the State of California, nor has he performed any acts or caused any effects in said State. The motion will be based on this notice of motion, the declaration of defendant, and memorandum of points and authorities attached hereto, the papers and records on file herein, and such other evidence both oral and documentary as may be presented at the hearing of said motion.

DATED: ________________, 19___.

____
Attorney for Defendant

****

The defendant on or before the last day of his time to plead may move to quash service of summons. C.C.P. §418.10. The notice must designate the time for making the motion, which shall be not less than 10, nor more than 20 days after filing the notice. Service and filing of the notice extends defendant's time to plead until 15 days after service upon him of a written notice of entry of an order denying his motion. C.C.P. §418.10(b).

CAPTION	Case No. ____________
	DECLARATION OF DEFENDANT IN SUPPORT OF MOTION TO QUASH SERVICE OF SUMMONS

I, __________________, declare:

I am the defendant in the above-entitled cause.

On _______________, 19___, I was served with a copy of the summons and complaint in the within action in the following manner: (Set forth manner of service).

At the time of the service of the summons and complaint and at all times pertinent to the alleged cause of action in the complaint and at present, I am and have been a resident of the State of Rhode Island.

On _________________, 19___, I entered into a written contract with the plaintiff in Rhode Island, wherein it was agreed that I would manufacture a quantity of bushings for an engine which plaintiff was designing and building.

I witnessed plaintiff's activites in the State of Rhode Island with respect to the project, and at no time was it indicated to me that any of the manufacturing activities would take place in California.

I manufactured the products as agreed and shipped them to _______________ Street, in _______________, Rhode Island, and was not aware until the receipt of the complaint that the goods were thereupon shipped to California for assemblage.

EXECUTED at _________________________, California, on ____________, 19___.

I declare under penalty of perjury that the foregoing is true and correct.

____
Defendant

****

A California court does not have jurisdiction over a corporation who does not manufacture anything in California, and where its activity has nothing to do with the cause of action in question. Annestead vs. Beech, 521 F.2d 1298; Spokane vs. Superior Court, 63 C.A.3d 548.

CAPTION)   Case No.__________
)
) COMPLAINT IN EQUITY TO SET ASIDE
) JUDGMENT WITHOUT JURISDICTION
____________________)

Plaintiff complains:

1. On________, 19____, in the__________court of ________________, an action was commenced entitled___________ vs________________. Said case had number_____________. Plaintiff herein was the defendant in that matter and defendant herein was the plaintiff in that matter.

2. On_________, 19____, in said court, a judgment was rendered against plaintiff in the amount of $____________. A copy of the judgment is attached hereto, marked Exhibit "A" and incorporated herein.

3. Said judgment was, and at all times has been, and is now void and of force and effect because the court had no jurisdiction to render such judgment. That there was filed in said action a purported declaration of service by one____________ purportedly showing service on the plaintiff herein on________, 19____. Plaintiff was not, in fact, served with summons and complaint in said action at that date or at any time and said affidavit was wholly false and fraudulent. By reason thereof, the judgment is wholly void.

4. Plaintiff has a meritorious defense to the action and still has defense which is as follows, (state defense). Plaintiff herein had no knowledge of the commencement of the action or the entry of the judgment until___________, 19____, at which time he first learned that judgment had been rendered against him.

5. Plaintiff desires that said judgment be declared null and void and that the enforcement of the same be enjoined until the within action is adjudicated.

WHEREFORE plaintiff prays:

1. That the judgment dated________, 19____, in case number________, in the__________court of__________county be declared null and void.

2. That it be adjudged that plaintiff herein was never served with process in said action and that the court has no jurisdiction over the defendant.

3. That defendant be enjoined from enforcing said judgment or claiming any rights thereunder.

4. For costs of suit and such other relief as the court deems just.

____
Attorney for Plaintiff

****

The plaintiff in the new case must show that he has a meritorious defense to the old case. Matson vs. Batto, 173 Cal. 800.

The filing of a false return of service is extrinsic fraud. Richert vs. Benson, 139, C.A. 671.

CAPTION)
)
______________)

NOTICE OF MOTION FOR
SEPARATE TRIALS

TO THE ____________________________PLAINTIFFS AND TO THEIR ATTORNEYS AND TO THE ______________________________ DEFENDANTS AND THEIR ATTORNEYS:

YOU AND EACH OF YOU are hereby notified that on ____________________, 19__, at the hour of _________________a.m. in Department _________ of the above entitled court, plaintiff will move for an order for separate trials in the following actions:

________________________vs.__________________________.

________________________vs.__________________________.

Although said actions have previously been joined pursuant to the provisions of CCP §379, the ends of justice would require separate trials for the reason that _____________ will be put to undue expense.

The motion will be based upon this notice of motion, the declaration of ______________________ and points and authorities attached hereto, the records and papers on file herein and such other evidence, oral and documentary, which may be presented at the hearing on the motion.

Dated:________________________

____
Attorney for Plaintiff

****

The court may, to prevent any party from being embarrassed, delayed or put to undue expense, order separate trials if the parties have previously been joined. CCP §379.5.

CAPTION)
)
)
)
__________________)

Case No.____________

COMPLAINT FOR SPECIFIC PERFORMANCE OF SALE OF PERSONAL PROPERTY

Plaintiff complains:

1. At all times herein mentioned, defendant was and now is a resident of the County of__________, State of California.

2. On________, 19____, in the City of___________, California, plaintiff and defendant entered into an agreement wherein defendant was to manufacture the following described goods, (describe) which plaintiff agreed to accept and pay for, upon delivery.

3. The contract was evidenced by a series of writings and specifications and letters executed both by plaintiff and defendant. They are attached hereto and marked Exhibits "A" through "F".

4. The item which was to be manufactured by defendant is unique in the operation of plaintiff's business for the following reason, (describe).

5. Pursuant to the agreement, defendant was to retain title to the property until plaintiff paid the purchase price and accepted delivery. Defendant was and now is, the owner of said property and retains title thereto.

6. On__________, 19____, plaintiff tendered to defendant the sum of $______________ and demanded that defendant execute and deliver a bill of sale and the above-described items and all other documents necessary to pass title to plaintiff. Defendant has failed and refused and still fails and refuses to execute and deliver the documents of title and the above-described goods to plaintiff.

7. Plaintiff has duly performed all conditions and convenants on his part required of him under the terms of the agreement.

8. Plaintiff cannot obtain similar property in substitution for the property which is the subject matter of this action, and plaintiff has no adequate remedy at law and will suffer irreparable injury unless specific performance is granted.

WHEREFORE, plaintiff prays:

1. That defendant be ordered to specifically perform the agreement and sell and deliver the property.

2. That defendant be ordered to execute and deliver all documents necessary to transfer title to the property to plaintiff.

3. For costs of suit and such other relief as the court deems just.

____
Attorney for Plaintiff

****

When goods are unique, specific performance may be granted, Commercial Code §2716(2).

Hunt Foods vs. O'Disho, 98 Fed. Supp. 267.

Commercial Code §2716 also provides buyer with the right of replevin, if after a reasonable effort, he is unable to acquire other goods.

CAPTION) Case No.____________________
)
) COMPLAINT FOR BREACH OF EXPRESS WARRANTY,
) IMPLIED WARRANTY OF FITNESS, IMPLIED
________________) WARRANTY OF MERCHANTABILITY

Plaintiff complains:

1. On or about_____, 19____, in the City of ___________, County of__________, California, defendant sold and delivered to plaintiff the following described goods, (describe) for which plaintiff paid the sum of $______________.

2. At the time and place of the sale and with the intention of inducing plaintiff to purchase the above-described goods, defendant warranted and represented as follows, (describe express warranties). These representations and warranties were part of the basis of the bargain and sale made between the parties and in reliance upon said warranties, plaintiff was induced to and did purchase the goods.

3. The representations and warranties of defendant were false in the following particulars, (describe).

4. The goods at the time of delivery to plaintiff were of the value of $________________and if the representations and warranties of defendant had been true, the goods would have been the value of $_________________.

5. On or about________, 19____, plaintiff discovered that the representations and warranties were false and immediately thereafter gave defendant due and timely notice, as required by Commercial Code, §2607.

6. By reason of the foregoing, plaintiff has sustained damages in the sum of $___________, the difference between the actual value of the goods and the value they would have had as warranted. (For other aspects of damages, see Commercial Code §2714 and §2715.)

7. (Allege this paragraph if breach of warranty by sample.) At the time and place of the sale, defendant, in order to induce plaintiff to purchase the goods, displayed to plaintiff, a sample of the goods and warranted and represented to plaintiff that the goods sold, would in all respects, conform to the quality and design of the sample. The representations and warranties made by defendant were part of the basis of the bargain, and in reliance thereon, plaintiff was induced to, and did, purchase the goods as herein alleged.

8. The representations and warranties made by defendant were false and the goods did not conform to the sample in the following respects, (describe).

9. (Allege the following for violation of warranty of merchantability). At all times mentioned herein, defendant was and now is, a merchant engaged in the sale of the following-described goods, (describe). At the time and place of the sale, defendant impliedly warranted that the goods were of merchantability quality.

10. The goods were not of merchantability quality and, in fact, were defective in the following ways, (describe).

11. (Allege if implied warranty of fitness is violated). At the time and place of the sale, plaintiff made known to defendant the particular purpose for which the goods were to be purchased. The purpose was, (describe). Plaintiff at the time and place of the sale, relied on defendant's skill and judgment to select suitable goods for plaintiff's purpose, all of which was well known to defendant. At the time and place of the sale, defendant impliedly warranted that the goods were fit for the purpose for which plaintiff intended to use them. The goods were not fit for plaintiff's purpose, but were in fact unsuitable for the purpose in the following particulars, (describe).

WHEREFORE, plaintiff prays:

1. For judgment in the amount of $_________.

2. For incidental damages in the amount of $______________.

3. For costs of suit and such other relief as the court deems just.

____
Attorney for Plaintiff

****

Commercial Code §§ 2312 through 2315.

The buyer must notify the seller of the breach within a reasonable time. Commercial Code §2607.

CAPTION)   Case No.____________
)
) COMPLAINT FOR DAMAGES
) (Failure of Delivery)
____________________)

Plaintiff complains:

1. Defendant now, and prior to the commencement of the action has been a resident of the County of____________, California.

2. On or about________, 19____, in_____________, California, plaintiff and defendant entered into a written agreement wherein defendant agreed to sell and deliver and plaintiff agreed to purchase and accept, the following described goods, (describe) for the sum of $____________. A copy of plaintiff's purchase order is attached hereto, marked Exhibit "A" and incorporated herein.

3. On ___________, 19____, by letter, defendant informed the plaintiff that the goods would be delivered on or before_________________, 19____ and that plaintiff was to pay defendant the sum of $__________________upon delivery.

4. Plaintiff has performed all conditions on his part to be performed.

5. Plaintiff was and now is, ready, willing and able to accept delivery and to pay for said goods and has performed all conditions and covenants on his part to be performed pursuant to said agreement.

6. On or about ___________, 19____, a date subsequent to the date of delivery, plaintiff requested defendant to deliver the goods, however, defendant has failed and refused, and still fails and refuses to deliver the goods as agreed.

7. On or about_________, 19____, plaintiff learned that defendant had breached said agreement and at that time the market price of the goods was the sum of $_________________.

8. On or about_________, 19____, plaintiff in good faith, purchased similar goods at a price of $___________. By reason of the foregoing, plaintiff has sustained damages in the sum of $___________, which is the difference between the market price of the goods, at the time plaintiff learned of the breach and the price plaintiff paid for similar goods.

9. (Alternate Paragraph) By reason of the foregoing, plaintiff has sustained damages in the sum of $____________, which is the difference between the contract price of the goods and the market price of the goods at the time plaintiff learned of the breach.

WHEREFORE, plaintiff prays:

1. For judgment in the amount of $____________.

2. For judgment in the amount of $__________as incidental and consequential damages.

3. For costs of suit and such other relief as the court deems just.

____
Attorney for Plaintiff

****

Commercial Code §2711 permits a buyer to recover the difference between the market price and contract price.

Commercial Code §2712 permits a buyer to cover and have damages for the difference between the newly purchased goods and the contract price, plus incidental or consequential damages.

Incidental and consequential damages are discussed in §2715.

Loss of business good will may be a proper element of damage, Stott vs. Johnston, 36 Cal 2d, 864.

CAPTION)   Case No.______________
)
)   COMPLAINT TO RECOVER PRICE OF
)   GOODS SOLD
________________)

Plaintiff complains:

1. At all times herein mentioned, defendant was and now is, a resident of the County of___________, State of California.

2. On or about_______, 19____, in the City of _________________, California, plaintiff and defendant entered into a written contract wherein plaintiff agreed to sell and deliver the following described goods, (describe) and defendant agreed to accept, purchase and pay for the goods upon delivery. The agreed sum was $_______________. The agreement was evidenced by a purchase order, a copy of which is attached hereto, marked Exhibit "A" and made a part hereof.

3. On or about_______, 19___, plaintiff delivered the goods and performed all other conditions on his part under the terms of the agreement.

4. The goods were accepted by defendant, but defendant has failed and refused and still fails and refuses to pay for the goods, although demand has been made thereof. The sum of $_____________is now due, owing and unpaid.

WHEREFORE, plaintiff prays:

1. For judgment in the sum of $_______________.

2. For interest at the rate of_______% per annum from______________, 19____.

3. For costs of suit and such other relief as the court deems just.

____
Attorney for Plaintiff

****

The buyer may recover the contract price of the goods, plus incidental damages. Commercial Code §2709.

If goods have not been accepted, seller must make a resonable effort to resell them and then may sue for the price, or the difference between the resold price and the contract price. Commercial Code §2709(b).

CAPTION)   Case No.___________
)
)   COMPLAINT FOR DAMAGES
)   (Buyer's Repudiation of Goods)
_____________________)

Plaintiff complains:

1. At all times herein mentioned, defendant was and now is, an individual doing business as ____________, under the fictitious firm name and style of _______________ in the City of _______________, California and is engaged in the retail business of____________.

2. At all times herein mentioned, plaintiff was and now is, engaged in the business of selling and furnishing to retail establishments, at wholesale, the following described goods, (describe). On or about_________, 19____, plaintiff and defendant entered into an agreement whereby plaintiff agreed to sell and deliver the following described goods, (describe) and defendant agreed to purchase, accept and pay for the goods on plaintiff's delivery in the sum of $_________________.

3. Pursuant to said agreement, defendant on _______________, 19____, mailed to plaintiff a purchase order which on__________, 19____, plaintiff received. A copy of the purchase order is attached hereto, marked Exhibit "A" and made a part hereof.

4. On__________, 19____, plaintiff delivered the goods to defendant and performed all other conditions on his part to be performed under the terms of the agreement. Upon tender of delivery, defendant failed and refused, and still fails and refuses to accept delivery of the goods.

5. As a result of defendant's breach of the aforementioned contract, plaintiff was obliged to retrieve the goods and sell them at the market price of $_______________, an amount less than the price to defendant of $________________.

6. In addition, as a result of defendant's breach, plaintiff suffered incidental damages in the form of payment of shipping charges to return the goods to plaintiff's place of business in the amount of $____________.

WHEREFORE, plaintiff prays:

1. For actual damages in the amount of $__________.

2. For incidental damages in the amount of $____________.

3. For costs and such other relief as the court deems just.

____
Attorney for Plaintiff

****

A seller may recover the difference between the market price and the price defendant was going to pay, plus incidental damages. Commercial Code §2708 and §2710.

______________________)
)
) (Caption)
)
______________________)

No.

COMPLAINT FOR SPECIFIC PERFORMANCE OF CONTRACT TO CONVEY REAL PROPERTY

Plaintiff (or petitioner) alleges:

I

(Allegations of fictitious entities, capacity of parties, unknown parties, agency, residence, venue and jurisdiction must be set forth in separate paragraphs if appropriate.)

II

At all times herein mentioned defendant was and now is the owner in fee simple absolute of that certain real property in the County of Los Angeles, California described as follows:

III

On or about ______________, 19__ plaintiff and defendant entered into a written agreement wherein it was agreed that defendant would sell to plaintiff, and plaintiff would purchase from defendant, the above-described real property for a purchase price of $___________, payable on the following terms:

A copy of the agreement is attached hereto and marked Exhibit "A" and made a part hereof by reference.

IV

The purchase price set forth in said contract was a fair and reasonable price for the purchase of said property.

V

On _______________, 19__, in accordance with the terms of said written contract, plaintiff deposited with _____________, the designated escrow company, the full amount of said purchase price, together with executed escrow instructions, a copy of which is attached hereto and marked Exhibit "B" and made a part hereof by reference.

VI

Plaintiff has performed all the terms, convenants and conditions on his part to be performed under the terms of said written contract.

VII

Although demand has been made on the defendant to consummate said sale and to execute and deliver a deed, as provided in said written contract, defendant has failed and refused and still fails and refuses to consummate said sale.

VIII

Plaintiff still remains ready, willing and able to consummate the sale and purchase of said real property and to pay the purchase price agreed upon.

IX

Plaintiff is informed and believes and on such information and belief alleges that the reasonable rental value and the reasonable value of the use and occupancy of said real property is the sum of $______________ per month. Plaintiff has been wrongfully deprived of the reasonable rental value and the reasonable value of the use and occupancy of said real property since ____________, 19__.

X

Said written contract attached hereto as Exhibit "A" is as to defendant in all respects fair, just, reasonable and equitable.

WHEREFORE, plaintiff prays judgment against defendant as follows:

1. For a decree of specific performance upon the payment to defendant of the sum of $__________;

2. Defendant be ordered and directed to convey the hereinabove described real property to plaintiff and to perform all other conditions of said written contract to be performed by him;

3. That plaintiff have judgment from defendant for the amount of $___________ for damages for the wrongful withholding of said real property; and

4. For costs of suit herein and for such other relief as the court deems just and proper.

____

Attorney for Plaintiff

	)	
	)	Case No. ____________
	)	NOTICE OF MOTION FOR SUMMARY JUDGMENT [C.C.P. §437(c)]
CAPTION	)	
	)	Date: ____________________
	)	Time: ____________________
	)	Dept: ____________________
____________________________	)	

TO THE ____________________, DEFENDANT, AND TO ______________, HIS ATTORNEY:

YOU AND EACH OF YOU WILL PLEASE TAKE NOTICE that on ____________________, 19____, at the hour of _________A.M., or as soon thereafter as the matter may be heard, in Department ______of the above-entitled court, plaintiff will move the court for an order granting judgment for the plaintiff on the complaint herein.

Said motion will be made on the ground that the answer of defendant has presented no triable issue of fact.

The motion will be made and based upon this notice, and the affidavit and points and authorities attached hereto, the papers and records on file herein, and such other evidence, oral and documentary, as may be adduced at the hearing on the motion.

DATED: ________________________.

____
Attorney for Plaintiff

****

10 days' notice must be given for a hearing on a motion for summary judgment. Poochigian vs. Layne, 120 C.A.2d 757.

Either party may move for summary judgment.

If there is a triable issue of fact, the motion must be denied. Rader vs. Thrasher, 22 C.A.3d 883.

Declarations must allege facts within the declarant's personal knowledge except that the former verified statement of the opponent may be relied upon. Desney vs. Wilder, 46 C.2d 715; Joslin vs. Marin Water District, 67 C.2d 132.

CAPTION)))))))))	Case No. ______________
	DECLARATION IN SUPPORT OF MOTION FOR SUMMARY JUDGMENT

I, __________________, plaintiff declare:

I am the plaintiff in the above-entitled cause, which seeks an amount unpaid on a promissory note.

On July 1, 1974, defendant herein in my presence executed the promissory note which was in payment for services that declarant, the plaintiff, rendered to him in connection with the preparation and drafting of a set of blueprints for the construction of defendant's dwelling house.

The face amount of the note, to-wit, $700.00, remains unpaid.

EXECUTED at Los Angeles, California, on January 4, 1976.

I declare under penalty of perjury that the foregoing is true and correct.

____
Plaintiff

CAPTION	)	Case No. _______________
	)	DECLARATION OF DEFENDANT IN OPPOSITION TO MOTION FOR SUMMARY JUDGMENT

I, ___________________, declare:

That I am the defendant in the within cause. That I did, in fact, execute the promissory note which is incorporated as Exhibit "A" to plaintiff's complaint, and did execute it on the day mentioned in plaintiff's declaration.

Prior to executing the note, there was a conversation between your declarant and the plaintiff in which it was agreed that if your declarant could not secure a building permit for the construction which was the subject of the plans and blueprints, that the project would be abandoned and that your declarant would have no liability on the promissory note.

There were frequent and diligent efforts made by your declarant to obtain the building permit, and due to unstable soil conditions, the application for the permit was denied.

EXECUTED at Los Angeles, California, on _____________, 19____.

I declare under penalty of perjury that the foregoing is true and correct.

____
Defendant

	)	Case No. __________________
	)	
	)	ORDER DENYING PLAINTIFF'S
	)	MOTION FOR SUMMARY JUDGMENT
	)	
CAPTION	)	
	)	
________________________	)	

Plaintiff's motion for an order granting summary judgment came on regularly for hearing before the undersigned on ____________________, 19____.

_________________________appeared as counsel for plaintiff, and_________________________appeared as counsel for defendant. The court examined the declarations submitted in support of and in opposition to the motion, and the matter was argued and submitted.

The court being fully advised herein, and good cause appearing therefor,

The court finds that there is a triable issue of fact, and it is ordered that plaintiff's motion for summary judgment is denied.

DATED: ____________________, 19____.

____
Judge

CAPTION ______________________	No. ________________ NOTICE OF THIRD PARTY CLAIM

TO ________________________, JUDGMENT CREDITOR:

PLEASE TAKE NOTICE that a third party claim of ownership in the following-described property (set forth description) upon which the undersigned levied execution at your request has been filed by ____________________, whose address is______ ______________________.

Pursuant to C.C.P. §689, the undersigned will release the property from levy unless within 5 days from the date hereof you give me an undertaking executed by at least 2 good and sufficient sureties in double the amount of the value of the property levied upon.

DATED: ________________________.

____
Sheriff, Marshal or Constable

CAPTION ______________________	No. ____________ THIRD PARTY CLAIM

TO SHERIFF, MARSHAL OR CONSTABLE OF THE COUNTY OF ____________:

PLEASE TAKE NOTICE that you are holding under writ of execution the following-described personal property: (Set forth description.) Said property has a reasonable value of $________________.

At the time of the levy of the writ of execution, the property belonged to ___________________, the undersigned, and he is presently entitled to the possession of said property. He acquired said property and possession thereof from ________ ________________, the defendant, by purchasing same from him on ________________, 19___.

WHEREFORE, demand is made upon you for the immediate release of said described property to the undersigned.

____
[Name, Address and City and State of Third Party Claimant]

****

This document must be verified.

	)	No. ____________________
	)	
	)	PETITION TO DETERMINE TITLE
CAPTION	)	
	)	
	)	
______________________________	)	

The petition of ______________ respectfully shows:

That on ________________, 19_____, the above-entitled court rendered a judgment in favor of plaintiff and against the defendant for the sum of $_______________ together with costs and interest.

That pursuant thereto, on the _____ day of ___________, 19____, the sheriff of the County of _________________ at the request of plaintiff levied a writ of execution on the following described property: (Set forth description.)

On _______________, 19____, a verified third party claim was filed with the sheriff of the County of ____________ asserting ownership of the property hereinabove described. A copy of said third party claim is attached hereto, marked Exhibit "A" and made a part hereof by reference.

Petitioner is informed and believes and therefore alleges that the defendant claims ownership of said property for the following reasons: (Set forth reasons.)

Petitioner alleges that defendant has no right, title or interest in said property, that petitioner has a superior claim for the following reasons: (Set forth reasons.)

WHEREFORE, petitioner prays that it be determined that the title to the property hereinabove described is in _____________________ and that the sheriff be ordered to release said property from levy.

DATED: ____________________________.

____
Petitioner

****

C.C.P. §689 provides that this petition may be filed by the plaintiff or any person in whose favor the writ runs, the third party claimant or the defendant. The petition must be filed within 15 days after the delivery of the third party claim to the officer. The hearing must be had within 20 days from the filing of the petition. 10 days' notice of the hearing must be given to the officer, the plaintiff, the third party claimant, or the defendant.

	)	No. ____________
	)	
CAPTION	)	NOTICE OF SECURED CREDITOR'S CLAIM
	)	TO PROPERTY UNDER EXECUTION
	)	
___________________________	)	

TO THE SHERIFF, MARSHAL OR CONSTABLE:

PLEASE TAKE NOTICE that the undersigned hereby makes to you a claim as a mortgagee on the following-described property: (Set forth description.)

Interest of Claimant: Mortgagee

Total amount of sums due: (Set forth amount of sums due or to accrue under the contract or mortgage above setoffs with interest to date of tender.)

Address for Purpose of Service by Mail

(Set forth address within this state.)

DATED: ________________________.

____
Third Party Claimant

****

C.C.P. §689(b). This claim must be verified.

CAPTION	)))))))	No. ________________ STATEMENT OF INVALIDITY OF SECURED CREDITOR'S CLAIM

TO THE SHERIFF, MARSHAL OR CONSTABLE:

THIS IS TO NOTIFY YOU that the mortgage claimed by _______________ to be valid and outstanding in a statement heretofore furnished to you is invalid for the following reasons: (Set forth the reasons.) The undersigned hereby tenders the undertaking required by law.

DATED: _______________________.

____
Plaintiff

****

Neither the plaintiff nor the third party claimant is entitled to a hearing to determine the validity of the mortgage. To obtain a hearing, a petition should be filed similar to the petition to determine title that must be filed for an ordinary third party claim. The same time limits apply. C.C.P §689(b)(10).

CAPTION	)))))	No. ____________________ NOTICE OF FILING OF UNDERTAKING

TO ____________________, THIRD PARTY CLAIMANT:

PLEASE TAKE NOTICE that on ________________________, the judgment creditor levying the writ of execution on property as to which you filed a third party claim, has filed with the undersigned an undertaking to prevent the release of said property in accordance with your third party claim. Said undertaking was filed within 5 days of demand by me pursuant to to C.C.P. §689. The undertaking is in the amount of $__________ and lists as sureties ______________________ and ______________ ____________. Said undertaking is available for examination at the offices of the undersigned.

DATED: ________________________.

____
Sheriff, Marshal or Constable

CAPTION

No. ____________

NOTICE OF MOTION TO INCREASE UNDERTAKING

Date: ____________
Time: ____________
Dept: ____________

TO ____________, PLAINTIFF AND TO HIS ATTORNEY, ____________, AND TO ____________, DEFENDANT AND HIS ATTORNEY, ____________:

YOU AND EACH OF YOU WILL PLEASE TAKE NOTICE that on ____________, 19___, at the hour of ______ A.M., in the courtroom of Department ______, of the above-entitled court, the undersigned will move the court for an order establishing the valuation of the property subject to levy and for an order increasing the amount of the undertaking heretofore posted by the plaintiff.

Said motion will be made upon the grounds each and all that the undertaking furnished by plaintiff is insufficient to protect the moving party. The motion will further be based upon C.C.P. §689 and upon the affidavit of ____________, all the papers, records and documents on file herein, and such other evidence, oral and documentary, that may be adduced at the hearing.

DATED: ____________.

____
Attorney for Third Party Claimant

****

This motion must be accompanied by points and authorities and an affidavit setting forth the value of the subject property.

CAPTION

No. ____________

ORDER INCREASING UNDERTAKING

The motion of ____________, the third party claimant in the above-entitled action having come on regularly for hearing before the undersigned on ____________, 19_____, and evidence having been presented on the value of the property,

IT IS HEREBY ORDERED that the motion of the third party claimant for an increased undertaking is hereby granted, the value of the property having been established at $____________. Plaintiff is required to file with the sheriff of this County within 5 days hereof an undertaking in the amount of $____________. Failure to post the increased undertaking will result in the levy of execution being released.

DATED: ____________.

____
JUDGE

CAPTION) No. ____________
) NOTICE OF MOTION TO SELL PERISHABLE PROPERTY
) Date: ____________
) Time: ____________
) Dept: ____________
____________)

TO THE FOLLOWING PARTIES AND THEIR ATTORNEYS: (Set forth appropriate parties.)

YOU AND EACH OF YOU WILL PLEASE TAKE NOTICE that on ____________, 19___, at the hour of ________, A.M., in Department _____ of the above-entitled court, ________ ________ will move the court for an order directing the sheriff to sell the following-described property: (Describe property.)

The motion shall be made on the ground that the above-described property because of its nature will perish and become valueless unless sold before the hearing on the petition to determine title.

The motion shall be made on the basis of C.C.P. §689, upon the affidavit of ____________, and all the papers, records and documents on file herein, and upon such other evidence, oral and documentary, as may be presented at the hearing on this motion.

DATED: ____________.

____
(Moving Party)

****

C.C.P. §689 provides that the court may order the sale of any perishable property. If destruction of the property is imminent C.C.P. §689 does not forbid the acquisition of an order to sell by an ex parte application.

CAPTION) Case No.____________
)
) COMPLAINT FOR PERMANENT INJUNCTION,
) PRELIMINARY INJUNCTION, TEMPORARY
__________________) RESTRAINING ORDER AND INTERFERENCE WITH
PROSPECTIVE ADVANTAGE

Plaintiff alleges as follows:

1. Plaintiff is, and at all times herein mentioned was, a California corporation, with its principal place of business in ____________, California, and owns and operates a car wash business in the City of______________, California.

2. All the acts complained of herein took place in _______________, California.

3. Plaintiff does not know the true names and capacities, whether individual, corporate, associate or otherwise, of the defendants sued herein as Does I to XX, sued herein pursuant to Code of Civil Procedure 474, and plaintiff will amend this complaint to show their true names and capacities when the same have been ascertained.

4. Within the year last past and continuing until the present time and thereafter to continue, defendants, and each of them, without compensation, wrongfully and unlawfully have either allowed or conducted car wash activity on their premises without a car wash business license in violation of the___________City business license requirement and have failed to comply with several requirements such as a sump for runoff, a backflow prevention device, a canopy, and other violations of the City Code all in direct interference with plaintiff's right to conduct his lawful car wash business.

5. Defendants said conduct was wrongful and malicious and with the intent to injure plaintiff financially.

6. As a proximate result of said wrongfull conduct of and threatened by defendants, and each of them, and of the conditions wrongfully created thereby as aforesaid, and defendants' threats to continue said conduct, the plaintiff has lost customers and income and will continue to do so.

7. Defendants, and each of them, have threatened to continue said conduct and have refused to stop their conduct and unless and until defendants' said wrongful conduct is forthwith enjoined by this court, plaintiff will continue to suffer said detriments and injuries and infringements of his rights.

8. Defendants' said threatened wrongful conduct and conduct to date, unless and until the same is forthwith enjoined and restrained by order of this court, will cause great and irreparable injury to plaintiff in that defendants will continue to conduct said wrongfull activity thereby causing plaintiff to lose car wash customers and income to its business, thereby decreasing the value of plaintiff's car wash business.

9. Plaintiff has no adequate legal remedy at law for said injuries in that defendants will continue to conduct said wrongful activity resulting in a multiplicity of suits, irreparable damages will result to plaintiff in an undeterminable amount which will be extremely difficult to ascertain and for which plaintiff's remedy at law is inadequate because of the speculative damages.

10. As a further proximate result of defendants' said wrongful conduct, plaintiff's business has been damaged in the sum of $________ from the defendants' wrongful and malicious conduct. Plaintiff will be further damaged in like manner so long as defendants' said conduct continues; the full amount of such damage is not now known to plaintiff and plaintiff will amend this complaint to so state when the same becomes known to him, or upon proof thereof.

WHEREFORE, plaintiff prays judgment as follows:

1. For an order requiring defendants to show cause, if any they have, why they should not be enjoined as hereinafter set forth, during the pendency of this action.

2. For a temporary restraining order, a preliminary injunction, and a permanent injunction, all enjoining defendants, and each of them, and their agents, servants and employees, and all persons acting under, in concert with, or for them:

Defendants shall not permit any person, group, organization or club to use their business premises for the purpose of conducting a car wash fund raising project, without a valid business license issued by the City of_______, California.

3. For damages in the sum of $___________ plus damages in the further sum as may be sustained and as are ascertained before final judgment herein.

4. For costs of suit and such other relief as the court deems just.

____
Attorney for Plaintiff

CAPTION) Case No.______________
)
) COMPLAINT FOR DAMAGES BASED ON
) CONSPIRACY
_________________________)

Plaintiff alleges:

1. That at all times herein mentioned, defendant ________________was, and now is, a resident of the City of_________, County of___________, State of California.

2. At all times herein mentioned, defendant White was, and now is, a resident of the City of_________, County of _____________, State of California.

3. On or about_____, 19____, defendants Black and White, knowingly and wilfully conspired and agreed among themselves to do the following: (Allege what defendants did to create the conspiracy and what the conspiracy intended to achieve.)

4. Defendants Black and White engaged in the above-mentioned conspiracy willfully, knowingly and maliciously and with intent to destroy plaintiff's business and financial credit by further doing the following: (Describe acts.)

5. As a proximate result of the above acts, plaintiff has been damaged in the sum of $______________.

6. As a result of the above wrongful acts, plaintiff has been specially damaged in that the following vendors have refused, and continue to refuse to sell to plaintiff, merchandise on credit.

7. Defendants did the things above-mentioned maliciously and with the intent to oppress plaintiff. Plaintiff is therefore entitled to punitive damages in the sum of $___________.

WHEREFORE, plaintiff prays judgment as follows:

1. For general damages against each defendant in the sum of $______________.

2. For special damages against each defendant in the sum of $_______________.

3. For punitive damages against each defendant in the sum of $__________________.

4. For costs of suit herein and such other relief as the court deems just.

____
Attorney for Plaintiff

****

The conspiracy must consist of the unlawful act of two or more persons with the intent of injuring plaintiff. Southern Cal vs. Lonkin, 183 C.A. 2d 431; Tietz vs. Los Angeles, 238 C.A. 2d 905.

Other cases: Haris vs. Capitol Records, 64 Cal. 2d, 454, Prince vs. Harting, 177 C.A. 2d, 720, DeVries vs. Brumback, 53 Cal. 2d, 643.

CAPTION)
)
) COMPLAINT FOR NEGLIGENT
) INFLICTION OF EMOTIONAL
________________) DISTRESS

Case No.__________

Plaintiff complains:

1. (Allege cause of action for accident which serves as basis for plaintiff's observations.)

2. At all times herein mentioned, the plaintiff was in close proximity to the above-described collision and personally witnessed the collision.

3. As a proximate result of the collision, ______________ was seriously injured and dismembered.__________ was the only child of plaintiff.

4. As a proximate cause of defendant's conduct, plaintiff sustained great emotional disturbance and shock and injury to her nervous system, all of which has caused, and continues to cause great physical and mental pain and suffering, all to her damage in the amount of$__________.

5. Plaintiff was required to and did incur medical, psychiatric and other expenses for the examination, treatment and care of the physical and emotional injuries. Plaintiff will incur additional expenses for the treatment and care of said injuries and will ask leave to amend the complaint when the totality of the expenses has been ascertained.

WHEREFORE, plaintiff prays:

1. For damages in the sum of $__________.

2. For medical and incidental expenses according to proof.

3. For costs of suit and such other relief as the court deems just.

____
Attorney for Plaintiff

****

Dillo vs. Legg, 68 Cal 2d, 728

Powers vs. Sissoev, 39 C.A. 3d, 865.

CAPTION)
)
)
)
_______________)

Case No.___________

COMPLAINT FOR DAMAGES
(Interference with Economic Advantageous Relationship)

Plaintiff complains:

1. At all times herein mentioned, defendant Smith was, and now is, a resident of the County of_______________, State of California.

2. At all times herein mentioned, defendant Green was and now is, a resident of the County of________________, State of California.

3. On or about________, 19____, plaintiff and defendant Smith entered into an oral agreement wherein and whereby plaintiff agreed to procure for defendant Smith, a parcel of real property suitable for the operation of defendant Smith's business operation.

4. On or about______, 19____, plaintiff located the following described real property, (describe), which property belonged to defendant Green, and which property plaintiff considered to be suitable for the business operation of defendant Smith.

5. Plaintiff advised defendant Smith that plaintiff had located a suitable property and defendant Smith agreed with plaintiff that if plaintiff would negotiate with defendant Green for the sale of said property, that defendant Smith would pay plaintiff the sum of $________________.

6. Pursuant thereto, plaintiff did negotiate with defendant Green for the sale of said property.

7. Upon learning of defendant Smith's interest in said property, plaintiff is informed and believes, and upon such information and belief, alleges that defendant Green thereafter personally contacted defendant Smith and arranged directly with defendant Smith for the sale of the above-described property.

8. Defendants Smith and Green agreed and conspired to consummate the sale of the above-described property and with knowledge of the existence of the agreement between defendant Smith and plaintiff, entered into such conspiracy for the purpose of consummating the sale to the exclusion of plaintiff's fee.

9. As a proximate result of the conspiracy between the defendants, defendant Green induced defendant Smith to breach his contract with plaintiff, all to plaintiff's damage in the sum of $________________.

10. Said acts were done willfully and maliciously and with the intent to injure the plaintiff and by reason thereof, plaintiff is entitled to punitive damages in the sum of $________.

WHEREFORE, plaintiff prays:

1. For damages in the sum of $______________.

2. For punitive damages in the sum of $________.

3. For costs of suit and such other relief as the court deems just.

____
Attorney for Plaintiff

****

Buckaloo vs. Johnson, 14 Cal. 3d, 815.

CAPTION) Case No.______________
)
) COMPLAINT FOR DAMAGES
) (Invasion of Privacy)
____________________)

Plaintiff complains:

1. At all times herein mentioned, defendant was and now is, a resident of the County of ___________, State of California.

2. On or about__________, 19____, the defendant without the consent of plaintiff leased to________________ magazine, a photograph of plaintiff, who at the time was depicted in the photograph as being engaged in the following activity, (describe).

3. In the year________, plaintiff was engaged in the activity of ____________________and in the course of said activity engaged in the activity as depicted in said photograph. Subsequently, plaintiff rehabilitated himself and assumed a place in respectable society with many friends who were unaware of the incidents of his earlier life.

4. As a proximate result of the publication of said picture, plaintiff's friends learned for the first time of plaintiff's past activities and abandoned him and plaintiff was exposed to contempt and ridicule causing him great mental anguish, embarrassment and humiliation.

5. As a proximate result of the acts and conduct of defendant, plaintiff has been damaged in the sum of $____________.

6. Plaintiff is informed and believes and upon such information and belief alleges that defendant's conduct was willful, deliberate and malicious with the sole intent to harm plaintiff and thus plaintiff is entitled to punitive damages in the amount of $____________________.

WHEREFORE, plaintiff prays:

1. For general damages in the amount of $____________.

2. For punitive damages in the amount of $____________.

3. For costs of suit and such other relief as the court deems just.

____
Attorney for Plaintiff

****

Melvin vs. Reid, 112, C.A. 285.

California Constitution, Article I, §1.

Stilson vs. Reader's Digest, 21 C.A. 3d, 270.

CAPTION) Case No.____________
)
) COMPLAINT FOR DAMAGES
) (USURY)
____________________)

Plaintiff complains:

1. Defendant at all times herein mentioned, was and now is, a resident of the __________County, State of California.

2. On or about________, 19____, defendant loaned and advanced to plaintiff, the sum of $_____________.

3. As a condition for making the loan, defendant required plaintiff, at said time and place, to execute and deliver to said defendant a promissory note, dated ________, 19____, in the face amount of $____________. The face amount of the loan was greater than the amount of the loan by the sum of $_________. The note was payable to defendant or order, together with interest thereon at the rate of ______% per annum. A copy of said note is attached hereto, marked Exhibit "A" and made a part hereof.

4. On_________, 19____, plaintiff paid to defendant the full amount of the note, to wit; the sum of $__________, together with interest thereon at the rate of _____________% per annum from the date of said note to the date of payment in the total amount of $_______________.

5. By reason of said payment, defendant has received the sum of $______________in excess of the amount of the principal of the loan, said amount being the difference between the face amount of the note and the amount of the loan, and also has received interest on the full face amount of the note, at the rate of _______% per annum, making a total of $__________received by defendant as interest on the loan.

6. Said sum of $____________, the total amount of interest paid, received by defendant as interest, is in excess of the amount of maximum interest allowed by §_______of the ____________Code of the State of California. The difference between the amount of the loan and the face amount of the note was a method of defendant to conceal the usury.

WHEREFORE, plaintiff prays:

1. For the sum of $_______________which is treble the amount of all interest paid within the year previous to the filing of the action.

2. For costs of suit.

3. For such other relief as the court deems just.

____
Attorney for Plaintiff

****

Terry vs. Barsky, 210 Cal. 428.

Milana vs. Credit Discount, 27 Cal. 2d, 335.

CAPTION	Case No. ______________
	NOTICE OF MOTION FOR CHANGE OF VENUE
	Date:__________
	Time:__________
	Dept:__________

TO THE PLAINTIFF________________AND TO HIS ATTORNEY:

YOU AND EACH OF YOU ARE HEREBY NOTIFIED that on ______________, 19___, at the hour of ______A.M., in Department ____ of the above-entitled court, defendant will move the court for an order transferring the action to the Superior Court of the County of __________.

The motion will be based on the ground that the convenience of witnesses and the ends of justice would be promoted by the change of venue.

The motion will further be based on this notice of motion, the declaration of merits attached hereto, points and authorities submitted herewith, the records and papers on file herein, and such other evidence, oral and documentary as may be adduced at the hearing on the motion.

DATED: ______________________.

____
Attorney for Defendant

****

The court may change the place of trial in the following cases:

1. Where the court designated in the complaint is not the proper court;
2. Where there is reason to believe that an impartial trial cannot be had;
3. Where the convenience of witnesses and the ends of justice would be promoted by the change;
4. Where there is no judge of the court qualified to act;
5. Certain dissolution proceedings.

C.C.P. §397.

See also C.C.P. §392 through §395.5.

	)	
	)	
	)	Case No. _______________
	)	
CAPTION	)	DECLARATION OF MERITS
	)	
	)	
	)	
______________________	)	

I, ____________________, declare:

That I am the defendant in the above-entitled action.

The convenience of witnesses and the ends of justice would be promoted by a change of venue for the following reasons: (Set forth reasons, including names and numbers of witnesses, and addresses of witnesses and materiality of their testimony).

Your declarant further states that at all times mentioned in the complaint and at the present time, he resides in the County of _____________.

EXECUTED at________________, California, at ________________, 19___.

I declare under penalty of perjury that the foregoing is true and correct.

Your declarant further states that he has fully and fairly stated the case and all the facts and circumstances connected therewith to______________, attorney at law, admitted to practice in the Courts of California, and after such statement, he is advised by said attorney, and he believes that he has a good and valid defense upon the merits to the alleged causes of action set forth in said complaint.

____
Defendant

****

Plaintiff's own convenience cannot be considered on defendant's motion for change of venue. Maxwell vs. Murray, 190 C.A.2d 440.

An affidavit of merits must be filed. A general affidavit does not satisy the statutory requirement. Peterson vs. Mueller, 178 C.A.2d 280.

CAPTION	Case No. ________________ DECLARATION OF JURISDICTIONAL FACTS [C.C.P. §396(a)]

I, ________________, declare:

I am the plaintiff in the above-entitled action. The within action is an action for breach of contract involving the sum of $____________.

The contract was entered into in the City of________, which is in the ____________Judicial District.

The contract is not a retail installment contract or the contract for the purchase of a motor vehicle which is subject to the provisions of either Civil Code §1812.10 or §2984.4.

EXECUTED at Los Angeles, California, on __________, 19___.

I declare under penalty of perjury that the foregoing is true and correct.

____
Plaintiff

****

Where actions are commenced in Municipal or Justice Courts and are subject to Civil Code §§1812.10 or 2984.4, plaintiff must state facts in the complaint under oath or in an affidavit showing that the action has been commenced in the proper court. When the affidavit is filed with the complaint, a copy must be served with the summons. C.C.P. §396(a).

CAPTION	Case No. ___________ NOTICE OF MOTION TO TRANSFER ACTION [C.C.P. § 396] Date: ______________ Time: ______________ Place: ______________

TO THE PLAINTIFF______________AND TO HIS ATTORNEYS:

YOU AND EACH OF YOU SHALL PLEASE TAKE NOTICE that on __________________, 19___, at _____A.M., in Department___ of the above-entitled court, defendant will move the court for an order to transfer the action to the Superior Court of the State of California for the County of______________.

The motion will be made on the ground that the Municipal Court lacks jurisdiction of the subject matter herein and will be based further upon the provisions of C.C.P. §396, the affidavit of____________and the points and authorities attached hereto and other papers and records on file herein, and upon such evidence oral and documentary as may be presented at the hearing on this motion.

DATED: _________________________.

____
Attorney for Defendant

****

This motion may be used where the court lacks jurisdiction over the subject matter or where the amount sought in the complaint exceeds the jurisdiction of the court.

Where a court lacks jurisdiction over the subject matter, either by virtue of the complaint or cross-complaint, the court can do nothing but transfer the action to the Superior Court. Eveleth vs. American Brass & Iron, 203 C.A.2d 41.

CAPTION	Case No. ______________
	ORDER TRANSFERRING ACTION

The motion of______________, defendant, for an order to transfer the action to the Superior Court for the County of ______________came on regularly for hearing before the undersigned on ______________, 19___, upon notice duly served. The defendant appeared by______________, his attorney, and plaintiff appeared by______________. The matter was argued and submitted, and good cause appearing therefor,

IT IS ORDERED that the action herein be transferred to the Superior Court of the State of California for the County of ____________ , and that defendant pay the transfer fees herein.

DATED: ________________.

____
JUDGE

CAPTION	Case No. ______________
	NOTICE OF TRANSFER OF ACTION

TO____________________, PLAINTIFF:

YOU ARE HEREBY NOTIFIED that the above-entitled action has been transferred to the Superior Court of the State of California for the County of ______________.

DATED: __________________.

CAPTION)
)
)
__________)

No.__________

COMPLAINT FOR WRONGFUL DEATH

1. Plaintiff was appointed Executor of the Will (or Administrator of the Estate) of ______________,deceased, in the Superior Court of _____________County in case #__________, on________19___ and is presently acting in such capacity. A true copy of Letters of_________________is attached hereto and made a part hereof. Plaintiff is bringing this action on behalf of all the heirs of the deceased.

(Alternate) Plaintiff___________and__________are the sole heirs of______________deceased and are bringing this action in that capacity.(If there are additional heirs who refuse to join as plaintiffs, allege: Plaintiff__________and_________are heirs of ________________deceased and are bringing this action in that capacity. Defendant____________is the only other heir who has refused to join as a party plaintiff and for that reason he has been made a defendant).

2. The sole-surviving heirs of the deceased are as follows: (Set forth names and relationship to decedent of additional heirs.)

3. __________and ___________ are named herein as defendants pursuant to C.C.P. §382 since their consents to be joined as plaintiffs could not be obtained for the following reasons. (Set forth reasons.)

4. Defendant now is, and at all times herein mentioned was a resident of _________County, California.

5. On ______, 19_____, the decedent was the owner of the following-described motor vehicle. (Set forth description.)

6. At all times herein mentioned, defendant was the owner of the following-described motor vehicle. (Describe vehicle.) and on_________, 19_____ was operating said motor vehicle.

7. At all times herein mentioned __________and _________________streets were intersecting public highways in the City of_______, County of__________, California.

8. On or about______, 19_____, at or about the hour of __________A. M., decedent was operating his automobile on _______ street in a general______direction at or near the intersection of____________street.

9. At said time and place, defendants and each of them, so carelessly and negligently entrusted, managed, operated and drove their motor vehicle along________street in a general________ direction so as to approximately cause it to collide with decedent's automobile. As a direct and proximate result of said negligence, decedent on__________, 19___, died.

10. Immediately prior to his death, decedent was an adult in excellent physical and mental condition and was a faithful and dutiful husband and father to__________and __________ and was their sole source of support.

11. As a proximate result of said negligence of defendant and the death of said decedent, the above-mentioned heirs have been deprived of the society, comfort, protection, services and support of said decedent and have thereby sustained pecuniary loss in the sum of $_______________.

12. As a further proximate result of said negligence of defendants and the death of said decedent, __________has paid from the estate of said decedent, funeral and burial expenses in the sum of $________________.

WHEREFORE, plaintiff prays judgment as follows:

1. For damages in the sum of $__________________.

2. For funeral and burial expenses in the sum of $______________________.

3. For costs of suit herein and for such other relief as the court deems just.

DATED: _________________, 19____.

____
Attorney for Plaintiff

****

C.C.P. §377 provides that when the death of a person is caused by the wrongful act of another, either the heirs or personal representatives may maintain an action for damages against the person causing the death.

The action may be joined with an action under Probate Code §573 which is an action that decedent could have maintained had he survived. In a personal injury case, cause of action for special damages such as property loss and loss of earnings, survives, but a cause of action for general damages such as pain and suffering does not survive.

In a wrongful death action, all the heirs should be joined in the action and may be joined as defendants under C.C.P. §382. Watkins vs. Nutting, 17 Cal. 2d, 490.

The judgment recovered in the wrongful death action is in a lump sum and no recovery can be had by an heir who has not sustained a loss. Cross vs. Pacific Gas, 60 Cal. 2d, 690.

After judgment the court in a separate proceeding will apportion the amount of the recovery.

CAPTION)
)
)
____

NOTICE OF MOTION FOR CONSOLIDATION
(CCP §377)

TO THE DEFENDANT _________________________ and to his attorney:

TO _____________________________, administrator of the estate of _____________________________, deceased and to his attorney:

YOU AND EACH OF YOU will please take notice that on _____________________ 19___, at the hour of ________ a.m., in Department _____ of the above entitled court, plaintiff will move the court for an order consolidating the following actions:

____________________ vs. _________________________, the within action.

A _________________________ administrator vs. ______________________________________, an action commenced under Probate Code §573 bearing Case No. ____________________.

The motion will be made upon the grounds that the issues and facts in both actions are substantially the same and that the ends of justice would best be served by consolidation.

The motion will also be based upon this notice of motion, the declaration and points and authorities attached hereto, and upon all the papers and records on file herein and such other evidence, oral and documentary, as may be presented at the hearing on the motion.

Dated: ___________________

____
Attorney for Plaintiffs